ASCII SHRUG

¯_(ツ)_/¯

An Overview of the History, Basics, and Challenges of Computer Science

BING WANG

*With love and thanks to my husband,
daughter, dad, mom, and brother*

ASCII SHRUG
AN OVERVIEW OF THE HISTORY, BASICS, AND
CHALLENGES OF COMPUTER SCIENCE

iUniverse books may be ordered through booksellers or by contacting:

iUniverse
1663 Liberty Drive
Bloomington, IN 47403
www.iuniverse.com
844-349-9409

ISBN: 978-1-6632-4721-6 (sc)
ISBN: 978-1-6632-4722-3 (e)

Library of Congress Control Number: 2022919990

Print information available on the last page.

iUniverse rev. date: 06/19/2023

To my dearest, truthiest, kindest and purest ABC daughter, Nali.

To those old friends who shaped me but I am no longer see them because they moved away and let me move on.

To those who have learned but constantly question themselves.

To those expecting yesterday once more and wanting to back starting from zero.

To those too young to know how the ASCII was born.

I know one thing: that I know nothing. – Mr. Socrates

PROVERB

Computer science has created careers, roles and employment for people that we could never have imagined. As a software engineer, my goal is to join with all company IT professionals to:

Well done is better than well said. - Benjamin Franklin

Help both company and company's customers prosper.

Act based on believing that everything we do should be simple personal fair.

Storm, norm and form aspects.

Fatal production issues to minor ones out.

Flat out working style, in a blunt or direct manner, black or white, flat out revolution

CONTENTS

Preface..xv

Acknowledgment xix

I.   Trail Without Shrugging..1

II. Languages Skeleton Shrug...19

     2.1 Machine Language..20

     2.2 Assembly Language 26

     2.3 High-level Language (HLL)..33

          2.3.1 Imperative Language..............................35

          2.3.2 Declarative Language..............................40

          2.3.3 Functional Language 42

          2.3.4 Object-Oriented Language...............................46

     2.4 Very high-level language (VHLL)..............................47

III. Languages Computing Shrug..48

     3.1 Compiled and Interpreted Languages
          and JIT Compiler..48

     3.2 Computer Languages Basics.....................................53

          3.2.1 Bool...56

          3.2.2 Numbers 59

               3.2.2.1 Integer 61

               3.2.2.2 Floating Point..............................68

3.2.3   Text 72

    3.2.3.1   Character 72

    3.2.3.2   String 75

3.2.4   Object 76

3.2.5   Operator 79

3.2.6   Value type and Reference type 87

3.2.7   Generic Type 91

3.2.8   Type Conversion 102

3.2.9   Function Overloading 110

3.2.10 Iteration 114

3.2.11 Recursive 119

3.2.12 Delegate 124

IV. Object-Oriented Programming Shrug 128

   4.1   Object-Oriented Philosophy 128

     4.1.1   Object 128

     4.1.2   Object relations 130

   4.2   Object-Oriented Programming (OOP) 133

     4.2.1   Object-oriented programming paradigm 133

     4.2.2   Object in object-oriented programming 137

     4.2.3   Class in object-oriented programming 142

     4.2.4   Object oriented programming principles 149

   4.3   Object-oriented expression 160

   4.4   The pitfall of object-oriented programming 163

V. Computing World Development Shrug 166

   5.1   Data 166

   5.2   Database 170

   5.3   SQL Server 177

     5.3.1   SQL Server Architecture 179

5.3.2 SQL error analysis 185

    5.3.2.1 transaction log 185

    5.3.2.2 SQL timeout 187

    5.3.2.3 Deadlock 190

5.4 Data Modeling 193

  5.4.1 Guid 195

  5.4.2 Binary Large Object (BLOB) 196

5.5 OLE DB vs. ODBC vs. ADO 197

  5.5.1 Data Set to Data Model 200

    5.5.1.1 Serialization 201

    5.5.1.2 Linq 202

    5.5.1.3 Reflection 203

    5.5.1.4 Attributed Mapping 204

    5.5.1.5 Entity Framework 205

5.6 Windows Desktop Interface 207

  5.6.1 Windows Form 217

  5.6.2 Windows Presentation Foundation (WPF) 218

5.7 Web Services 225

  5.7.1 XML-RPC 229

  5.7.2 SOAP 230

  5.7.3 WSDL and UDDI 232

  5.7.4 NET Remoting 235

    5.7.4.1. NET Remoting Client and Service ... 238

    5.7.4.2 Communication Stack 241

  5.7.5 ASP.NET Web Service and IIS 250

    5.7.5.1 ASP.NET Web Service Sample 254

    5.7.5.2 ASP.NET Web Service Security 259

5.8 Secure Communication 263

  5.8.1 ASP.NET Web Service Authentication 266

  5.8.2 ASP.NET Pipeline 269

5.9 Windows Communication Foundation.....................271

    5.9.1   Service Contract 272

    5.9.2   Data Contract.....................................273

    5.9.3   Operation Contract...........................274

    5.9.4   Message Contract 275

    5.9.5   Windows Communication
          Foundation Behaviors.....................277

          5.9.5.1   Service Behavior 277

          5.9.5.2   Endpoint Behavior............279

          5.9.5.3   Contract Behavior.............287

          5.9.5.4   Operation Behavior 288

    5.9.6   Communication Stack 291

    5.9.7   WCF Data Service 292

    5.9.8   WCF Web Service Model 293

    5.9.9   WCF AppFabric AutoStart................297

    5.9.10 WCF Hosting 298

5.10 Windows Service, Microservice and Messaging 303

5.11 RESTful Service 312

5.12 WEB API Service 321

5.13 Miscellaneous..331

    5.13.1 MIME Type and Content Type.....................331

    5.13.2 Serialization and Deserialization 333

    5.13.3 Http Basic Authentication and
            Digest Authentication 337

    5.13.4 Bootstrapping....................................339

VI. Challenges of Tomorrow Programming.............347

   6.1   High-level programming language 348

   6.2   Database development................................352

   6.3   Windows operating system 356

   6.4   Windows user interface.............................358

References...363

Afterword 365

PREFACE

I kept a file called *Developer Note* when started to work for a new company, or on a new project, or in a new business domain, or in a new industry world. For a long time, I keep an invisible lingering in my mind to crave for a chance to re-learn some basics, some history, some present and some future. Now I think the opportunity is coming, I put all I assimilated in my *developer note* in a book. I'm learning some history, some basics. I'm reviewing some coding, some problem solutions. I'm expecting tomorrow, continuing to think and work. And at the same time, I am writing, here is my bigger compact of developer note, my book: *ASCII Shrug*.

Why call the book name *ASCII Shrug*? The born of ASCII makes almost every computing feature possible, GUI interface, networking, machines communication, data management and transaction, and many others. The born of ASCII transforms computing and our lives in such an easier way, sometimes we may finish a job with just a shrug. Computer is more friendly to users, and computing is more nature to human being.

But all these came not easy, countless computing scientists and engineers have devoted to, forgetting day and night, they ever suffered, failed, even went into disaster, just because of these failures created a series of milestones. *Chapter I: Trail without shrugging* brings you to hundred years ago, even ancient time when civilization just sprouted. How number is generated? How mathematics and algebra developed? How mathematic related with computing? Who implemented the first program in the world? How first computing machine was built? many. many... The trail can shed you some lights to see the history reflections.

Basically, I am a programmer, after years of programming, I want to pause to review all the languages from a higher-level point of view that how programming languages are classified? *Chapter II: Languages Skeleton Shrug* touches many basic concepts, and they are very common topics. I explained them from my personal understanding along with the diagrams to illustrate my summaries. *Chapter III: Languages Computing Shrug* goes into a deep further to explain some basic and popular topics in language computing. For all these topics, all software developers need tackle them during their programming time, but have you ever thought about the basics. For example, you know how to write loop statements, but what exactly is iteration? How computer performs iterative statements? You are very clear about float data type, especially for financial software, we need play a lot with currency represented as decimal number, but have you ever thought about how important floating point is? Why the supercomputing machines speed-competition in the world use floating point calculation speed as a gauge?

If philosophy can help us understand the world, we can trace back to Before Christ. Over thousand years, philosophy gradually immerse into the life of human being, the power nature, and the abstract sciences. The same apply to computing and programming. *Chapter IV: Object-Oriented Programming* tries to illustrate the very important programming paradigm from fundamental, from philosophy first. What is object in the world? What is object-oriented way of thinking from philosophical point of view? Is object-oriented programming slow dying?

Chapter V: Computing Programming Development Shrug is a big chapter, it accumulates all the contents in my *developer note*, all my study and research. It covers data, database, data modeling, SQL server, and the evolvement of windows interface implementation and web services implementation over the years. We all know these highlights, we all tackle SQL server, GUI or web services almost every day. But have you ever thought about what's the SQL server architecture? Why the query can run through in SQL server? Have you seen those SQL reported errors before? What are fundamentals of windows form and windows presentation foundation? How to program GUI before those advanced GUI frameworks were born? We all know IIS in Microsoft server machine, have you ever investigated how IIS pipeline works? Why we browse an address sending to the server and can get a web page back?

We are too busy and have no time to think about tomorrow, the future. But we all know technologies development are quietly silently happening every day, tomorrow is indeed different from today. *Chapter VI: Challenges of Tomorrow Programming* pictures tomorrow's technologies in some computing areas, which directions are for programming languages development, big data, and user interface, at the same time, it lays out some challenges in some research areas. If tomorrow comes, we will have something new along with the difficulties, we will have lots of work and challenges, but we are full of hope, we will be looking forward to the coming of each tomorrow.

October. 1st, 2022

ACKNOWLEDGMENT

Before presenting my book to you, my readers, some important words I want to say beforehand, that is expressing my deeply appreciations to someone who live in my life, in my heart.

My daughter, my flesh and blood, my achievement, your birth first brought me deepest fears, then surprise joyful that I didn't realize my then slim body was such strong and powerful. Watching you grow up is an unimaginable and indelible journey. You are my mirror teaching me how to be frank, honest, humble and down to the earth. Thank you, my dear daughter! My husband Wei, Dad, Mom and brother, your encouragement and support go with me all the time, your being around color my life with laughs and tears. Thank you, my family members! To those my old friends, some I may no longer see, your compliments enlightened me, your criticizes shaped me, your encouragements strengthened me. Thanks for all your help, on my academic study, and on my career development.

Time is flitting, the old school days are still vivid in my memory. I want to thank the University of Pittsburgh, all the professors I know, especially those in Graduate School of Computer Science, some are retired, some still stand at the podium happily talk with youth. It is you who opened the gate of computer science dragging me in so that I could extensively learn, explore and fumble in the computing world. I also want to thank you for your wonderful C programming projects that made me glue on the Sun SPARC workstation so much. Today, I code C# in Microsoft Windows 10 operation system, but I don't have today without my old C days, thank you!

My career path is a bumpy road, from a fledging C++ programmer to a skilled C# developer, I have learned and worked in many fields of the computing. I want to thank for all the companies I worked and work for, Oil & Gas giants ExxonMobile and BP, historically reputational financial firms Wellsfargo and Santander, real estate authority firms Stewart Lender Service and Aegis, Software service providers GC Service and Cubic, consulting service companies Sogeti and Tata Consultant Service. Thank you for providing the projects and giving me the opportunities to learn and work with different business domain knowledges and different application contexts designed in the Microsoft framework ecosystem. Thanks for all my previous managers, colleagues and my current managers and teammates, I learned a lot from you! My developer notes and my book have your knowledge traces.

Finally, I want to thank for the iUniverse publisher, your editorial evaluation, your book cover design and interior formatting, going to present my book to the readers. Without your work and help, everything about my book is impossible. Thank you!

TRAIL WITHOUT SHRUGGING

I came, I saw, I conquered.

– Julius Caesar

I'VE BEEN TO BRAZIL TAKING the boat flitting on the amazon river. I've seen the two-color water clearly distinguished by a zigzag demarcation line. I've seen the jungled rainforest besides the river. Walking into the old days of computer world, as if I'm trailing in the ten-thousands years of amazon indigenous forest. I wish I'm rather a naturalist, archeologist, and historian than a computer programmer. I'm approaching the adventure, from see nothing to gradually observe something. The rough narrow road, the extruding branches and leaves, the extreme pitch sounds and the buzzy noises ringing at my ears. I heard the talks from some philosophies, mathematicians, physics and astronomists who built the milestones. I was collecting the variety of forms from the very beginning Sumerian's number system to powerful floating-point notations, from the embryonic form of calculator calibi to super computer with astronomical figures of calculation speed, from the first equation represented by language to big data machine learning algorithm, from external punch card to omnipresent cloud computing. Computer is not an overgrown human pocket-calculator, it is a revolution history of human being civilization.

Computing history is not only the collected ancient forms, but also a metaphor of despair and delight. It was such a long-long bumpy road full of puzzle, thoughts, questions, idea strike, failure, even sometimes intrigues and disaster. Incomparable to computing history, what I try to approach is such tiny, even not mention achieved, perhaps that is why I want to trail on the history of computing world to come to my nature of nothing.

The spirit is the inspiring for human life and the universe, the knowledge is based on the hierarchical levels of organized elements, on the first level, along with language, is to find the number and the calculations. From 3300 BCE, the Sumerians, who settled in Mesopotamia, part of what is now Iraq, started to treat number order based on the size and shape of object. They began to call it calculi to symbolize the object. Thousand years later, we have number machine calculi, further override as calculator. All ancient regions had invented numbers and even some elementary algebra concepts. Babylonians could solve equations with first and second degree. Ancient Chinese invented abacus doing the notational calculations similar to the modern approach of matrix and determinants. We call the Chinese abacus as 算盘, which is so popular in old China time that it passes from generation to generation. Designed by the wooden tabulate frame with at least seven cords. Each cord has seven wooden beads with two at the top deck and five at the bottom. Beads move up and down doing calculation and even carry over. Similarly, the ancient Egyptian counting instrument depicted on the wall, the ancient Greece's marble count board, the ancient Room's *Jetons*, the ancient Russia's *Schoty*, the ancient Japanese *Soroban*, and the Native Americans' *Nepohualtzintzin*, they laid out the foundation for number positional notation and computing.

However, if you think carefully, all the numbers, no matter written in what kind of symbol, you cannot find number **zero** **0**, the ° in Babylonians, *Nefer* in Egyptian, μηδέν in Greek, 零 and *empty space* in Chinese, ᛥ᛬ in Arabic, ᥱ᛬᛬ in India, *Nulla* in Roman. Let's step on zero's path walking back to the very origin. You seem to see nothing at the beginning, but actually you see the world after you stepped into the contour. Sumerians recorded used space to be absence, they used one vertical stroke as the unit symbol to represent number one, one wedge as the ten numerical to represent number ten, one wedge and two vertical strokes as twelve, two wedges to represent number twenty. Mesopotamia has first recorded zero around 3 B.C, and the first person documented zero as a number was the astronomer and mathematician Brahmagupta in 628 CE. India first developed the concept of zero as a written digit. How can nothing be something? Everyone knows it plays a crucial role in mathematizing the world. The discovery of zero pushed arithmetic calculation forward. The emerge and development of algebraic symbol and notation set off a new chapter in the history of mathematics.

The first gnawing bone in my study of Computer Science was reviewing and correcting the Pascal code from students. The dazzle ASCII string repelled me outside the door of computing world. Now I understood why, because at that moment I had no idea that in 1600s, a French mathematician named Blaise Pascal created the first calculator in the world, *Pascal Calculator* or *Pascaline*, which is a mechanical machine that can add or subtract two numbers and can also do multiplication through repeated addition and subtraction. I was even completely blind that dozens of years before Pascaline's born, an English mathematician named William Oughtred invented the slide rule which uses two scales to slide to do multiplication and division, the predecessor of our calculators. There were more before Pascaline, German astronomy Wilhelm Schickard constructed the *Rechenuhr*, a clock calculator can do six-digit number addition and subtraction even ring with overflow. Scottish mathematician John Napier proposed the idea of logarithmic that can be used as a device to aid the mathematical calculation.

Now sometimes when I am easily coding C# on top of the most cutting-edge .NET Core platform in the powerful Visual Studio 2022 editor, I shrug myself that programmer is not a hard job. But I'm still not sure if I stepped into the 0 contour to see the world, see the universe, both physical and mental universe, standing from the philosophy point of view, nothing was self-evident. Some computing historians could see the world and universe as a mathematician, as a physicist, as an astronomist, as an engineer, and as a philosopher.

The first computer programmer, Ada Lovelace, who engaged her whole life to mathematics and finally wrote the first program in the world, an Analyst Engine in 1800s. Ada, a lovely girl easily caught illness at early childhood never stop her keen interests on science and mathematics. When grew to twelve years old, this "Lady Fairy" was so eager to fly that she constructed wings mechanically and materially. Years later, this full blossom flower did not indulge the court dance and romance, on the contrary, she was fascinated to get acquainted with scientists and engineers. She self-purposely educated herself, her devoting to mathematics dominated her whole life. In 1830, her met with Mr. Charles Babbage changed her life completely. Mr. Babbage, the father of modern computers, introduced her his difference engine whose name derived from the mathematical difference. This engine is an auto mechanical calculator that can tabulate polynomial functions. It's a huge machine pretty like the heat exchanger in the chemical engineering refinery plant and right now sits in the London Science Museum. The No.2 difference engine was completed in 1990s.

Ada and Charles developed a very intimate relationship, she became fascinated with this difference engine and wrote notes described her thoughts as an analyst engine. She declared that her engine has no pretension from any origin but can follow any order and demand. She also dismissed artificial intelligence saying no engine can predicate analytical relations and truth, which raised questions from many scientists, especially Alan Turning, who objected this statement in his published paper *Computing Machinery and Intelligence*. Ada in her last note wrote the first program in the world, an algorithm in her analyst engine to compute Bernoulli numbers.

A flash in an instance, Ada died at young age of 36 from cancer. But her first program manifested to the world that a series of simple instructions can compose to be a program that run in a computer ordered to do complex mathematical calculation. *Ada*, the first object-oriented language developed in US Department of Defense in 1980s, was named in memory of Ada Lovelace, the perpetual blooming flower.

More and more young IT professionals today love to talk about fast computing, speedy memory and I/O access. It's true that today, a typical 7200 RPM HDD could reach read write speed up to about 160 mb/s, and a typical SDD could reach read write speed up to roughly 550 mb/s. But at your leisure, let us flip the computing pages back to 1890 US census, when the first punch cards, 12 rows and 24 columns, size of a dollar bill was the first machine readable media used as data collection. Mr. Herman Hollerith, the data processing pioneer, his tabulating machine opened the window for data reading writing and laid the foundation for IBM. The punch cards, also called IBM cards, can be traced back even as early as 1830s, Mr. Semen Korsakov who worked for the Russia's government used the cards for information storage and retrieval.

The punch card was designed to have holes presence or absence at the predefined position to represent digital data. The reader got the card input, reading from top left down to bottom and then went to the next column. The card reader was also the computer input device, it could take optical sensing or electrical sensing. When taking optical, the lighting passed through when there was a hole or not so that represents bit 1 or 0 respectively. When taking electrical, it would break the circuit and reconnect again if there was a hole so that represents bit 0 or 1 respectively. Therefore, in both cases there were timing and sensing resolutions to read card column based on the typical IBM 80 column punch card format.

Now more than a century has passed, the punch cards are gradually deprecated, but the ideas of reading cards carried on for quite long. Think about our current RFID, the contactless radio frequency identification technology, simply just tap or wave the card in front of the reader. Think about QR code, barcode, many systems now still keep the idea of using passive radio or optical sensor and reader to get data input. With the born of magnetic media, punch cards, the piles of stiff papers were replaced by HDD. Now with faster and faster HDD and SDD, I/O read and write are gradually no longer the bottle neck. With the born of cloud computing and cloud drives, someday I/O will step off from the world computing stage.

If it is said that war brings catastrophic damage to human being and our earth, from another narrow view, it also pushed for the technology development, especially during world war II, inventions from medical, electrical, mechanical, and computing, changed human life dramatically. Flu vaccines, penicillin, blood plasma transfusion, jet engine, radar, and electronical computing, etc. The world war II brought the computing a leap jump in America and Europe.

ENIAC, acronym for Electronic Numerical Integrator and Computer, was the first programmable, electronical general-purpose digital computer built in 1943. It is more than 30 short tons and occupies over 1800 square feet. It used IBM card reader as input and an IBM card punch as output, these punch cards were used for external memory storage. Its clock speed is 100KHz doing about 5000 10-digit number addition per second, compared with current fastest supercomputer Fagaku with 2GHz clock speed able to do quadrillions float point calculations within one second. ENIAC was the first electronic simulated machine to run the program of neutron decay during neutron fusion, which cannot be solved through traditional mathematics. At that time, some female programmers emerged such as Klara Dan, Betty Jean Jennings and Fran Bilas, etc. They studied the machine's logic, physical structure, operation, circuitry, not only able to understand the machine computation but also the ENIAC machine itself. The difficulties and problems with the machine ENIAC served as a catalyst to the research result in a decisive chapter in the history of automation calculation.

In 1944, a project to create an analytical calculator, given the name of Electronic Variable Automatic Computer (EDVAC). A solution of gradually emerged during this project was the stored program. It was stated in *the First Draft of a Report on EDVAC*, published by von Neumann, a Hungarian-American mathematician, physicist and computer scientist. This was the first scientific document to highlight an overview related with the new system of programming and the theories of numerical and sequential automata through stored program. Later on, computer scientists predicted the future major components of the computer systems: the arithmetical logic unit (ALU), the control unit, the memory to record the numerical data and instructions, input devices and output devices. As Claude Bernard (a French physiologist) noted: *"Sciences are studies analytically, they are taught synthetically... When Science cannot be taught synthetically because it's not sufficiently developed. A science is not science until it is synthesized."*

Von Neumann's essential contribution was to demonstrate a programmable sequential automatic numerical calculator with a stored program. While the Turing Machine, an idealized and abstract model of a computer invented by Alan Turing in 1936, denoted by TM, is a collection of the following things:

A finite set of conditions q1, q2 ... qn, m-configurations, supplied by an one-way infinite or one-dimensional tape divided into a sequence of squared numbered cell, each carrying a symbol.

1. A tape head, a read write head, can read content of the cell in one step that the machine scanning the content of the cell bearing either a symbol or a blank.
2. The machine is automatic, that is, in any given moment the behavior of the machine can be decided by its current state and the symbol it scanned. It typically can do three actions: print symbol S_i on the tape-by-tape head, the tape moves one square to the left L and goes to state q_j, print symbol S_i on the tape-by-tape head, the tape moves one square to right R and goes to state q_i.

3. A state register stores a finite of states including exactly one *Start* state when begin execution, one or more *Halt* state that execution terminates. The other states have no functions except only names: q1, q2, q3, ..., qn.

4. A set of rules tell machine based on the configuration of the tape head, the active cell: how to change state, what to write on the tape, and where to move the tape. The rules are analogous to the machine code instructions in the computer. The machine is like a black box, given a certain input. The rules decide what kind of operations the black box need to perform.

Alan dedicated his research on computing machine from mathematics. In his famous paper *On Computable Numbers with an Application to the Entscheidungsproblem*, which was the first to show that there exist classes of problems having no algorithmic solution. After this paper was published, he went to Princeton and got chance to know von Neuman. In his other famous paper *Computing Machinery and Intelligence*, Alan denoted the idea of digital computer, which is a human computer following a set of fixed rules that human has no authority to deviate from them in any detail. It is analogous to a human who has unlimited paper supply to do the calculations. Alan's digital computer, as he wrote, consists of the three parts: Store, Executive and Control. It was universally classified as discrete-state machine that in this machine a quite finite of state could jump to another state, even though strictly speaking there is no such machine because everything moves smoothly.

Characterized the family of analytical calculator with a stored program, this machine is a computer structure that eliminate the defect of Babbage's machine and external program made the leap from family of analytical calculator to von Neumann's machine. The revolutionary of artificial logic automata was born, capable, without human intervention, execute any kind of algorithmic program within the physical limit of this machine. The concepts of universal Turing machine possess the large capacity of memory characteristics, it has a limited set of precisely defined instructions that makes the programs translated into machine readable code understanding the algorithm of the program. The instructions are automatic sequential operations with symbol-manipulations capability, large problem-solving capability and the capability to simulate any other Turing machine when programmed. These mathematical notions of Turing's universal algorithmic automation obviously provide the theoretical model for all the computers in the future.

The *Rube Goldberg Machine*, well known throughout the world, fascinates millions of youths to create and image their owns. In United States, there are even Rube Goldberg machine contests in high schools and colleges. The ideas of the event are to encourage youths to invent the fancible machines designed from human imaginations and beyond, the machines also indicate foolable inefficiency at the same time. Counterparts the Rube Goldberg, a famous English cartoonist William Heath Robinson, his masterpiece, or the dictionary recognized term *Heath Robinson Contraption*, is an inventive machine that is creative, ingenious, and over-complicated. In order to honor Heath Robinson, the first machine engineered to compare all the possible starting positions of the two tapes named *Heath Robinson*, it was used in world war II to break a high-level German Enigma Code generated by a teletypewriter in-line cipher machine called Lorenz SZ40/42. With the many incredible hindsight, Thomas Harold Flowers, an English engineer, recognized the downsize of a simple batch job. He proposed a more advanced sophisticated replacement using a completely electrical design through thermionic valves, or vacuum tubes. It was a device with the capability to control the electrical current flow in high vacuum between electrodes. This new breakthrough machine is called *Colossus*. In this machine, the number were stored in bi-quinary registers, the operations were synchronized through an internal clock, the conditional branching logic can be accomplished through hardware. *Colossus* is the forerunner of the modern computer at that time, it proved to be faster and more efficient than the Lorenz cipher SZ42 machine.

The *Heath Robinson Machine* and the *Colossus Computer* propelled the electrical machine design and engineering. However, they are all programmed through either punched tape, or complex hardwired machine's basic components. A new chapter of computer design, compute memory systems, has emerged after lots of researches and explorations. More and more computer engineers realized that main memory design was the controlling factor in machine's architecture, the constructing of large reliable storage devices was one of the hurdles in modern computer design. It was recognized very earlier that computer's memory should have the following properties: erasable and overwritten by new data, long period of time storage, inexpensive and easy to construct, possible getting the stored data in short period of time.

The first idea is thermal memory tried by Mr. Andrew Donald Booth, a British electrical engineer, who joined the early developing of magnetic drum memory. This thermal memory consisted of a small drum whose chalk surface can be heated by a series of small wires. It is two inches long and two inches wide and able to hold 10 bits of data per square inch. The cooperation with his father led the production of disk-pin that is able to store the data. Furthermore, during the manufacture process, a simpler system of using fine wired was produced. But ultimately the thermal mechanism memory was replaced for subsequent machines.

The first reliable memory system gained widespread acceptance was acoustic delay line. It has been used in many early machines. The basic concept is using a circuit designed to delay a series of pulses into the transmission of a signal, the pulse represents a binary number and it fed back to the delay line to store the data for a short period of time. The numerous repetitive short delays add up together to accomplish the long-term storage. Mercury, alcohol and water have been tried as the medium, but finally nickel wire had been detected to have the great advantage of good carrying low frequency sound. A later version of the delay line applies the magnetostrictive effect by transducers, the magnetic core replaced delay line but the device can only apply for short-term memory, and information could not be immediately available, the first high-speed random-access memory designed by Frederic William to overcome this defect. William adopted the idea of cathode ray tubes (CRT) as a memory device. The William tube, or William-Kilburn tube, depends on the effect of second emission happened on CRT, the electron beams strike the phosphor causing illumination.

When the beam energy is reaching a certain threshold, the electron is out of phosphor and their travel generates the positive and negative charge, which subsequently accomplishes the write and read operation. The electron beam moves anywhere on the CRT and the compute access at any location, this is the basic concept of random-access-memory. William-Kilburn tube was widely used in early computers and some IBM machines because it can be built from known technologies and component. However, during this process, engineers had noticed the problem that the reading beam focuses on one of the tubes but electron tends to move around over adjacent areas. Another form of electrostatic storage tube of complete digital electrostatic was developed in RCA laboratory, it is called *Selectron*. It was a vacuum tube with the same design principal as William-Kilburn tube, but it stores the digital data as electron charge in William-Kilburn tube storage device, it had been started massive commercial production after the magnetic core memory becomes universal.

The magnetic-core memory, or core memory, was the first predominant form of random-access memory proving the foundation for large-scale reliable memory with economic cost. It uses hard magnetic materials as transform coil called toroid, the insulated or enameled wire threads through the core and more wires pass through each core, all the magnetic flux is contained in the core material. The state of each core is remembered by magnetic hysteresis, the smaller cores and wires, the more density of the core memory. With the design and development of the first semiconductor memory chip, static random-access memory (SRAM) was initially created followed by dynamic-random-access-memory (DRAM). The fast development of semiconductor led the rapid increase of storage capacity. Core memory dominated the market in the 1970's. For example, the mission-critical control system, Apollo Guidance Computer for NASA's successful moon landing used core rope memory.

Starting from vacuum tube to solid state transistor to integrated chips, the large-scale integration (LSI) technology drove the development of semiconductor memory and then microprocessor, the computer primary memory was moving away from magnetic memory to solid state and dynamic semiconductor memory. The cost, size and power varied dramatically over the years.

The real electrical computer development started from World War II. Konrad Zuse, a German civil engineer and computer scientist pioneer, invented and designed electromechanical computer in 1941. It was the world first fully automatic digital and programmed computer. Built with 2600 relays, it could do floating point binary arithmetic with 22-bit word length for aerodynamic calculation. Z3 is Turing complete, it can construct loop but no conditional branch, the simple binary operation coming from the book *Principals and Mathematic Logic* brought a big success. Z3 was destroyed during World War II, Zuse supervised to reconstruct it to display to the future generation years after the war.

Conceived by Harvard physics professor Howard Aiken, a pioneer in computing, the Automatic Sequence Controlled Calculator (ASCC) was built also called Harvard Mark 1. It is a room-sized and fully relay-based calculator. Von Neumann used this machine working on Manhattan project, he run the first program on Mark I. Similar to the ancient *Analytical Engine* designed by computing father Charles Babbage hundreds year ago for example, it used the function library to print a brief extract mathematical functions table, Harvard Mark 1 could calculate massive mathematical tables, a type of table could show various mathematical operation results.

Years later at the other side of Atlantic Ocean, a Small-Scale-Experimental-Machine (SSEM), initially better known as Manchester baby and later developed as Manchester Mark 1, was born in Manchester University research center. It was developed by Frederic Williams, Tom Kilburn, Geoff Tootill and other research students. As the first fully electronic machine, it had an initial memory of 32 words with each 32 bits stored on a single William's tube cathode ray tube and can execute stored program. With the more design and evolvement, it can do more complicated calculation with more memory added. The input and output hardware had more improvement with more circuits. The electrostatic memory had more words with more bits stored on CRTs. Kilburn wrote the first program in history consisting of seventeen instructions that can run on the electronic, digital and stored-program machine like Manchester Mark 1. However, during the operation of the Mark I, design problems were gradually emerged like the drum and the power supply.

By the time the World War II was over, the development of digital electronics in America was advanced in a steady and fast pace. The University of Pennsylvania Moor School has produced an all-electronic calculating machine, the Electronic Numeric Integrator and Computer (ENIAC). It laid out the foundation of stored-program computer. The Turing Complete, a machine given enough time and memory and instructions can solve any computational problems, accomplished extensive numerical problems calculations, especially for United States Army's ballistic research. ENIAC can do loop, condition and subroutine, except it needs the program originally hard wired into the machine. The Moore School team had conceived the idea of the Electronic Discrete Variable Automatic Computer (EDVAC) while constructing ENIAC. The initial design of EDVAC was constructing a mercury delay-line memory, a binary serial processed bit by bit one bit at a time. Von Neumann proposed the idea of separating memory and computing units that data movement and computing works happen simultaneously, so bits need be processed in parallel to speed up the calculation. But the final decision was to seek a simple version with a serial electronics machine rather than parallel machine. However, Von Neumann submitted a report title as *First Draft of a Report on the EDVAC*, it lays out the design concept of automatic digital computing system and embodies the stored-program principals.

The Institute of Advance Study (IAS) computer, the Binary Automatic Computer (BINAC) and the Universal Automatic Computer (UNIVAC), all played very important roles in the computer machine development. The Whirlwind computer developed by MIT could be classified as one of the most important projects. Whirlwind I was a vacuum tube computer with digital electronic computing and real time output. It also was the first computer calculating in parallel on magnetic core memory.

Whirlwind II was designed to serve United State Air Force Sage air defense system. Whirlwind operated on 16-bit word every cycle in bit parallel mode, it was sixteen times faster than other machines in that era. It laid out foundation for future CPU architected in bit-parallel mode. Years later, IBM developed and was commercial a series computer machines: Model 650 magnetic drum calculator, Model 701 electronic data processing machine, 7000 series of mainframe computers are the company's first used transistors. 7030 stretch, played a major role in the design of later IBM System/360. It is the most successful computer family in IBM history.

Look back first before looking forward. The electronic technology revolution and booming during World War II and after the war pushed the computer industry development throughout the world. Wrapped up the computing history trail, as a software developer, let me back to the programming world to depict my understandings and summaries on the programming languages.

Code for fun! Let me walk down the deep to try to fumble if I can gain something both important and interesting.

LANGUAGES
SKELETON SHRUG

There are only two kinds of languages: the ones people complain about and the ones nobody uses.

- Bjarne Stroustrup

AS A HUMAN BEING, WE cannot separate from language. Human language is composable, is an aspect of the mind that makes us unique human. It is also the most complex cognitive function that our brain execute. Its main purpose is expressing, "I like C#", three words jumped out from my mouth yet composing of subject, verb and object. It tells us many: "I" maybe a programmer, "C#" maybe attractive and is not hard to learn, "I" might be enthusiastic on programming, and "I" might not be a dumb person, etc. That's the powerful of human language, it is creative, it is productive, it is imaginative, it is systematic and it is also abstractive. Human language can be classified as written, oral and nonverbal based on the formality. Based on the geographic region on the earth, they can be categorized into different language families: Indo-European language, Afro-Asiatic languages, Altaic languages, Sino-Tibetan languages, Austro-tai languages, Dravidian languages, Caucasian languages, Niger-Congo languages, Austronesian languages, Amerindian languages, etc. Comparable to human language, computer languages can be categorized as machine languages, assembly languages, and high-level languages from algebraic view.

2.1 Machine Language

At the very beginning, machine was built on the hardest way, we can think of CPU is packaged through sets of registers connected by wires, CPU execution is actually the state transition, the electrical switch signals are changed from on to off back to on, or the presence and absence of voltage. The specific on and off states can be represented by corresponding bit 0 and 1, the presence of voltage denoted by 1 and the absence of voltage denoted by 0, this is positive logic or vice versa the negative logic, this is machine language. The language of the machine, which CPU reads, understands and speaks. No matter how basic the machine is built up, as long as we have input devices that can input mixed strings of 0s and 1s, we can control CPU execution to generate the desired output. The long sequence of zeros and ones represent instructions to order the CPU to perform specific tasks, such as load, store, jump, or arithmetic logic unit (ALU) operation on one or more units of data in the registers or memory. Machine language is the oldest, lowest level and the only one language that digital computer can understand. It also called machine code, a string of binary digit or bit of 0 and 1. The ASCII value for letter "A" is 01000001 but displays "A" on the monitor screen. For text "Hello!", it is "01001000 01100101 01101100 01101100 01101111 00100001". Different operating systems translate the programming languages to different machine binary code, different digital machine typically "speak" and "understand" different machine language, different computer may have different size of the machine code instructions such as 32-bit still in use and 64-bit is very common now.

The computer was divided into three basic components by computer scientist von Neumann decades ago but still remains today: The processor is the brain of the computer, the memory is the bones of the computer, and the input output are the arms and legs of the computer. The processor, the CPU, is further divided into the computation, which is the Arithmetic and Logic Unit (ALU) performing the arithmetic and logical operation, and control unit. All these components are wired connected. The below diagram shows the very basic information of the computer components:

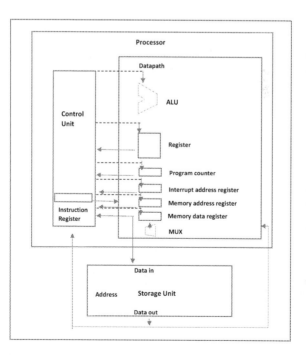

Figure 2.1.1: CPU components

The "arithmetic" organ is datapath, it consists of execution unit like ALU, the registers and communication path between them, it contains most of the states of the processor. The state includes the program counter, interrupt address register, and the program status register. The implementation of the hardware sets the clock cycle time. The clock cycle time is determined by the slowest circuits operating during a clock cycle period within the processor.

Input bits are fed into one at a time, one per clock cycle, for example: 000111000:

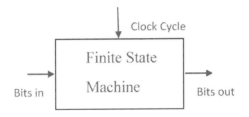

Figure 2.1.2: FSM Bits flow

The circuit is designed that have output for one clock cycle when input bits changes from 0 to 1. We can draw the below state transition diagram:

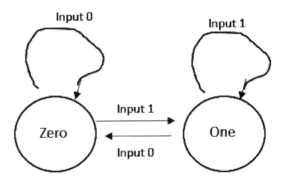

Figure 2.1.3: State transition diagram

The state transition of 0 and 1 drives machine running, consider the following example:

constructing a Turing Machine for language $L = \{0^n 1^n \mid n \geq 1\}$

This represents a language composed of 0s and 1s, if w is the string, and w = 000111, Turing Machine should accept it. First this machine is in state "0" with input 0, it circles by itself with same input 0 until input changes to 1. It moves to right changes to state "1", it circles itself with same input 1 at state "1" until input has 0 and changes to state "0". It follows the same pattern again and again keep computing until it enters the halt state. The finite memory of the machine and any input number breaking the flow control can stop the machine. In usual case, the machine can run without errors until reaching the maximum number n and no more inputs.

Yes, it is true that we can write machine language directly with string of bits code since both program and I/O data can be represented by 0s and 1s, and program does not need translator step from higher level language convert to machine code, the program runs faster one step reaching the goal. However, it is just too tiresome, error prone and difficult to read and debug. Besides, machine language is not portable, it depends on computer platform and architecture. Different machine, the instruction format, data format, ALU logic instruction and branch instruction, all maybe different, one bits-string pattern represents addition and may represent subtraction in another machine. That's why IBM adopted the method of series PC production when they were designing IBM360 in 1960s. Series PCs may have here and there hardware difference, but the instruction format, data format and I/O system are almost the same, in this way it reduced the issues of software compatible. Series PC is also called compatible machine. In addition, when a machine language runs, the operating systems such as Windows, Linux, MacOS act as hosting environments providing services like I/O. Different operating systems have different service programs, the machine language is more focused on the system running the program than on how the program solves a problem. Almost all programming languages finally compiled into machine recognizable machine code to execute. There are some languages compiled into bytecode, a specific pseudo instructions not native machine languages, such as Object-Oriented language Python and interpreted language PHP.

.NET C# application is strong type managed source code, it is compiled into Microsoft Intermediate Language (MSIL), which is a set of CPU-independent instructions, then feed to Just-in-time compiler (JIT) to be compiled again to against the Common Language Runtime (CLR) to generate CPU-specific machine code. Below is a sample of another way to generate machine code through Native Image Generator (ngen.exe). Ngen.exe is a tool to create C# application executable native image, usually an *.ni.exe file containing compiled CPU-specific machine code.

A very simple C# console application program:

```
static void Main ()
{
        Console.WriteLine("Welcome to read my book.");
        Console.ReadLine();
}
```

Compile the code in Visual Studio 2017 to generate ConsoleApp.exe. Ngen.exe can install the executable into the native image cache on the local computer location:

C:\WINDOWS\assembly\NativeImages_v4.0.30319_32\ConsoleApp\7c450a61e8b1c5db3fbbcb3b1843b84a\ConsoleApp.ni.exe

C:\WINDOWS\Microsoft.NET\Framework\v4.0.30319>ngen install "C:\TestCode\ConsoleApp\ConsoleApp.exe"

Microsoft (R) CLR Native Image Generator - Version 4.8.4320.0

Copyright (c) Microsoft Corporation. All rights reserved.

1> Compiling assembly C:\TestCode\ConsoleApp\ConsoleApp.exe (CLR v4.0.30319) ...

Below image is part of the machine code stored in file ConsoleApp.ni.exe

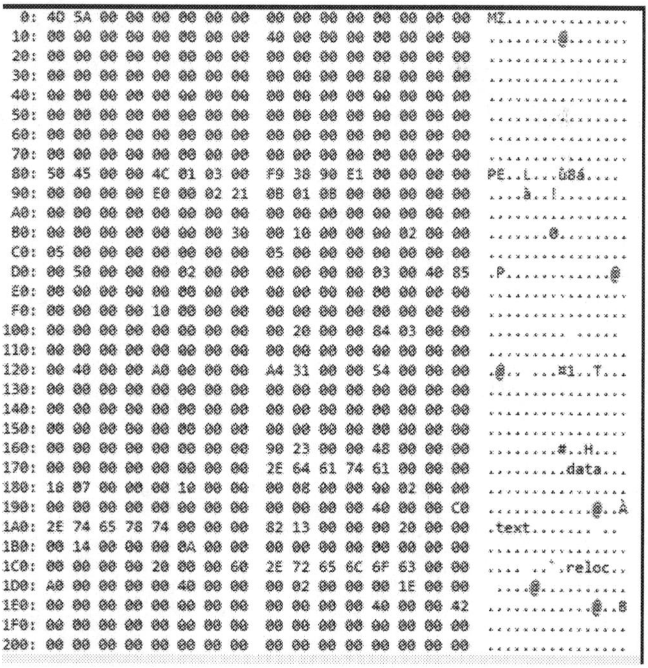

```
  0: 4D 5A 00 00 00 00 00 00  00 00 00 00 00 00 00 00  MZ..............
 10: 00 00 00 00 00 00 00 00  40 00 00 00 00 00 00 00  ........@.......
 20: 00 00 00 00 00 00 00 00  00 00 00 00 00 00 00 00  ................
 30: 00 00 00 00 00 00 00 00  00 00 00 00 80 00 00 00  ................
 40: 00 00 00 00 00 00 00 00  00 00 00 00 00 00 00 00  ................
 50: 00 00 00 00 00 00 00 00  00 00 00 00 00 00 00 00  ................
 60: 00 00 00 00 00 00 00 00  00 00 00 00 00 00 00 00  ................
 70: 00 00 00 00 00 00 00 00  00 00 00 00 00 00 00 00  ................
 80: 50 45 00 00 4C 01 03 00  F9 38 90 E1 00 00 00 00  PE..L...ù8.á....
 90: 00 00 00 00 E0 00 02 21  0B 01 0B 00 00 00 00 00  ....à..!........
 A0: 00 00 00 00 00 00 00 00  00 00 00 00 00 00 00 00  ................
 B0: 00 00 00 00 00 00 00 30  00 10 00 00 00 02 00 00  .......0........
 C0: 05 00 00 00 00 00 00 00  05 00 00 00 00 00 00 00  ................
 D0: 00 50 00 00 00 02 00 00  00 00 00 00 03 00 40 85  .P............@.
 E0: 00 00 00 00 00 00 00 00  00 00 00 00 00 00 00 00  ................
 F0: 00 00 00 00 10 00 00 00  00 00 00 00 00 00 00 00  ................
100: 00 00 00 00 00 00 00 00  00 20 00 00 84 03 00 00  ......... ......
110: 00 00 00 00 00 00 00 00  00 00 00 00 00 00 00 00  ................
120: 00 40 00 00 A0 00 00 00  A4 31 00 00 54 00 00 00  .@.. ...¤1..T...
130: 00 00 00 00 00 00 00 00  00 00 00 00 00 00 00 00  ................
140: 00 00 00 00 00 00 00 00  00 00 00 00 00 00 00 00  ................
150: 00 00 00 00 00 00 00 00  00 00 00 00 00 00 00 00  ................
160: 00 00 00 00 00 00 00 00  90 23 00 00 48 00 00 00  .........#..H...
170: 00 00 00 00 00 00 00 00  2E 64 61 74 61 00 00 00  .........data...
180: 18 07 00 00 00 10 00 00  00 08 00 00 00 02 00 00  ................
190: 00 00 00 00 00 00 00 00  00 00 00 00 40 00 00 C0  ............@..À
1A0: 2E 74 65 78 74 00 00 00  82 13 00 00 00 20 00 00  .text........ ..
1B0: 00 14 00 00 00 0A 00 00  00 00 00 00 00 00 00 00  ................
1C0: 00 00 00 00 20 00 00 60  2E 72 65 6C 6F 63 00 00  .... ..`.reloc..
1D0: A0 00 00 00 00 40 00 00  00 02 00 00 00 1E 00 00   ....@..........
1E0: 00 00 00 00 00 00 00 00  00 00 00 00 40 00 00 42  ............@..B
1F0: 00 00 00 00 00 00 00 00  00 00 00 00 00 00 00 00  ................
200: 00 00 00 00 00 00 00 00  00 00 00 00 00 00 00 00  ................
```

Figure 2.1.4: Machine code of C# ConsoleApp.exe application

2.2 Assembly Language

If the bits 0, 1 and hexadecimal code of machine languages are coded for machine, the assembly and high-level languages are coded for human because they are designated readable by humans. The bit stream of 0s and 1s binary instructions change the state be "off" and "on" of the electricity trans-flowing in the machine wire circuit. Certain bit streams represent a certain of instructions. CPU and register keep working when receiving the instruction. It is very hard to write machine binary code directly, computer engineers write in a language that intuitive to human being easy to understand, high-level language. The language has logical keyword "*And*" "*Or*", same as some operators "*&&*" "*||*", but how to convert the human-understandable language context to the machine code? Assembly language plays the role. It is a bridge to translate and convey the high-level language to the machine-speaking binary code. Assembly languages did not exist at the time of the stored-program computer was introduced. The first assembly language was developed in 1940s, at that time the first modern electrically powered computer was also created, that's why the history of assembly language is closely mingled with the history of stored program computer because from then the communication and what language usage have become the main research and development direction for computing software engineers. The beginning computer's limited speed and memory drove computer programmers to have to write the difficult and manually tuned assembly language, it is written in paper first, then manually "compiled" into punch card. Both David Wheeler and Kathleen Booth and many other computer engineers devoted an inventible contribution to the assembly language design and growing.

Assembly language, abbreviated as asm, runs in stored-program machine that generated from languages compilers, in which the conversion process is called assembly. It uses text as input to CPU, register and ALU instead of ancient ways of wiring, plugging and switch flipping. Since assembly depends on the machine code instruction, it might specific to the computer architecture, it might also specific to the computer operating system. The below diagram shows the flow among from assembly language to processor and memory:

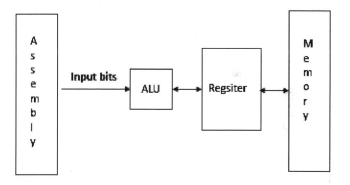

Figure 2.2.1 Assembly to processor

The assembly language covers the following concepts:

Mnemonic: Mnemonic originally means a device assisting in remembering something. In assembly language, it needs to remember the "operations" a machine can do, like "add", "st" and "mov" etc.

Bing Wang

Opcode: the machine language instruction specifying the operation to be performed.

Architectural register: the quickly accessible and fast storage location available to computer's processor.

Operands: the objects of a mathematical operation.

The machine code 0010 0001 0010 0011 is translated from the assembly language: add r1 r2 r3

meaning	operation type	source register	other source	destination register
machine binary code	0010	0001	0010	0011
assembly (opcode)	add (operand)	r1 (operand)	r2 (operand)	r3

Operation type has arithmetical logic such as "add", "sub", "mult", "and", "or", memory load and store such as "ld", "st", control transfer such as "jmp", "bne", complex such as "movs". Operands can be registered that values in register such as "add", and memorize that values stored into or loaded from memory such as "st". The above operation adds numbers in register 1 and register 2 and pushes the summation to register 3.

The type of internal CPU has stack, accumulator and register. The instructions set for stack are "push", "add" and "pop", for accumulator are "load", "add" and "store". For example, 8086 CPU has four general purpose registers: AX: the accumulator register divided into AH and AL, BX: the base address register divided into BH and BL, CX: the count register divided into CH and CL and

DX: the data register divided into DH and DL. The main purpose of a register is to keep a number, variable or operand. The size of the above registers is 16-bit:0011000000111001b in binary form, or 12345 in decimal form. These four general purpose registers are made of two separate 8-bit registers, for example if AX= 0011000000111001b, then AH=00110000b and AL=00111001b. When any of the 8-bit registers has been modified, the 16-bit register is also updated, and vice-versa. "H" is for high part and "L" is for low part.

The high-level code: z = x + y would need the following 8086 instruction sets:

```
LOAD r1, x      - load operand x to register r1
ADD r1, y       - add value of operand y to register r1
STORE z, r1     - store the value in register r1 to operand z
```

Look at another example of instruction sets:

```
ADD r1, r2, r3      - add the values of operands in r1 and r2 to the operand
                      in register r1: r1 ← r2 + r3
ADDI r1, r2, #1     - add immediate operand 1 to the value in register 2 and
                      store the summation in register r1: r1 ← r2 + 1
LHI r1, #42         - load high immediate value 42: r1 ← 42##0¹⁶
```

The below is an example of 8086 assembly print out a message:

```
org 100h
. DATA
msg DB 'Welcome to read my book$' - string need terminated as '$' to be
printed
. CODE
MAIN PROC
        MOV AX, @DATA   - move the data msg to register AX
```

```
        MOV DS, AX     - move the value in register AX to register DS
        LEA DX, msg    - load effective address is a shift-and-add
                         instruction. string msg will be load into
                         DX register
        MOV AH, 09H    - call the interrupt with function code 9 in
                         AH, DOS function 09h: display a string of
                         characters whose offset is specified by DX
        INT 21H        - call the interrupt handler 0x21 which is the
                         DOS Function dispatcher
        END MAIN
Ret
```

Writing a good assembly language can give you complete control over machine's system resources: CPU and register. The language touches memory address directly to push the value to register and retrieve the value from memory address. Robust assembly code is good for performance optimization such as touching device driver, low-level and embed system. Assembly languages have four types based on machine architecture: complex instruction-set computer (CISC), reduced instruction-set computer (RISC), digital signal processor (DSP) and very long instruction word (VLIW). CISC is a computer architecture that a single instruction can execute several low-level operations or is capable of multi-step operations or addressing modes. Examples of CISC processors are System/360, VAX, AMD, and Intel x86 CPUs. CISC assembly language is complicated that often executed by a little program called microcode. RISC designs the uniform instruction length for almost all instructions, and employs strictly separate load and store instructions. Examples of processors with the RISC architecture includes SPARC, MIPS, HP-PA, PowerPC, etc. RISC assembly language is designed to be pipelined in order to make the common operations as fast as possible. DSP is designed specifically for signal processing algorithms. It takes real-world signals like voice, audio, video, temperature, pressure, or position that have been digitized and then mathematically manipulate them. Its operations of "add", "subtract", "multiply" and "divide" are very fast. DSP assembly language often written by hand with substantial instruction-level parallelism. Conventional central processing units allow programs to specify instructions to execute in sequence only, while VLIW processor allows programs to explicitly specify instructions to execute in parallel.

In old days programming, computer engineers were very good at assembly languages and implemented them in all sorts of programming. In recent dozens of years, in order to improve programming productivity, assembly languages were gradually supplanted by higher-level languages, even though the debates have been on-going for quite a long time on pros and cons of assembly language over the high-level languages in terms of efficiency and performance. But if you understand the assembly, you will know how to write compilers for your high-level language. Sometimes we have to resolve an application bug and if the only input you have is a core dump, which is assembly code, at that moment you definitely need to know assembly. For unmanage source code like C / C++, creating an executable is a multistage process divided into two components: compilation and linking. The compilation is the processing from source code file to create object file, the object file contains a translation of source code into a machine language. Linking is the creation of single execution file from multiple object files. Compilation and linking are separate steps, they are independent functions where for large complex program, developers do not need do the whole recompilation if only part of the code need change, those unchanged object files can still use for linking. For managed code like .Net C#, the source code is compiled into Microsoft intermediate language (MSIL) and metadata generated along the way. A portable executable (PE) file contains the MSIL and metadata, just-in-compiler converts it to CPU-specific code. During the program execution, the common language runtime (CLR) locates and extracts the metadata from the PE file as needed, then the machine code is generated on demand when the assembly content is loaded and executed. Below is an example of C# code converted to JIT assembly:

C# code:
```
using System;
public class Program {
    public void Main () {
        Console.WriteLine("Welcome to read my book.");
    }
}
```

JIT assembly:

L0000: push ebp
- *preserves esp, the previous stack frame pointer, so it can be returned to at the end of the function.*

L0001: mov ebp, esp
- *moves the current stack position into ebp which is the base of the stack.*

L0003: push eax
- *push eax on the stack.*

L0004: mov [ebp-4], ecx
- *move content in ecx into the bytes at memory address ebp+(-4).*

L0007: cmp dword ptr [0x1dabc190], 0
- *read the 32-bit value from address [0x1dabc190] and do a subtract operation with immediate value 0, save the flags but do not save the result.*

L000e: je short L0015 — *short jumps, near calls, are jumps whose target is in the same module*

L0010: call 0x0ff14e50 — *call near procedures through a full pointer.*

L0015: nop — *does nothing.*

L0016: mov ecx, [0x8dfebcc] — *move content of address [0x8dfebcc] to register ecx.*

L001c: call System.Console.
WriteLine (System.String) — *call system function.*

L0021: nop — *does nothing.*

L0022: nop — *does nothing.*

L0023: mov esp, ebp — *move content of register ebp to esp.*

L0025: pop ebp — *pop ebp cleaning up the stack.*

L0026: ret — *pops the return address off the stack.*

You can use online tool called sharplab, type your C# code on the left, JIT assembly automatically shows up on the right:

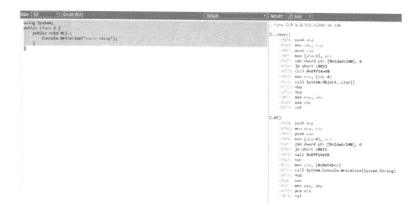

Figure 2.2.2 sharplab converting C# to assembly code

2.3 High-level Language (HLL)

Low-level programming languages deal with computer register, memory address, call stack and scalar operation, they are more understandable to machine. High-level programming languages refer to high level abstraction from machine languages and is designed for independent of computer system architecture. The language context is more user-friendly programming toward problem solving through logics and algorithms rather than how to deal with the underlying machine architecture. Sometimes when I was coding, I feel like I am talking with my computer, I was using English statements and symbols to create sequence of commands: hello, could you do this? Is my logic clear? Is my algorithm too convoluted? Coding in this pattern is better understandable or that pattern is more code maintainable? I am thinking, talking with my computer while typing the code in editor. It's a challenge and enjoyable process. The data types, objects, variables, complex arithmetic and logic expressions, functions, recursive, multithreads and memory garbage collection, etc. many aspects of the language you need to learn, think, apply to the specific problem solving. The higher abstraction allows for more advanced powerful techniques and provides better results such as slick GUI, 3-D animation, real time control, concurrency and multi threads background executions, etc. The languages have more safeguards preventing programmer from issuing commands that could potentially damage a computer, it doesn't give you too much control as low-level languages do. They are closer to human language and more understandable to human. Therefore, for programmers we always say: code for human not for machine. The first high-level languages were developed in the 1950s, today, they are still widely used. I believe all developers heard about BASIC, COBOL, FORTRAN, C, C++ and work on C++, Java, C#, PHP, Python and Ruby, etc.

High-level programming languages are grouped by paradigm. A paradigm is a way of thinking and solving problem. In science and philosophy, a paradigm is a distinct set of concepts or thought patterns. From paradigm point of view, we can divide the high-level languages as imperative languages, declarative languages, functional languages and object-oriented languages. Below diagram shows the layered structure of computer language:

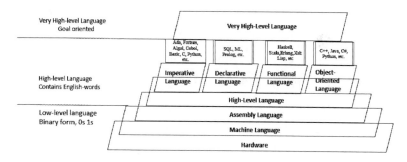

Figure 2.3.1 Language hierarchy structure

2.3.1 Imperative Language

Imperative language, from Latin, imperare is command, also considered as procedure languages, is the oldest programming paradigm. Imperative, from human nature language point of view, it is expressing command. The imperative mood in general used to give an order, give a warning, give an instruction.

Please join the team meeting every Monday, it is very important.
– give an order

Please continue monitor the server log, the transaction is too slow.
– give a warning

Please install the software based on installation guide. – give an instruction

From computer language, imperative language is designed to solve a problem through step-by-step statements or commands, the statements change the program's states. Ada, Fortran, Algol, Cobol, Basic, C, Python etc. are imperative languages. The hardware implementations for almost all machines are imperative. Each computer hardware is designed to execute the code in an imperative style. The earliest imperative language was machine language. The corresponding high-level language uses variable and expression to follow the imperative paradigm style. The program state is defined as memory content. The statements of changing computer's state also can be grouped into sections, originally called code blocks, then compound statement, finally today's procedure. One procedure is an imperative statement of execution. So, if I can use one expression to specify the imperative language, that is f(state) = statements.

Below is a simple C example program containing the comparative and print command:

```c
#include <stdio.h>
int main()
{
    int num1, num2;
    int *pnum1, *pnum2;
    printf("Please input number1: ");
    scanf("%d", &num1);
    printf("Please input number2: ");
    scanf("%d",&num2);
    pnum1 = &num1;
    pnum2 = &num2;
```

```
if(*pnum1 > *pnum2) {
        printf("%d is the larger", *pnum1);
}
else {
        printf("%d is the larger", *pnum2);
}

return 0;
}
```

The program reads two numbers and uses pointers through conditional logic, it conditional flows to determine the larger number to print. Imperative languages like C can provide a simple but computing efficient solution to the problem. Usually, each procedure needs to run from top to bottom to execute each statement. Programmers sometimes are criticized for writing spaghetti code.

Computation is performed as a direct change to program state. Imperative style is especially useful when manipulating data structures and produces elegantly with simple code. It focuses more on *how* a program operates. Programs change state information as needed in order to achieve the goal. Below is an example using numlist in Python:

```
summation = 0
for num in numlist:
    summation += num
print(summation)
```

The value of summation changes with each iteration of the loop. As a result, summation has state. The variable is tied to a specific register to maintain the state.

The basic unit of abstraction is the procedure, whose basic structure is a sequence of statements that are executed in succession, abstracting the way that program counter is incremented. Below is an example of C# with procedure call as one statement:

```
class Program
{
        static void Main()
        {
                Console.WriteLine("Enter a string with letter character
                only.");
                String text = Console.ReadLine();
                If (InputValid(text))
                {
                        Console.WriteLine(text);
                }
                else
                {
                        Console.WriteLine("${text} is invalid input.");
                }
                Console.ReadKey();
        }
        static bool InputValid(string text)
        {
                return Regex.IsMatch(text, @"^[a-zA-Z]+$");
        }
}
```

The above examples show many similarities of the basic structure of most high-level language and scripting language. The flow charts below illustrate decision-making algorithm very common in high-level language: conditions and loops.

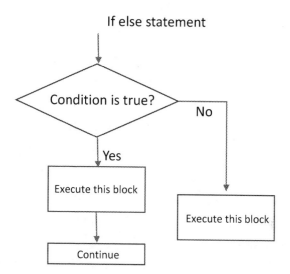

If else statement

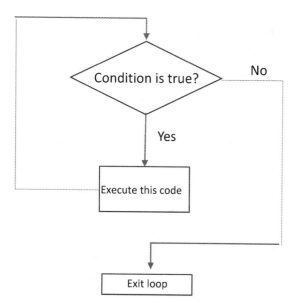

Loop statement

Figure 2.3.1.1 Flowchart of condition and loop

2.3.2 Declarative Language

If imperative language is how a problem can be solved, declarative language is what needs be achieved. It builds the program statements with computation or logic expression without specifying the control flow in the program. The declarative language is an umbrella term that it includes some language paradigms such as constraint programming that the relationship between variables is in a constraint to specify the target of solution. The declarative languages, varied by the domain they design to work with, also called design-specific language (DSL). Some other declarative languages include hybrid language like "makefile", logic programming and declarative modeling languages.

The structure query language (SQL) is one of the declarative languages. SQL works with relational database management system. The code is declared to what the result should be and ignore how the result is generated. For example, searching a data record from a table: select * from person where LastName = 'lewis'. This line of code is trying to get the result of person record whose last name is lewis, it declares what program wants to know and not intend to know how the result carries out. So, declarative languages are context free, or context independent. Other examples like meta language (ML), pure Lisp and pure Prolog, etc. Declarative language focuses on expressions that are what without adding how. For example, html code <button type="button">Click Me</button> tells the browser to display an button with the text "Click Me" on it but without telling browser how to display the button, so Html is not Turing-complete language, it only allows you do specific thing. Declarative language is also usually simple to write and read, so they are more popular in web user interface declaration. For example, the below javascript library React uses JSX for defining components:

```
const demoComponent = props => {
        <h1>{prop.message}</h1>
};
```

The above React example does not actually touch a Document Object Model (DOM) element. It simply declares that an element should be rendered without actually manipulate the DOM itself. Writing React code helps you think of what the component should look like instead of how to accomplish the result. It helps you understand the control flow of how a series of predictable and replicable mutations drive the state goes, how the principals apply to state changes of components. It additionally helps you understand that no explicit computation and condition instructions are needed. Declarative language does not place emphasis on the order of execution and control flow. It is the compiler who plays the role to make decision.

Below C# example code line declares remove all the items that have no children from the list:

```
var dataList = list.RemoveAll(i => i.HasChildren == false);
```

Below C# code lines implement the same logic in an imperative way:

```
bool foundMatch = true;
while(foundMatch)
{
      foundMatch = false;
      foreach(var item in list)
      {
            if (!item.HasChildren)
            {
                  list.Remove(item);
                  foundMatch=true;
                  break;
            }
      }
}
```

Declarative and imperative have their own pros and cons, which one to use and how to use them really depend on the software application complexity, but they all have their unique features.

2.3.3 Functional Language

Functional language is a type of declarative language. It is a way of constructing software application through creating pure functions. It emphasizes on the expression and declaration of functions instead of statements of execution inside of the functions. We need back to the invention of *lambda calculus*, or λ-calculus by Alonzo Church. Functions have been a critical part of calculus since it emerged in the 17th century. In the programming, functions can be sent to functions as arguments or returned from functions as results. Anything is computable if it can be computed by lambda calculus, which is equivalent to the computing ability of the Turing Machine. If imperative languages list instructions in sequential order to be executed by the computer, one at a time from start to end, functional programming focuses on processing input and output through a sequential of function calls starting from the top. We would like to say that the entire program is a big function composed of a chain of functions, evaluating first input and return first value, then second input with second return value, then continues, until no more value needs to be computed, and program terminates. For example, lisp language invented by John McCarthy in 1958 was a constant effort to find a straightforward and symbolic syntax for *lambda calculus* and its Turing complete. A lambda-expression is a list with the following syntax:

(lambda *lambda-list . body*)

The first element must be the symbol lambda. The second element must be a list, lambda-list, the *body* may then refer to the arguments by using the parameter names, it consists of zero or any number of forms.

The below lisp code samples denote the lambda expression:

```
(write((lambda (a b c d)
   (+ (* a b) (* c d)))
   1 2 3 4)
)
```

The output is 14

```
(write ((lambda (a b c d)
   (+ (* a (* d d))(+ (* b d) c)))
   1 2 3 4)
)
```

The output is 27

Lisp allows you to write anonymous functions to be evaluated only when needed in the program. These functions are called *lambda* functions. Many artificial intelligence software programs are written in lisp due to its quick and effective processing of symbolic information.

Functional programming has gradually taken on new approach and it shows more and more importance in the programming world. The ideal in functional programming is pure functions. A pure function is a function whose results completely depend upon the input parameters, and whose operation does not produce shared state and mutable data. The pure function's only result is the value it returns. They are deterministic, you can see from the following simple pure function:

```
sum(a, b)
      return a + b
```
sum function does not modify variables a and b, but only returns a + b as a result.

The following function is impure:

```
int x;
function impure()
{
      x = x + 100;
}
```

Another important of functional programming philosophy is immutability, that is not to modify data outside the function. Beyond the pure function's ideal, the functional programming hinges on first class functions and higher-order functions. A first-class function is a function that is treated as *a thing in itself*, capable of standing alone independently, high-order function is a function that operates upon a function, such as the following code sample for passing function as argument:

printsum(f)
print(f);
printsum(sum(1,2))
printsum is declared as taking argument f, which is another function sum, so it's a function passing to another function.

Big data is coming and functional programming is great for big databases, in-demand tasks, data analysis and machine learning.

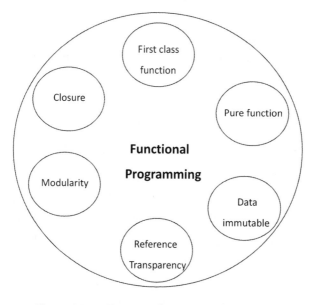

Figure 2.3.3.1 Functional Programming Features

2.3.4 Object-Oriented Language

Object-oriented programming (OOP) is a programming paradigm that relies on the concepts of object, which contains data and code, a modular design. Data is in the form of fields and code is in the form of procedures. We can say the world is composed of objects. An object is anything we can name and describe, it is "thing" that we want to encapsulate it to become an entity in our program domain, such as "Account", "Inventory", "Employee", etc. The goal of objects is to represent the business world through the application domain. Objects in the application domain collaborate each other through sending and receiving messages. The four principals of OOP paradigm are encapsulation, abstraction, inheritance and polymorphism:

- Encapsulation: the object's data fields are private, other objects can only access them through procedure call.
- Abstraction: the complexity of object is reduced through hiding the relevant of the data.
- Inheritance: sub-class can inherit properties and methods from one or more parent classes.
- Polymorphism: the ability of object to take on many different forms, such as a method with the same name can have different implementations in different classes.

OOP was developed to increase the reusability and maintainability of source code. I'll illustrate more detail in the next chapter.

2.4 Very high-level language (VHLL)

Very high-level language (VHLL) is a high-level programming language with a high level of abstraction, it is generated as a productivity tool designed to reduce the complexity and amount of source code. VHLLs are domain specific language incorporating higher data and abstract control, it limits to a dedicated purpose of task, so it is also known as a goal-oriented programming language. It does not require typical variable declaration like other high-level language, and it supports autotyping. Although it is designed for limited and specific use, in the modern programming language world, very high-level languages may have a broad and diversity usages for software products and services.

LANGUAGES COMPUTING SHRUG

Ideas are the source of all things.

– Plato

THE LANGUAGES I HAVE BEEN working on so far can divided into two categories: compiled languages and interpreted languages.

3.1 Compiled and Interpreted Languages and JIT Compiler

Compiled languages are languages that got translated into runnable binary machine code through a program called compiler. The compiler statically compiles the source code into object code, which is machine instruction, then linked by a linker into an executable. Once the binary code is generated, you can run it without looking at the source code again, just like most software are delivered as compiled generated binary codes. The generated binary code through compiler is destined to run faster than those generated at run time involving the translation process overhead. Interpreted languages, interpreter, is a computer program executing instructions directly written in the programming or script languages without compiling it into machine binary code to execute. Compiled languages are targeting the machine itself, while interpreted languages are generally read and executed by other programs. Think about your teenage child has a packet of pieces and need to assembly into a gadget, and the user instruction is written in Chinese. If your child does not understand Chinese and eager to build a gadget, you could provide two offers. One is if you understand Chinese, you could translate the instruction into English and hand over to him. He will try to assembly, connect the pieces by themselves based on the translated instructions. Each assembled part is preprocessor after compilation, then linked the complete parts, output object files to final gadget, also the product, the dll or executable file. The built gadget is the compiled version. During the process, your child has full control of the pieces and parts, he will think and try more just like controlling the memory usage and CPU resources. If he wants to change to build another gadget by adding or reducing some pieces, you could just simply write another version of instruction and handover to him, he will rebuild again quickly. Another offer is that instead of translating the instructions, you site besides him while he is assembling the gadget, you tell him how to do it in English based on the Chinese instructions, line by line, step by step, like a second command program. Finally, he still can produce the gadget but with longer time and limited maneuvers on the pieces and parts. This gadget is an interpreted version. If your child wants to build another gadget, you don't need tell all the instructions to him again, just that part of instructions need to add or reduce pieces, he may only need redo that part to build a different gadget based on your partial instruction. During the process, your child simply process based on your instruction like not having full controls of memory and CPU of machine.

Compiled language gives the excellent performance and complete OS access but also difficult to program. Traditional Fortran, C, C++, etc. are all compiled languages. Javascript language is a very good example of interpreted language, the source code is read and executed by the running browser program. Some early languages like Lisp, Basic and Perl, etc. are also interpreted languages.

Compiled and interpreted languages are two main mechanisms by which the languages are implemented, they are not mutual exclusive. Some languages are compiled ahead of time stored as machine independent code and then linked at run time to be executed by an interpreter or compiler. We call this mingled of compiling and interpreting the Just in time system (JIT). JIT originally was a philosophy in economic management not a technique. It first started in Japan in post-world-war-II era in many Japanese motor manufactories. The manager level sought minimum waste in all production lines. Kiichiro Toyoda, the founder of Toyota and the father of JIT, adapted the way at Toyota to handle small batch size but with more variety of parts that could be used to construct the assembly line. In its pure theory, just in time is a method where material arrives just on or in time when it is needed. Software industry has been using just-in-time compilation since 1960s. It is dynamic compilation that the program translation only occurs after a program begins execution. JIT compiler has the ability to store the already compiled machine code without translating it each time. The languages are compiled into bytecode during compiling time and generated machine native code through JIT compiler during run time. Bytecode, also portable code or p-code, is a form of instruction sets that have one-byte opcodes followed by optional parameters. A bytecode program can be executed by parsing or the instructions are directly executed. Just-in-time compilation improves the performance of interpreted program, because there is a runtime environment which profiles the application while it is running to generate more optimized code. Some examples of JIT are Java Virtual Machine (JVM), Common Language Runtime (CLR) and Android Run Time (ART), etc.

In 1996, Sun announced the first just-in-time compiler for Java platform, javac compiler converts java code into bytecode .class files. Java Virtual Machine (JVM) internally verifies class file at load time so that it needs little parsing or verification when it is time to compile. Java-based JIT compiler takes .class files as input converted into machine code that CPU executes directly.

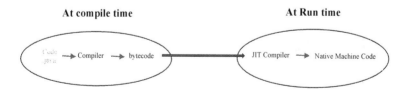

Figure 3.1.1 Java JIT Compiling

Microsoft has created several managed language compilers that target common language runtime CLR: C++, C#, J#, F#, and an intermediate IL assembler. These compilers check syntax analyzing the source code, regardless of which compiler you use, the output is a managed module, windows portable executable files PE32 and PE32+ for 32-bit and 64-bit windows. Part of the managed module is intermediate language code IL, at runtime, the JIT compiler compiles the IL into CPU instructions. The managed compiler knows more execution environment than unmanaged compiler. It gives the application a performance boost. If the application is running on Intel CPU and produces native code for Intel CPU, the managed compiler takes advantage of any special instructions offered by the CPU. The JIT compiler also smart to know where the code block does not need to run so it will not generate CPU instruction. The CLR can profile the execution environment and recompile the IL to native code when application is running.

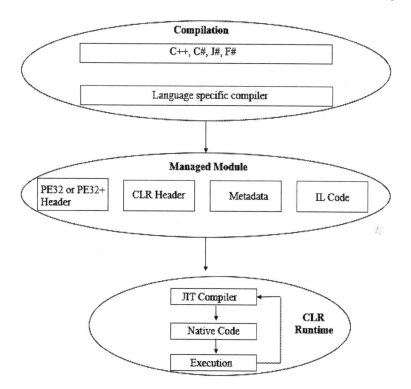

Figure 3.1.2 .NET JIT Compiler

3.2 Computer Languages Basics

When we were toddlers crawling on the floor or staggering to walk, the great thing we accomplished at that moment is babbling. That's our mother language we all first spoke even though we did not know what we were talking about. Out little brain CPU assimilate the surrounding inputs and process them to produce the "yaya" language. At grammar elementary school, we accepted formally language study and practice: characters, sentences, grammars, speaking and writing. Chinese characters are hieroglyphs, the most difficult characters to learn among all languages in the world. Likewise, the first computer language I learned is C in Unix at school, the Sun SPARC workstation was a huge magnet attracting me. Writing C language was just so enjoyable like writing Chinese characters that you may forget clock.

So, what's computing language basics? How it asks computer to work? Learning human language can help you express your thoughts, ideas, emotions, or maybe suffering, computer language is a kind of dull because you are talking with machine. What the language can produce are just a sequence of statements to instruct machine to execute to generate output that you can do further analysis. For example, the below simple language statements in C:

```
int a = 10;
int b = 20;
int c = a + b;
```

The below diagram tells you how the program asks computer to do the job:

Memory (RAM)	CPU
int a = 10; - declare variable a and store value 10 in the a's address	Fetch value from a's address and store in a register
int b = 20; - declare variable b and store value 20 in the b's address	Fetch value from b's address and store in a register
int c = a + b; - declare variable c, do the calculation of a + b and store the summation in the c's address	CPU do the mathematic of a + b

Figure 3.2.1 Computer Basic Work

Computer input is from connected devices: keyboard, mice, microphone, digital camera, etc. It is stored in the memory to wait for CPU processing. The final output flows to the devices in a human readable format. The output device includes monitors, printers, graphic output devices, speakers, etc. It is all about data and computation. Input and output are deal with data, arithmetic, conditional and looping are processed through computation. They are five basic elements of programming. For example, you purchase a book from online, you can select which book, quantity and your payment information from the browser running in your laptop or mobile device. Once the online book store processed your request, a confirmation of purchasing will be displayed on the screen and an order confirmation will be emailed to you. The total price plus tax calculation will be arithmetically calculated in the web server and data stored in the backend database. It is required a certain condition that check whether the book is in stock, otherwise will not execute the function mentioned above. It is also required to repeat perform the task of checking all the current stores to see if can locate the book until the condition no longer holds that finally shows "out of stock" on the screen.

Data can be number or text, the data types tell program how to deal with the data, it is an attribute of data. All languages have a finite set of build-in primitive types. Why called primitive? Primitive preserves the characters of the early stage in the evolution or historical develop of something. Primitive types can be extended to use to build the user defined types. Primitive types are atomic that cannot be decomposed into simpler types. They are part of core language and their elements got special treatment during compiling. The structured modeling language (SML) has five basic primitive types: bool, int, real, char, string, summarizing into two sections: logic and data. The size of data type is decided by compiler, or the machine architecture, 32bits or 64 bits. Computer memory, just like part of human brain, stores a sequence of cells, and the smallest addressable unit called byte. Each byte is identified, stored or accessed in memory as memory address. If the total bytes in memory is n, the addressable address is enumerated from 0 to n-1.

For computer language basics, let us start from data and data type.

3.2.1 Bool

> The binary is the underpin of all the science,
> culture and history. – binary philosophy

Truth, Veritas, Harvard's motto, the entire chapter of Philosophy is pursuing it. Does the truth exist or is defined contingently against false? Can a proposition be both true or false, or has to be either true or false? Is it absolute truth or false, or relatively?

Boolean data type is named after George Boole, a self-taught English mathematician, philosopher and logician, who first defined an algebraic system of logic in 19th century. In his famous book *The Law of Thought*, he wrote: *"The design of the following treatise is to investigate the fundamental laws of those operations of the mind by which reasoning is performed; to give expression to them in the symbolical language of Calculus, and upon this foundation to establish the science of Logic and construct its method; to make that method itself the basis of a general method for the application of the mathematical truth brought to view in the course of these inquiries some probable intimations concerning the nature and constitution of the human mind."* Boole was trying to take the logical principle in the form of algebra mathematical calculation, the boolean algebra. In the boolean algebra, all formula variables are truth values, true or false, denoted by 1 or 0 respectively. The set of these truth values are boolean domain. The basic operations of boolean algebra are conjunction, disjunction, and negation, the same as our logic operator *and, or, not* respectively. For example, the following boolean algebra formula:

$$x \wedge y = x \cdot y$$

x and y have the following probability inputs:

$1 \wedge 1 = 1 \cdot 1 = 1$
$1 \wedge 0 = 1 \cdot 0 = 0$
$0 \wedge 1 = 0 \cdot 1 = 0$
$0 \wedge 0 = 0 \cdot 0 = 0$

It is also the *and* logic operation:

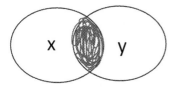

$$x \vee y = x + y - (x \wedge y) = x + y - (x \cdot y)$$

x and y have the following probability inputs:

$1 \vee 1 = 1 + 1 - 1 = 1$
$1 \vee 0 = 1 + 0 - 0 = 1$
$0 \vee 1 = 0 + 1 - 0 = 1$
$0 \vee 0 = 0 + 0 - 0 = 0$

It is also the *or* logic operation:

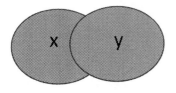

$\daleth x = 1 - x$

x has the following probability inputs:

$\daleth 1 = 1 - 1 = 0$
$\daleth 0 = 1 - 0 = 1$

It is also the *not* logic operation:

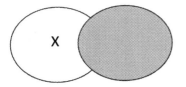

Boole strengthened the role of logic in symbolic algebra mathematic, which had profound influence in the algebra and philosophy. He is the founder of the algebra tradition in logic.

Almost all computer languages have bool logical type that can have only the values true or false. By default, the bool type is set to false. Some scripting languages do not have bool type such as Perl, which *if statement* returns true or false directly. Boolean logic can also be used to describe electromagnetically charged memory or circuit states that either charged, 1 or true, or not charged, 0 or false. The logic operations also apply to ALU's AND gate and OR gate processing. Bool type is actually one byte, but memory alignment may cause 4 bytes to be used on a 32-bit platform, or even 8 bytes on a 64-bit platform. This is faster to push around a four-byte Int32 than it is to work with individual bytes or bits. The below picture denotes boolean logic flow:

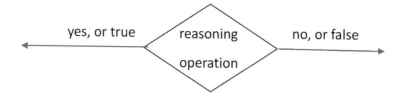

Figure 3.2.1.1 Boolean logic flow

3.2.2 Numbers

Our growing up are accompanied by numbers starting from counting 1,2,3… using our little fingers when we just learned to say "Mama" and "Papa". Numbers are the origin of mathematics, without numbers, there is no mathematic kingdom. Plato claimed that numbers exist in some mind-independent abstract heaven, it is ideas in people's minds. Pythagoreanism, a cult of ancient Greece, believed that numbers were the basis of the entire universe, and the whole universe ran on numerical harmony. The evolution of numbers developed in different ancient regions and times: Egyptian, Babylonians, Hindu-Arabic, Mayans, Romans, etc. Discovered evidence indicates that numbers and counting began with the number one, they came into being with the rise of cities. The counting history could be traced back to 4000 BC in Sumeria, one of the earliest civilizations. The ancient people tried to keep track of the livestock, crops by carving tally marks into cave walls, bones and stone, which led to the introduction of numbers, and the invention of arithmetic also started. This counting system extended to early numerals system with the civilization developing, then started to develop writing down large numbers. The large number system requires to write down many symbols to record a single number and create new symbols for each large number. Finally, the numerals were later developed to 1,2,3,4,5,6,7,8,9 with the time. A position system developed in Babylonians allowed you to reuse the same symbols by assigning the symbols different values based on their positions in the sequence. Indian mathematicians developed a decimal of base ten position system. Today, we mostly take our number system for granted. Number system has been grown up to be one of the mature academic branches. Numbers are mathematical entities whose function is to express the size, order or magnitude of something or other. The earliest written records denote the positive integers:1,2,3..., then extended to rational numbers, the most venerable one other than integer number. In computing ecosystem, number can be integers or decimals with fractional parts, or floating points. But why not make all numbers be floating point with decimal part be 0 for integers? It just cannot be thought that way, because one is that somethings in real world are just not fractional, a running animal, even with 4 legs, it is still a whole animal not fractional. The second is that integer is also used for program flow control, by counting, or by condition true or false, converted to number is 1 or 0, so it jumps from one value to another. The third is that integer used in computing is far predominant than float point and is much faster in CPU processing.

The world is not ruled by numbers, it is ruled by the physics who is expressed by the abstract concepts and numbers. A man does not live in a car, but use it as a transportation tool to take him to anywhere he desires, similarity, human is not playing with numbers, but use the numbers to understand and express all the science and technologies, in turn scientists seek the simplicity of calculation. Therefore, ultimately going against Plato's philosophy idea: *Numbers Rule the World!*

3.2.2.1 Integer

You may have asked your naught kid that how many eggs in this box? How many candles Mom should buy for your birthday cake? How many different colors of crayon we should use to draw a tree? What you are asking, in effect, is teaching your eager-to-learn kids start to count and keep track of how many objects we are interested. The whole number, like us people, cannot be broken up into small pieces. Integer, from the Latin word integer, means untouched, whole. The symbol for integer is 'Z', the German word 'Zahlen' means numbers. It is the set of positive numbers, zero and negative numbers. But is 0.999…. is an integer? No, for 0.999… 9 goes to infinity, but there is another form of whole number, which is 1. So, in order to learn the history and concept of integer, let's find out how infinity was evolved? There are tons of books and articles describing infinity, which tells us that infinity is one of objects we scarcely understand. The universe, the vast collection of animate and inanimate objects, the immeasurable collection of observable and unobservable objects, is infinitesimally decomposable and infinite in expansion. When the universe started to exist or does it always exist? Would the universe go on forever or end at a finite point? If we stick on a direction, can we travel forever? We are living on the earth, we have star, sun, moon and other planets in the universe, is the space finite or go on forever? The symbol of infinity is the lazy eight curve, lemniscate, ∞, one can travel endlessly around this curve. But early Greeks questioned about infinity said that virtually any matter in the world can be divided into smaller and smaller pieces and will finally reach a tiny piece that cannot be divided further. Atomists believe that matter is composed of an infinite number of indivisibles. Over two thousand years ago, mathematician Euclid proved his famous theorem that the sequence of primes can go infinitely, even today, his theory stands as a terrific reasoning model. The positive whole number 1,2,3,4,5.... can go endlessness, which rarely historic mathematical recordings tell us who discovered it.

What about zero? Zero was invented independently by the Babylonians and Indians, an India mathematician who is said first endorsed the number 0. Before zero, it was a dark space for how to calculate a problem if there was nothing there. But the India mathematician struggled with how to make zero respect the usual operations of arithmetic. As Bhaskara II suggests that if a number divided by 0 equals infinity, then 0 times infinity must equal to every number n, then all number are equal. This is why in mathematics, number n / 0 = undefined, and in computing runtime, if the program encounters number n divided by 0, run time error will be thrown out. Zero is such a unique, special and controversial integer. What about negative number? The India mathematician used negative number when positive numbers were adopted to represent fortunes and negative numbers were used to represent debt. The ancient Chinese used rods to represent negative numbers. Negative numbers were finally accepted into the number system in the 19th century. There were numerous uses of notions for negative numbers: small circles before the number, a slash through the number, back rods, symbol m, and finally Europeans invented the symbol + and – to represent positive and negative numbers, which is popular till today we all use this way throughout the worlds.

Almost in all computing languages, you can find integer type to represent the whole numbers. It is supposed to match the natural "word" size on the given platform: 16 bits on 16-bit platforms, 32 bits on 32-bit platforms, 64 bits on 64-bit platforms. However, for backward compatibility purposes some compilers prefer to stick to 32-bit int even on 64-bit platforms. How the integer numbers be represented in the computer? The most fundamental unit of computer memory is the bit, which can be a tiny magnetic region on a hard disk or a tiny transistor on a memory stick. It is like a switch, either "on" or "off", value of 1 or 0. A collection of 8 bits is a byte, a collection of 4 bytes 32 bits is a word. An integer type is a normal 4-byte bits collection, 1 word. For example, integer 65 written in binary form is 01000001, or 01 000 001, where each 3-binary-digit is an octal because each digit represents a value from 0 to 7. Hexadecimal form is another way to represent memory, each digit represents a value between 0 and 16: 0100 0001., so it is 0x41 or #41. The following table denotes the values in different base: base 2, base 10, or base 16:

Binary	Decimal	Hexadecimal
0000	0	0
0001	1	1
0010	2	2
0011	3	3
0100	4	4
0101	5	5
0110	6	6
0111	7	7
1000	8	8
1001	9	9
1010	10	A
1011	11	B
1100	12	C
1101	13	D
1110	14	E
1111	15	F

The block of computer memory for integer 65 is represented as three columns: offset column, a number indicting the which byte is shown first on the row; memory content column, a hexadecimal form; and a value column, the interpretation of the memory content, either text or numeric value. So as the following shows:

0 (offset column) | 00 00 00 41 (memory content) | 65 (values)

Since each bit has two possible states, for n bits combined to 2^n possible states, so we could represent numbers from 0,1,2... to $2^n - 1$. For 32-bits unsigned integer, computer could represent value from 0 up to $2^{32} - 1$. Considering negative number, computer sacrifices one bit to indicate whether the number is positive or negative, so the 32-bit signed integer range becomes -2^{31} ..., 1,0,1, ...2^{31}

The difference between signed and unsigned numbers is the maximum precision that the value may hold. Unsigned numbers are always positive that no negative numbers allowed and can use the maximum range of positive values. Signed numbers may be positive or negative, but their range is more limited than an unsigned positive value.

For the example of number +65 and -65, the below is 1's complement representation of signed integer. For +65, the representation rules are the same as signed integer representation, for -65, we can follow the below approaches:

I. -65 in 1's complement:

+65 = 01000001

-65 = 10111110

II. unsigned representation of $2^n - 1 - X$ for -X, so -65 for n = 8

-65 = $2^8 - 1 - 65$ = 256-1-65 = 190 = 10111110 = $2^1 + 2^2 + 2^3 + 2^4 + 2^5 + 2^7$ = 190

The following table shows the binary form changes for 1's complement:

Most Significant Bit	Magnitude	Decimal	Most Significant Bit	Magnitude	Decimal
0	000	0	1	000	-7
0	001	1	1	001	-6
0	010	2	1	010	-5
0	011	3	1	011	-4
0	100	4	1	100	-3
0	101	5	1	101	-2
0	110	6	1	110	-1
0	111	7	1	111	0

For the same +65 and -65, the below is 2's complement. For +65, the representation rules are the same as signed integer representation, for -65, we can follow the below approaches:

I. -65 in 2's complement:

+65 = 01000001

-65 = add 1 in 1's complement 10111110 = 101111111

II. unsigned representation of $2^n - X$ for -X, so -65 for n = 8

$-65 = 2^8 - 65 = 191 = 10111111 = 2^0 + 2^1 + 2^2 + 2^3 + 2^4 + 2^5 + 2^7 = 191$

The below table shows binary changes in 2's complement:

Most Significant Bit	Magnitude	Decimal	Most Significant Bit	Magnitude	Decimal
0	000	0	1	000	0
0	001	1	1	001	-1
0	010	2	1	010	-2
0	011	3	1	011	-3

0	100	4	1	100	-4
0	101	5	1	101	-5
0	110	6	1	110	-6
0	111	7	1	111	-7

The representation of integer is a string of bits. The order or sequence of bits in memory is called endianness, further expressed as big-endian (BE) or little-endian (LE). A big-endian store the most significant byte at the smallest memory address, on the contrast, a little-endian store the least significant byte at the smallest memory address. For example, a four-byte integer 0A0B0C0D storing in address a, a+1, a+2, a+3, the big-endian stores 0A in address a, the little-endian stores 0D in address a. Big-endian is network byte order, the communication protocol such as transmission control protocol (TCP) and internet protocol (IP) use this order for integer field, such as IP address and port numbers. On the other hand, the processor architecture of intel processors uses little-endian byte ordering, such as x86, RISC-V implementation. The difference of big and little endian sometimes may bring issues when data transfer in network with source and destination computers have different endian, or the memory content transmitted in computers with different endian.

Integer overflow is a very severe and easy prone programming error in computing world. For example, for an 8-bit machine, when integer 127 added 1, it results in -128, violating program assumption and leads to unexpected program behavior. For some critical real-time systems, the integer overflow compromises the program's reliability and security and may cause irreparable loss. One example is that European Space Agency fired rocket Ariane

5 On June 4 1996, but the integer overflow on 16-bit system led to the final explode of the rocket. A board of inquiry investigated the causes of the explosion and got the conclusion that the cause of the failure was a programming error in the inertial reference system. A 64-bit floating point number representing the horizontal velocity of the rocket was converted to a 16-bit signed integer. When the number was larger than 32,767, the maximum integer allowed in a 16-bit signed integer, the conversion failed and throw run time exception, software failed and rocket launch has disaster as the consequence.

3.2.2.2 Floating Point

Floating-point arithmetic is a very esoteric subject even though floating-point is ubiquitous in computer system, but many early minicomputers and microprocessors did not directly support floating point in hardware, none of the processors had a built-in floating-point capability until 1980s, when many hardware manufactures have their own type of floating point. Intel 8086, a co-processor also called floating-point unit FPU was designed to do the floating-point instruction. In later years X86 CPU production, a X87 FPU was also produced to team with the new CPU. Floating-point (FP) data type represents numbers with a fixed number of significant digits and scaled to an exponent with a fixed-numbers of digits. There're two floating primitive types: float and double. Float is also called "single-precision floating point", double called "double-precision floating point". We focus "precision" when dealing with floating-point numbers. Floating point numbers are represented by humans as the following:

$123.45 = 12345 \times 10^{-2}$
$12345 = 1.2345 \times 10^{4}$
$-123.45 = -12345 \times 10^{-2}$
$-12345 = -1.2345 \times 10^{4}$

The above examples tell us that a floating-point number is represented by using two numbers, the exponent and the mantissa, and two signs, one for exponent and one for mantissa. Mantissa is old terms for significant. 123.45 is logarithm, 123 is significant, 10 is base, -2 is exponent, 0.45 is mantissa, decimal point. The decimal point .45 tells the compiler to represent the value using a floating-point primitive type. Conceptually, a floating-point number has a sign, an exponent, and a significand (mantissa) allowing the representation of the form $(-1)^{sign} \times$ significand $\times$ base^{exponent}. So, for 64-bit double precision, the sign bit is bit 63 either 1 for negative or zero for positive, the exponent bits are the bit range from bit 52 to bit 62, the significant bits are range from bit 0 to bit 51. For 32-bit float type single precision, we have the sign bit 31, 8 bits after sign bit for exponent and remaining 23 bits for mantissa. In base 10, a number 0.12345 represents $1/10 + 2/100 + 3/1000 + 4/10000 + 5/100000$, it is the power of the base 10. The number 0.11111 represented in binary is: $1/2 + 1/4 + 1/8 + 1/16 + 1/32 = 31/32$, it is the power of base 2. So for fraction 31/32 represented in binary form would be 0.11111, normalizing this number $0.11111 = 1.1111 \times 2^{(-1)}$, sign of mantissa is 0, mantissa = 1111, excess 7FH exponent = 01111110 in binary, so the binary representation of the number is 0 01111110 1111000000000000000000000, regroup becomes

0011 1111 0111 1000 0000 0000 0000 0000, Hexadecimal representation of this number is 3F780000.

So why call it floating point? Because for number 123.45, the decimal portion .45 can "float", it can be placed anywhere relative to the significant number 123, there's no fixed number of digits before and after the decimal point. Thinking about in computers, numbers are represented in units consisting of a fixed number of binary digits. If we want to represent an integer, it is easy for us to just write down the number in its binary format and put it in register. But when treating decimal number, we could do it in a couple of ways. One is that splitting the register into two parts in which one part stores the digits before the decimal and another part stores the digits after the decimal, this is fixed point and digit never moves anywhere inside the register. The problem with this method is that it is not flexible and sometimes wasteful because what about when you are trying to store a decimal number with a very big integer number but a very small decimal number? The second technique is with floating point that allow the point to flow around. If it is a very big integer number, then decimal part float to the right, the opposite way the decimal part float to the left if a very small integer number with a big decimal number. The floating way may not as accurate as a fixed way, but it's very flexible, it could express the same unit of length when trying to measure the distance between galaxies and the diameter of an atomic nucleus.

The speed of floating-point operations is usually measured in terms of FLOPS, which is a critical characteristic of a computing system especially when involving intensive mathematical calculations. Because the mathematics with floating-point numbers require a great deal of computing power, many microprocessors come with a math or numeric coprocessor, a chip, specially carries out the operation on floating-point numbers.

Floating-point computing has been carried on for over a hundred years. Leonardo Torres Quevedo first started the floating-point arithmetic computing concept when he was designing an electro-mechanical version of Charles Babbage's Analytical Engine. Then Konrad Zuse of Berlin completed Z1, Z3, and Z4, continued to push the decimal floating-point numbers' computing forward. As of May 2022, Fugaku of Japan was superseded as the fastest supercomputer in the world, it can reach the speed of 442 quadrillion calculations per second, 442 petaFLOPS defeating the Summit system. Since June 2022, USA's Frontier debuts becoming the most powerful supercomputer in the world, it reaches 1102 petaFlops with additional energy efficient under the liquid-cooling system.

Floating-point also requires scientists cautious and diligent calculation, a tiny mistake may bring catastrophic error. The Spain's S-80 submarine program is one of the vividly example. Officials in Spain had a big and fat problem that A new submarine built in the county has to receive a major tummy tuck because it is overweight by more than 70 tons. Scientists worried that it would not resurface once waterborne. The hefty problem was traced to a miscalculation, someone apparently put a decimal point in the wrong place.

3.2.3 Text

Data can be expressed as qualitative and quantitative, or simply as word expression and number statistics. Text formatted data is one of the very important data types in computer languages. The text data type stores any kind of text data, can be both number and characters, can be both single-byte and multibyte characters that the locale supports. A *large object* type refers to an instance of a text or byte data type.

3.2.3.1 Character

The char data type represents character data in a fixed length filed, it takes 8 bits to form 1 byte storage size for one character and there are 255 variants for 8 bits. With char type, the values are ranged from -128 to 127 and unsinged char type the value ranged from 0 to 255. Before writing about char data type, let us review the ASCII and UNICODE. ASCII, American Standard Code for Information Interchange, is a character encoding standard for text data in computers and on the internet. Before the ASCII standard was born, computer manufactures had their numerous ways of representing characters in the computer systems, it is impossible for machine communicating to machine because different machines talked different languages. IBM engineer Bob Berner, the father and creator of ASCII, sent a proposal to the American National Standards Institute (ANSI). The main idea of the proposal is developing a standardized character set for the computer communication. Since computer can only recognize numbers, the basic 128 characters, including letters, numbers, punctuation marks, and control codes, each can be encoded as a standard numeric value represented in 7-bit binary form. The binary form consists of various sequence of 1s and 0s, 128 different possible combination of seven 1s and 0s. For example, letter 'a' is represented by the number 97 in the binary form 01100001. ASCII offers the easy compatible data communication based on a universally accepted character set system that can be understood by both humans and computer machines. ASCII brought a leap for the software design that developers can easily implement programs with text bits conversion. The ASCII table is divided into three different sections: The non-printable of system codes between 0 and 31, lower ASCII between 32 and 127, higher ASCII between 128 and 255.

Type the "format-hex" PowerShell command in windows 10 can display the ASCII encoding for a plain text file, which content is simply "ascii shrug!":

```
PS C:\Bing> format-hex plaintext.txt


        Path: C:\Bing\plaintext.txt

        00 01 02 03 04 05 06 07 08 09 0A 0B 0C 0D 0E 0F
00000000  61 73 63 69 69 20 73 68 72 75 67 21              ascii shrug!
```

Figure 3.2.3.1.1 ASCII encoding for plain text file content "ascii shrug!"

ASCII standard only has the ability to support 256 characters, which limits many languages like Asia languages not use Roman alphabets. To overcome this limitation, Unicode was created. It can represent many characters excluded in ASCII and quickly became the most common character encoding system in the computers communication. The standard is maintained by the Unicode Consortium, defines current version 14.0 covering 144,697 characters including letters, digits, diacritics, technical symbols for written languages throughout all of the world, emoji and non-visual control and formatting. It has three character-encoding-forms: UTF-8 with 8 bits mainly encode English characters, UTF-16 with 16 bits encoding the most commonly used characters and UTF-32 with 32 bits represents all of the characters. HTML 5 supports both UTF-8 and UTF-16. Major operating systems like Microsoft Windows utilize UTF-16. The code points are written as hexadecimal numbers and have a prefix of U+. For example, A is U+0041, a is U+0061 and á is U+0061U+0301. Emojis are Unicode astral plane characters, they provide a way to have images on your screen without actually having real images but just font glyphs. With the born of Unicode, all characters could be represented in a confirmed unified way, which across languages, platforms and machine architectures. It provides the foundation of building globalized software, it sets the milestone for people communicating through the software in their own languages. With the rise of web development, Unicode is especially vital for global communication, and the representation of text under the Unicode standard is no doubt push the internet waves to a new high peak.

But why we need encoding? When you hit the keyboard letter 'A', the input device sends an array of 65 to computer memory, then memory send to monitor convert bit array of 65 back to symbol 'A' and displays on the monitor, that is how the input and output transform and communicate through bit array digits of 0 and 1 but actually representing a character. Think about numbers can easily add, subtract, compare, search, sort, etc. because they have numeric values. What about characters? How to sort letter 'O' and 'P'? How to search a letter 'K' from texts? Through encoding, each character has a value of number, then we can compare, search or sort the letters the same way as we compare, search or sort numbers.

Some programming languages even start to make Unicode the default encoding, or include some features that enable Unicode throughout a single project. Older languages like C and C++ started in ASCII only and later added Unicode support. For example, C has actually two different char types: char and wchar_t. "char" may be one byte long, "wchar_t" may not necessarily. Most managed languages, like C# and Java, tend to be newer and have items like Unicode support built in from the ground up.

3.2.3.2 String

In mathematical logic, a string is a finite sequence of symbols that are chosen from a set of characters and numbers. In computer programming, a string is not a primitive data type but a very important data type in almost all modern languages. String is alphanumerical and used to represent and manipulate an array of data structure of bytes storing a sequence of characters through encoding. Since it allows the space in the sequence of characters, that's why string needs use quote at the beginning and the end. For languages C, C++, C# and Java, etc, they have char and string types respectively. For language javascript, python, swoft, etc., they treat char and string both as literal. Almost all modern languages support string literals with unlimited character length. Some old languages support string type with at most 255 characters. In the programming languages, string type can statically allocate computer memory for fixed number of character elements, or dynamically allocate the memory with a variable length of character elements.

String is immutable, or simply unmodifiable. The string object itself cannot be changed, but the reference of the string object can be changed. For example, string text = "hello"; you changed the reference of string object "text" be the string literal object "hello". Here the mentioned reference object will be described in detail in the following section. A string such as "123" is not the same as the number 123 because a string is a sequence of characters whereas a number is a sequence of digits.

3.2.4 Object

Charles Peirce, the father of pragmatism, defined the broad notion of "object" as anything we can think or talk about. In general sense, apple, air, juice, mood, disbelief, fear of dog. In strict sense, it refers to anything defined as "being", in philosophy, being is any existing thing either material or immaterial. In computer programming, an object is related with computing field, a variable, a data structure, a function. In this section, the object type is mainly illustrated.

Object-C, any Apple iOS developer knows, is a simple and small yet powerful language setting to the extensions to the standard ANSI C language designed to enable sophisticated object-oriented programming. It pushes out a new set of data types corresponding to the primitive types in ANSI C, such as NSInteger:

```
#if __LP64__
typedef long NSInteger;
#else
typedef int NSInteger;
#endif
```

From the above NSInteger implementation in Object-C, you will see that when developing in Object-C, you do not know the processor architect, 32-bit or 64-bit, you need use NSInteger. When building 32-bit applications, NSInteger is a 32-bit integer, when building 64-bit applications, NSInteger is a 64-bit integer, similarly, in the NextStep heritage, there're some similar data types such as NSString, NSNumber, etc. *Next* was the computer company that Steve Jobs formed after he quit Apple in 1985, and *NextStep* was a UNIX based operating system together with the Objective-C language and runtime, it became Mac OS X after Apple acquired *NextStep*. NS comes from *NextStep*. These types are treated as value types, in the object comparison call such as *isEqual* method, the bottom implementation is to compare two pointers' equality. The same apply to C++ language. Objective-C and C++ were first developed around the same time. The original developing goal of Objective-C was looking to extend C language with *SmallTalk*-like semantics, whereas the original developing thoughts of C++ was really trying to add *classes* to C language.

In Java JVM, there are a set of primitive class types wrapping the corresponding primitive types, such as Integer to int, Double to double, etc. Java is an object-oriented programming language, but its basic primitive values are not objects, they do not support some of the useful features of objects such as instance methods, subtyping and generics. As a workaround, the original standard library provided wrapper classes, each of which storing a single primitive value and presented it as an object. Each primitive object needs a primitive class, to which class the int values should belong. A lot of existing code assume that an object modeling a basic primitive value belongs to a wrapper class. By defining the basic primitive types with primitive class declarations, primitive types can be converted to objects and the objects back to the primitive types, and the useful features of objects such as instance methods, subtyping and generics can be applied.

A bit difference from Java on the build-in types is that all data types in .NET are inherited from System.Object, such as int is the alias of System.Int32, bool is alias for System.Bool, etc. and they are interchangeable as the following code snipe. There's no boxing and unboxing for the below cast.

```
int a = 123;
System.Int32 b = 123;
```

Unlike Java, there's a complete set of primitive wrapper classes which are reference types corresponding to the primitive value types, C# build-in types are value types with a certain of operations, such as ToString, Convert.ToInt32, GetHashCode, etc. Since C# represents all primitive data types as objects, it is possible to call an object's method on primitive data types. All the primitive data types in C# inherit from value type class and in turn from System.Object. This way you can treat value types as reference types. For instance, integer can be inserted to an array of object type through boxing. Everything in .NET world is object, an object of the *Integer* class can hold a sub-object int value through boxing, an int value can be extracted from *Integer* class through unboxing. You can think of this in terms of the Liskov Substitution Principle that an object and a sub-object must be interchangeable without breaking the program, actually this is more a semantic rather than merely syntactic relation. This unified type hierarchy is called the Common Type System (CTS). C# is also a statically strong typed language and its type and name of the variable must be known before they can be assigned to a value.

3.2.5 Operator

Operator in linguistic, is an auxiliary performing a grammatical operation modifying one statement to make a different statement, or join multiple statements together to form a more complicated statement, such as the word *and, or, not, since,* and *so,* etc. We think, speak, read, and write, we construct our expression statements through these conjunctions, we go through our cognitional reasoning and analysis. The series of repetitive reasoning, analysis and investigation produce conclusion: correct or wrong, good or bad, possible or impossible. It is pervasive and judgmental both in mind cognition and in our daily life context, from minds to machines. In logical world, the operator symbol is a connector linking two or more expressions to produce final statement, depends on the meaning of the operators, such as conjunction *and, or,* negation *not,* conditional *equal,* etc.

Similar with it, in the mathematical and programming domains, an operator is a symbol that represents a specific mathematical or logical action, it tells the compiler or interpreter to perform a certain mathematical or logical operation to generate output. The operators have tight connections with expressions. Many expressions cannot leave operators. Operator can be unary, binary, or ternary. Unary operator has one operand and its value changed after operation such as ^x, ++x, !x, etc., binary operator functions on two operands such as x + y, x != y, or x == y, etc., and ternary operator deals with three operands to produce output such as x = y == 0 ? m : n, "?" is ternary operator. From the view of computer architecture, the operation is an action carried out to perform a given task. There are five basic types of computer operations: store, control, input, process, output. The CPU, the brain of the computer, performs complex tasks by executing billions of individual operations per second. The ALU, the soul of the computer locates in the processor, performs arithmetic and logic operations on the operands based on the instruction. We have arithmetic operation and operators, logical operation and boolean relational operators, bytes bitwise operation and bitwise operators.

When we were studying elementary math, we learned that operators have precedence and associativity. Operators with higher precedence execute before operators with lower precedence, when precedence is the same, associativity plays the role, as the following:

$x + y * z$

$(x + y) * z$

The same precedence concept applies for logical operators, as the following:

x || y && z	equivalents to	x || (y && z)
x && y && z || h	equivalents to	((x && y) && z) || h
!x && y || z	equivalents to	((!x) && y) || z

Furthermore, bitwise operators for byte data calculation also have precedence:

~x << y & z ^ m | n	equivalents to	(((~x << y) && z) ^m) | n

With the example of language C++ and C#, the following table dictates the operators' kinds, descriptions, simple examples, whether can be overloadable and precedence:

operator kind	symbol	operator name	example	overloadable	precedence
Unary	.	member access	a.b	no	
	++	post-increment	a++	yes	
	--	post-decrement	a--	yes	
	+	positive value of	+a	yes	
	-	negative value of	-a	yes	
	!	Not	!a	yes	
	-	bitwise complement	-a	yes	
	++	pre-increment	++a	yes	
	--	pre-decrement	--a	yes	
	()	Cast	(int)a	no	
	*	value at address	*a	no	
	&	address of value	&a	no	
Binary	*	Multiply	a * b	yes	
	/	Divide	a / b	yes	
	%	Remainder	a % b	yes	
	+	Add	a + b	yes	
	-	Subtract	a - b	yes	
	<<	shift left	a << 1	yes	
	>>	shift right	a >> 1	yes	
	<	less than	a < b	yes	
	>	greater than	a > b	yes	
	<=	less equal to	a <= b	yes	

operator kind	symbol	operator name	example	overloadable	precedence
	>=	greater equal to	a >= b	yes	
	is	type is or is subclass of	a is b	no	
	as	type conversion	a as b	no	
	==	Equals	a == b	yes	
	!=	not equals	a != b	yes	
	&	logical and	a & b	yes	
	^	exclusive or	a ^ b	yes	
	|	logical or	a | b	yes	
	&&	conditional and	a && b	via &	
	||	conditional or	a || b	via |	
Ternary	??	null coalescing	a ?? b	no	
	?:	Conditional	a==true? b: c	no	
Unary	*=	multiply self by	a *= b	via*	
	/=	divide self by	a /= b	via /	
	+=	add to self	a += b	via +	
	-=	subtract from self	a -= b	via -	
	<<=	shift left self by	a <<= b	via <<	
	>>=	shift right self by	a >>= b	via >>	
	&=	and self by	a &= b	via &	
	^=	exclusive or self by	a ^= b	via ^	
	|=	or self by	a |= b	via |	
	=>	Lambda	a => a + 1	no	

Table 3.2.5.1 Language Operators

Bing Wang

ES6 Javascript provides a new operator called spread syntax (...). Its creation drives many programming language build spread operator (...). The spread operator allows an iterative such as array, vertex, map, set, string, or object to be expanded. It can be used when all elements from an array needed be included, such as the following code:

const a = [1,2,3];

let sum = sum (...a);

The rest parameter (...) collects the rest of elements in the array:

function myfunc (a, b, ...elements)

{ console.log(elements);}

myfunc(1, 2, 3, 4, 5);

the output is [3, 4, 5];

The spread-out operator (...) can spread out a string into the individual characters:

let array = ['a', 'b', ...'cd'];

console.log(array);

the output is 'a','b','c','d'.

So, the three dots (...) represent the spread operator, the rest operator and spread-out operator. The spread operator unpacks the elements of an iterative object, the rest parameter packs the elements into an array, the spread-out operator spreads the string into individual characters.

For object, the spread operator can be used to represent all elements of the object as arguments, such as the following:

myfunction(...obj);

let objectClone = {...obj};

For new operator, an array can be easily through new thanks to spread operator:

let mydate = [1910,1,1];

let newdate = new Date (...mydate);

With spread operator, we can easily concatenate two arrays and two objects:

let array1 = [1,2,3];

let array2 = [4,5,6];

let conarray = [...array1, ...array2];

let object1 = {name: 'jack', id: '100'};

let object2 = {name: 'john', id: '200'};

let mergeobj = {...object1, ...object2};

ReactJs by its language nature does not support self-by unary operator when the variable is declared in its state. We cannot program like the following:

this.setState({count:this.state.count++})

By doing this.state.count++, the state is mutated. Do remember, ReactJS's state is only transformed but not mutated. Besides, setState is an async function. Usually React batches a bunch of setStates. The value of this.state.count is the value at the time you make the request. A better solution is to call a function through lambda to get evaluated at the time the setState gets executed:

```
this.setState((pstate, props) => ({ counter: pstate.counter + 1 }));
```

Like C# and Java, the string interpolation operator wraps expression in {}: "The word is: ${expression}", ReactJS JSX also uses it frequently. Everything between "{" and "}" is javascript code, it is a replacing placeholder, the babel compiler translates specific JSX into javascript:

```
handleClick(e)
{
console.log ("click me");
}
<button onClick={handleClick()}>Click me</button>
```

The regular expression has a list of operators for pattern matching in a given text. The most frequent used are: matches any single character ".", matched at most once "?", matched zero or more times "*", etc. There are plenty of other operators in different languages. Python's floor division "//" and exponent "**", in the sequence "in" and not in the sequence "not in". TypeScript's bitwise right shift with zero >>> and Angular's two way bindings with model operator [( )], etc.

In programming language, operators are the major components predefined in the languages but different in syntactic or in semantic. At the same time, the compiling, overloading and operand coercion are functionalities also involved. Just like the linguistic operators penetrating into people's daily speaking and writing, the operators of programming languages will forever pervade to support the vivid and robust of the running programs.

3.2.6 Value type and Reference type

In .NET framework, value type is all primitive data types plus struct. They are simple structure, one int, one character, a lot of them accumulate in the program and occupying a small amount of memory. A value type derives from System.ValueType, the "light-weight" type holds the value in the static memory, the value is known at compile time. When a value type is created, a memory space is allocated to store that value, when this value assigns to another variable, another copy of data is created in another memory space to hold the exact same value with two variables work independently. When passing parameters with value types, the parameter passed by another copy of parameter data, thus the changes of parameter data in function will not affect the passing parameter value. Static memory is stack with LIFO mechanism. It is very easy to track the stack by pointer, when a block is freed, the pointer is just moved down to the next available block. Use stack only when you know the data size be allocated before compiling and not too big. In the multithreads programming environment, each thread has its independent stack to hold the data value and they are not shared. Garbage collector cannot access the memory in stack to free the memory space when deallocating.

Reference types are class, interface, array, data collection classes such as List, Dictionary, etc., reference type extends System.Object and holds the reference, or address of the object, not object itself. When reference type variable assigns to another variable, a copy of the reference assigns to create another reference but pointing to the same object. When passing reference type parameters, the values passed by reference, or address of the value, the changes to the reference type variables affect the passing parameters values. Reference types point to another area of memory called heap. The size of the value is dynamically allocated at run time. The access of heap is random without a specific order. You can allocate, access and free heap memory at any time, which makes the track of heap very hard. The size of heap memory is limited by the virtual memory size. In the multithread environment, the value in the heap is shared across threads, and it is application specific. The Garbage Collector erases the dangling reference objects to free memory during deallocation. Class is a very typical reference type. Its objects are created and accessed from heap and are pass-by-reference.

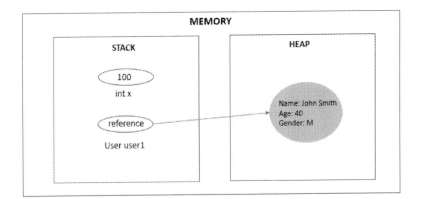

Figure 3.2.6.2: value and reference represented in memory

Memory is a set of word sequence each with an address and a content. The address is a value with fixed size and address length. The content is another value of fixed size and word length. Reading and storing content are through the load and store operations. An object is a concrete entity as a value in memory. It has its state, which is the value of some value type. You can see from the above picture that the name John Smith is a snapshot of this object user1's state. The state is mutable. Reference type is created at two memory location, one is location in stack holding the object user1's reference, or address, one is location in heap holding the composite data of user1 object "John Smith", such as his name, age, and gender, etc. Once the reference in stack is being deallocated, the user1 "John Smith" becomes orphan object, then it will be collected by garbage collector.

In .Net, value type inherits from System.ValueType, which further inherits from System.Object, the same for all reference types inheriting from System.Object. In Java, there is no a super type parenting both primitive types and reference types. It's not single rooted. The value type is intended to be the third form of data type available in the future version of Java. Beside the current primitive data types and object reference types, the future value type is "code like class but work as int", which indicates that value type will be a composite type - code like class, but lack the identity without object header - work as int. Reference types in Java are those types holding reference, or address of the dynamically created objects.

There's a simple litmus test for whether a language supports pass-by-reference semantics as a traditional swap function:

```
swap (Type a, Type b)
{
Type temp = a;
a = b;
b= temp;
}
a = ...;
b = ...;
swap(a,b);
```

If after calling this function, the value of a and b is swapped, then this language supports pass-by-reference semantics.

In C++, a value type is a type defined by its state and its state alone. Two integer variables with values 10 behave the same in terms of 0s and 1s bit sequence, assignment, expression and operation except for two different memory address. Value types are copyable that there are always copy constructor and copy assignments. Two shape objects may have same states such as color, texture, position, but may end up with two different shapes: circle and square. Such object type defined by both its state and behavior called polymorphic. Polymorphic type is about identity, what kind of object it is? If really want reference-like object, then the copy constructor and copy assignment need be explicitly disabled, like the below code snippet:

```
class ReferenceType {
private:
ReferenceType & operator= (const ReferenceType &);
ReferenceType (const ReferenceType &);
public:
ReferenceType () {}
};
```

The above copy constructor and copy assignment declared as private to prevent the caller calling constructor copying and object copy assignment.

In language C, the corresponding value types are basic types and enumerated types. The reference types are derived types such as pointer types, array types, struct types, etc. A variable definition has different meaning at the time of compilation and at the time of linking the program. Every variable is a memory location, which has an address can be accessed using ampersand "&" operator, it is an address in memory as a pointer. NULL value of a pointer variable, also called NULL pointer, indicates no exact address to be assigned. C's struct, class for C++', Java and C# are reference type, its property or state, and method or behavior, can be access by memory access operator ".". The object resources are dynamically allocated in memory when initialized and destroyed when object instance is no longer alive.

3.2.7 Generic Type

C++, Java and C# compilers all support generic feature. Generic uses the type parameter and has no specific data type. A type parameter is a placeholder for a particular type specified when creating an instance of the generic type. It also known as parametric polymorphism in some languages. With the more and more complex business concepts need be implemented in software, generic gains more and more substantial importance to help code reuse. So, what is reuse, if simply put, it is an item used more than once, whether it is reuse for the same function, or reuse for new function. From a broad philosophy view, reuse has long history that is more ostentatiously on resource preservation. We can use a cornucopia of phrases to describe this mindset: reuse, reusing, reuse recycling, reclamation, reused or reclaimed products, and reuse options. In software engineering, we have reused programs, or infrastructures. In global environment, we have cradle to cradle, zero waste, waste reduction, or waste reuse, the key to build green earth. Reuse concept is powerful, and analogues of the inheritance and polymorphism of object-oriented-programming.

Generic is primarily to have type parameters on your type, they are also called parameterized type or parametric polymorphism. It started from C++ templates, which has class template and function template. Template, just like documentation, has template to simply fill your content and become your version. Templates describe one technique to achieve the generic design. Template is a feature of C++ program that allows classes and functions operate with generic types:

template<class identifier> declaration;

template<typename identifier> declaration;

Below is a very simple C++ snippet showing generic programming:

```
#inlcude <iostream>
using namespace std;
template <typename T>
void print(T printedData)
{
      count<<printedData<<endl;
}
int main()
```

```
{
    print(100);
    print("ascii shrug");
    print(0.999);
    return 0;
}
```

Java generic was designed to add additional feature to Java's type system, it allows a type or method to operate on various types while provided compile-time type safety. It is different from C++ template, java has run time JVM but type validation happens at compile time, the run time does not need to know. Initiating a java class needs a call to constructor without knowing the parameterized typed. Java generic is bounded, or restricted, also called bounded type parameter. The bounded type parameter is followed by its upper bound, the super-class, such as the following:

public <T extends Animal> List<T> animalsCanRun(List<T> allAnimals) {}

A wildcard "?" can be used to relax the restrictions on a variable. A parameterized type is accepted with all its subclasses - the upper bound, and is accepted with all its super-classes - the lower bound, such as the below function declares an upper-class Animal bound with the *extends* keyword:

public void animalsRun(Collection<? extends Animal> animals) {}

the below declares a sub-class bound with the *super* keyword:

public void dogBark(Collection<? super Dog> dogs) {}

Java generic can also be unbound without restriction. The "?" is wildcard used for representing any type accepted as type parameter, such as the following unbound type is useful when you don't care about the actual type passed through:

```
public void printAll(List<?> list) {}
```

It can print list of integers, strings, or customized user types. So <?> tells us you know the generics and your code can work with any kind of objects. Then what's the difference between <?> and <object>? <?> is generic, is more restrictive. It represents some types but not necessarily type of object. From .NET point of view that every type is subclass of System.Object. List<object> can be the list composed of integers, strings, user types that need additional boxing and unboxing, such as ArrayList(). But List<?> can be list composed of the same types, can be list of integers, list of strings, or list of user types that avoid boxing, unboxing and explicit casting, thus improve the code performance. Java generic is a very powerful feature that it protects type safety and compile-time type checking, it avoids the casting among difference types. But it has its limitation, it cannot instantiate generic parametrized types, it cannot use casts or instanceof with parameterized types. It is because Java complier provides type erasure, it replaces all type parameter with bounded types, or object if type parameter is unbounded. The parameterized types are not stored in the compiled bytecode. During the load process, the explicit type annotations are removed before the program executes at runtime, when the program transformed to binary code, the parameterized type is just abstraction, a concrete type structure for its values existence.

.NET C# generic classes and methods combine reusability, type safety and performance that their non-generic counterparts cannot. Since .NET 2.0, it has new System.Collections.Generic namespace and the generic collection should be used whenever possible instead of the ArrayList, which requires additional boxing and unboxing when processing adding to list and retrieving from list. .Net generic has type constraints during declaration through "where" keyword, with the similar concept of bounded generic in Java. You can create a data structure of any type, or of any type that implements an interface and still is type safety during compiling time. For example, a list can take any type that implement *Employee* structure, if *Developer* and *Manager* both implement *Employee*, they can be added to the list, the *Employees* can be sorted as long as the type *T* implements *IComparable*.

in C#:

```
public class GenericList<T> where T : Employee, System.IComparable<T>
, new() {}
```

in Java:

```
public class GenericList<T extends Employee & Comparable<T>> {}
```

.NET C# generic has additional feature, which are covariance, contravariance and invariance. They only support reference type. Assume you have a base class Animal, a derived class Dog. Covariance allows you to use a more derived type than originally specified. So, you can assign an instance of Collection<Dog> to that of the Collection<Animal>. Contravariance allows to use a more generic type, a less derived type than the originally specified. Invariance specifies that you only use the type originally declared. So, you cannot assign an instance of Collection<Animal> to that of Collection<Dog>. During the assignment, a specific explicit cast is necessary, such as:

```
Animal[] a = { new Dog() };
Dog d = (a[0]) as Dog;
```

Covariance type parameters are used for some of the interface types, such as IEnumerable<T>, IGrouping<TKEy, TElement>, etc. The type parameters are used only for the return types of the members. Some generic interfaces have contravariant type parameters, such as IComparer<T>, IComparable<T>, or IEqualityComparer<T>, these type parameters are used only as parameter types in the member of the interfaces.

```
public interface IMyInterface<in TIn, out TOut>
{
TOut MyMethod(TIn param);
}
public delegate TResult Func<in TIn, out TResult>(TIn args);
```

The Func generic delegates Func<T, TResult> have covariant return type TResult and contravariant parameter type T, it is similar with ordinary delegate binding on the effects of covariance and contravariance.

.NET C# generic type or method is compiled into Microsoft intermediate language MSIL, which contains the metadata describing the parameterized type. From the below picture you can see that when generic supplied type is value type, each time an instance of Stack<T>, which is Stack<int> is created, it allocates an instance of Stack<int>. So, two instances stackone and stacktwo are created. Each instance has its own copy of method codes. When the supplied type is reference type, two instances of Stack<T> are created, but each parameterized type refers another instance of reference type, here is instance of inventory and instance of order. Both of the two instances share the same copy of method codes.

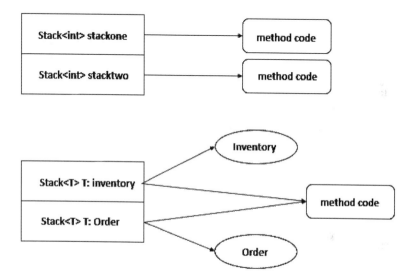

Figure 3.2.7.1 Type parameter is value type and reference type

When you declare Stack<Order> = new Stack<Order>(), the compiler is doing strong type checking and prevents non-Order type into the stack. So, C# compiler put Stack<Order> into IL metadata, during the CLR run time, the JIT compiler builds a new set of code for special stack containing type Order. This is one of the late binding in .NET.

Below is C# code snippet for type parameter be value type *int* and reference type *Order*:

Bing Wang

```
using System;
using System.Collections.Generic;

public class C {
    public void M() {
        Stack<int> numbers = new Stack<int>();
        numbers.Push(10);
        Stack<Order> orders = new Stack<Order>();
        orders.Push(new Order { Name = "book"});
        Print(numbers);
        Print(orders);
    }

    public void Print<T>(Stack<T> items)
    {
        foreach(T item in items)
        {
            Console.WriteLine(item.ToString());
        }
    }
}
public class Order
{
    public string Name { get; set; }
    public string ToString()
    {
        return Name;
    }
}
```

Below is the IL code for *M* method:
```
.method public hidebysig
        instance void M () cil managed
    {
        // Method begins at RVA 0x2050
        // Code size 63 (0x3f)
        .maxstack 4
        .locals init (
```

[0] class [System]System.Collections.Generic.Stack`1<int32> numbers,

[1] class [System]System.Collections.Generic.Stack`1<class Order> orders

)

IL_0000: nop
IL_0001: newobj instance void class [System]System.Collections. Generic.Stack`1<int32>::.ctor()
IL_0006: stloc.0
IL_0007: ldloc.0
IL_0008: ldc.i4.s 10
IL_000a: callvirt instance void class [System]System.Collections. Generic.Stack`1<int32>::Push(!0)
IL_000f: nop
IL_0010: newobj instance void class [System]System.Collections. Generic.Stack`1<class Order>::.ctor()
IL_0015: stloc.1
IL_0016: ldloc.1
IL_0017: newobj instance void Order::.ctor()
IL_001c: dup
IL_001d: ldstr "book"
IL_0022: callvirt instance void Order::set_Name(string)
IL_0027: nop
IL_0028: callvirt instance void class [System]System.Collections. Generic.Stack`1<class Order>::Push(!0)
IL_002d: nop
IL_002e: ldarg.0
IL_002f: ldloc.0
IL_0030: call instance void C::Print<int32>(class [System]System. Collections.Generic.Stack`1<!!0>)
IL_0035: nop
IL_0036: ldarg.0
IL_0037: ldloc.1
IL_0038: call instance void C::Print<class Order>(class [System] System.Collections.Generic.Stack`1<!!0>)
IL_003d: nop
IL_003e: ret
} // end of method C::M

Bing Wang

Below is the IL code for *Print* method:

```
.method public hidebysig
    instance void Print<T> (
        class [System]System.Collections.Generic.Stack`1<!!T> items
    ) cil managed
{
    // Method begins at RVA 0x208c
    // Code size 67 (0x43)
    .maxstack 1
    .locals init (
        [0] valuetype [System]System.Collections.Generic.Stack`1/
Enumerator<!!T>,
        [1] !!T item
    )

    IL_0000: nop
    IL_0001: nop
    IL_0002: ldarg.1
    IL_0003: callvirt instance valuetype [System]System.Collections.
Generic.Stack`1/Enumerator<!0> class [System]System.Collections.
Generic.Stack`1<!!T>::GetEnumerator()
    IL_0008: stloc.0
    .try
    {
        // sequence point: hidden
        IL_0009: br.s IL_0028
        // loop start (head: IL_0028)
            IL_000b: ldloca.s 0
            IL_000d: call instance !0 valuetype [System]System.Collections.
Generic.Stack`1/Enumerator<!!T>::get_Current()
            IL_0012: stloc.1
            IL_0013: nop
            IL_0014: ldloca.s 1
            IL_0016: constrained. !!T
            IL_001c: callvirt instance string [mscorlib]System.
Object::ToString()
            IL_0021: call void [mscorlib]System.Console::WriteLine(string)
            IL_0026: nop
```

```
IL_0027: nop
IL_0028: ldloca.s 0
IL_002a: call instance bool valuetype [System]System.
Collections.Generic.Stack`1/Enumerator<!!T>::MoveNext()
IL_002f: brtrue.s IL_000b
// end loop
IL_0031: leave.s IL_0042
} // end .try
finally
{
    // sequence point: hidden
    IL_0033: ldloca.s 0
    IL_0035: constrained. valuetype [System]System.Collections.
    Generic.Stack`1/Enumerator<!!T>
    IL_003b: callvirt instance void [mscorlib]System.
    IDisposable::Dispose()
    IL_0040: nop
    IL_0041: endfinally
} // end handler

IL_0042: ret
} // end of method C::Print
```

.NET world extensively uses late binding and improves performance dramatically, it also strengths type safety verification and reflection, but it doesn't support .NET version backward compatibility.

The algorithms of generic programming are written as the types going to specified later are instantiated when needed when provided as parameters. Suppose we have N kinds of data structures or functions or algorithms and M kind of data types, without generic, we may have to write N * M versions of application code even though the algorithms may be duplicate. The following example shows you the functions overloading with different type signatures to implement the N kind of different data structures using one algorithm *print*:

```
void print(int n) {}
void print(double n) {}
void print(string text) {}
.
.
.
```

With generic, at most we implement N algorithm(s) of application code:
void print(T data) {}

Both .NET C# and java compiled into the .dll or .class file and at runtime JVM or CLR build the specified type of code, on the contrary, C++ produces raw x86 binary code without underlying virtual machine needs to know about the type class, neither boxing or unboxing, so C++ compiler places no restrictions on template. However, C++ templates are much powerful than C# and Java counterparts as they evaluate the specialized type at compile time, which allows for template meta-programming during compiling process and it can truly compute like a Turing machine.

3.2.8 Type Conversion

Conversion, in Lat, conversion, in syllogistic, or in a traditional logical sense is a conclusion obtained directly from a single premise without the intervention of another premise or middle term. In computer programming, type conversion, casting, coercion, are ways of changing an expression from one data type to another under a certain rules and features, such as type hierarchies or data representations. The data types can be both primitive types or user defined data types. Each language library has its own rules for type conversion, strong typed languages like C++, Java and C# discourage the intervention of data representation through the language feature of generic. Weak typed languages like C force the compiler to interpret data items as different data representations, it needs very often deal with underlying hardware directly. Type conversion can do implicitly, or automatically and explicitly. Implicitly conversion, or coercion, is performed whenever a type T1 is used in the context but not accepted and other type T2 is accepted instead, but there exists one unambiguous implicit conversion sequence from T1 to T2. For the arithmetic operation, the destination type for the implicit conversions on the operands to binary operators is determined by the rule of arithmetic conversions. For the function or operator overloading, the overload resolution rule plays the decision which overload is compiled.

Implicit conversion has the following categories:

Identity conversion: type T expression converts to T itself. Type object and dynamic is a good example that they are considered equivalent, so an identity conversion exists between object and dynamic, such as: dynamic objectTodynamic = new { Property1 = "property1", Property2 = true};

this operation is suspended until run-time.

Numeric conversion: when the right value data of subtypes can be converted to a left value data of supertype as needed at runtime as below:

short s = 100;

```
int i;
i= s;
```

here the left value of s is promoted from short to integer without the explicit operator. This is standard conversion, which happens only in primitive types. On the contrary, if a right value data is supertype and left value data is subtype, the values may be truncated during conversion such as decimal part is removed, and if the result lies outside the range of the type, the conversion may lead to catastrophic error.

Interpolated string conversion: permits an interpolated string expression to be converted to System.FormattableString.

```
string text = "hello";
int number = 10;
```

for interpolated string expression $"{text}", the equivalent string is String.Format("{0}", text), the output is "hello". For interpolated string expression $"{number}", the equivalent string is String. Format("{0}", number), the output is "10". When this conversion happens, string value is not composed from the interpolated string, an instance of System.FormattableString is created.

Nullable conversion: implicit conversion of Nullable<T> to T is not allowed in C# because the conversion can fail if the nullable is actually null, but you can use coalescing operator to do implicit conversion:

```
int? x = 10;
int y = x ?? 0;
```

Reference conversion: one common example is user data type implicit conversion like for class. In C++, this is controlled through the following three member functions: single argument constructor allows the implicit conversion from another user type to initialize an object; assignment operator allows implicit conversion from a user type through assignment; type cast operator allows implicit conversion to a user type:

```
class Parent {};

class Child {
public:
Child (const Parent& p) {}
Child& operator= (const Parent& p) {return *this;}
operator Parent() {return Parent();}
};

// C++
int main ()
{
Parent parent;
// calls constructor
Child child = parent;
// calls assignment
child = parent;
// calls type-cast operator
parent = child;
return 0;
}

// C#
class Child : Parent
{
}
```

```
Int main ()
{
Parent parent;
Child child;
//convert from derived class to base class
parent = child;
return 0;
}

public class Bytes
{
private readonly byte b;

public Bytes(byte b)
{
this.b = b;
}

public static implicit operator byte(Bytes bytes) => bytes.b;
public static explicit operator Bytes(byte b) => new Bytes(b);
}

void Main()
{
var b = new Bytes(3);
// implicit conversion
byte number = b;
// explicit conversion
Bytes bytes = (Bytes)number;
}
```

Implicit reference conversion does not require check at run time. No matter implicit or explicit conversion, never change the referential identity of the object being converted, in another words, it never changes the type or value of the object being referred to.

Anonymous function and method group conversion: an anonymous method expression or lambda expression does not have a type, but can implicitly converted to a compatible delegate type or expression tree type, the same for method group:

```
Func<int, int, int> sum = static delegate (int a, int b) { return a + b; };
Console.WriteLine(sum(20, 30));
Func<int, int, int> constant = delegate (int _, int _) { return 10; };
Console.WriteLine(constant(20, 30));

public void Methodgroup()
{
}
Action action = Methodgroup;
Invoke(action);
```

Explicit conversion requires casting, otherwise compiling error occurs. A cast expression of the form (T)E performs an explicit conversion in the result of expression E to type T. It is applied when trying to convert a numeric value type down to a subtype that may lose precision, or from a base type down cast to a derived type. The conversion needs go through checked or unchecked context. In a checked context, the conversion succeeds if the value of the source operand is within the range of the destination type, otherwise throws overflow or invalid cast exception. In an uncheck context, the conversion always succeeds.

```
double x = 1.2345;
int a = (int)x;

public class Dog : Animal
{
}
Dog dog = new Dog();
```

```
Animal animal = dog;
Dog dog2 = (Dog)animal;
```

The following will throw invalid cast exception:

```
public class Cat : Animal
{
}
```

```
Animal animal = new Animal();
Cat cat = (Cat)animal;
```

The explicit enumeration conversion is given an enum type E with underlying type of int, a conversion from E to byte is processed as an explicit numeric conversion from int to byte:

```
public enum Color
{
Red = 1,
Black = 2
}
```

```
Color color = (Color)1;
```

A nullable conversion also has explicit conversion:

```
var nullableInt = new Nullable<int>(10);
int number = (int)nullableInt;
int number2 = Convert.ChangeType(nullInt, typeof(int));
```

An explicit dynamic conversion applies as an expression of type dynamic to any type T. The conversion is dynamically bound that the operation is evaluated at run-time. A run-time exception throws if no conversion is found.

```
class Operation
{
public static explicit operator Operation(string text)
```

```
{
return new Operation(int.Parse(text));
}
}
```

```
dynamic text = "100";
Operation operation = (Operation)text;
```

To convert between non-compatible types, such as boolean and integer, we can use helper class convert or parse method.

Type conversion looks simple in the code, no complicate logic and algorithm, but it sometimes plays a very critical role in the software programming. Any run-time error may lead to an irreparable consequence. During gulf war, when the Iraq Scud missile attacked USA base in Saudi Arabia, the wrong conversion: int clock = (int) timing caused the USA patriot missile defense system missed the time and targeted the empty sky. During the Spain's S-80 submarine program, Shanghai engineers mistook the decimal point that led to Spain's submarines overweight for 70 tons and cannot flout to the surface once is underwater. It also happened that in the calculation of unit system converter in Boeing software system, the wrong conversion from imperial to metric led to the gauge not working in fuel tank system. In 1628, one of the Sweden warship *TheVassa,* which two sides were measured in different measuring unit system, once attacked by strong wind, it leaned into one side and sank into the bottom of ocean. In 1996, European Space Agency fired rocket Ariane 5, an integer overflow on 16-bit system led to the rocket explode.

Type conversion, unneglectable!

3.2.9 Function Overloading

Overloading, place too much load, do not overload the car! In computer programming, we distribute the tasks to the multiple function signatures with the same function name but different parameter types, orders or return value type. We call it function overloading, or method overloading. Overloading, designed in the computer language concept, like a mysterious science of building a human machine, how the blind people can see? Why some animals can see in the dark? How does the brain control the body?

Overloading, is another way of polymorphisms. Unlike class inheritance and method overriding, which have the same function signatures but child class has a different function definition than parent class and they recognize the calling during runtime, function overloading maintains the same function name with different function definition. Overloaded function calling is resolved through the best-match algorithm, when a particular function call is accomplished in compile time through the matching of formal parameter types with the actual parameter types. The unconfusing compiler uses the number of arguments and their data types to distinguish one method from another, it can also recognize the designated function even though the parameter number and order are the same but with different data types. Therefore, in some languages like Java, C#, function overloading is also called compile-time polymorphism, however, the compiler does not consider the return type while differentiating the overloaded method, it throws error if two methods have the same method names and parameter types but different return types. Only when the methods have different signatures, the overloading is possible.

Function overloading has different categories and varies in different languages. The following category is function overloading with different argument types, number and order:

```
void print(string text);
void print(int number);
void print(string text, int number);
void print(string text, int number, char c);
```

The compiler creates the candidate functions for each argument, the candidate function is the function that the actual argument in that position can be converted to the type of the formal argument in that position. The "best-to-match" functions set are built for each argument, the final selected called function is the intersection of all the sets. If the intersection contains more than one function, it will generate compiling error of ambiguous functions, like the following:

```
void print(string text);
void print(string words);
```

The above two functions have the same argument type string, the compiler confuses and does not know which function should be selected. The process of matching function calls to a specific overloaded function is also called overload resolution.

Overloading can also happen in class constructor when multiple constructors needed, they implemented as overloading functions:

```
class Myclass
{
public Myclass() //default constructor
public Myclass(Myclass &instance)
}
```

An operator can also be overloaded by declaring an operator function. A user defined type can overload a language predefined operator. In the operator function, at least one of the operands must be the type in which the operator function is declared:

```
class Myclass
{
public int Number;
public Myclass() //default constructor
public Myclass(int number)
{
this.Number = number;
}
public static Myclass operator + (Myclass myclass, int number)
{
        return new Myclass(myclass.Number + number);
}
}
```

A user-defined type can define a custom implicit and explicit conversions from or to another type. The conversion is overloadable operator:

```
class Myclass
{
public int Number;
public Myclass(int number)
{
this.Number = number;
}
public static implicit operator int(Myclass myclass)
```

```
{
        return myclass.Number + 100;
}
public static explicit operator Myclass(it number)
{
        return new Myclass(number - 100);
}
}
```

Since predefined primitive type's implicit conversion always succeed and never throw exception, the same should be for user-typed implicit conversion. User-defined type's explicit conversion may lose information or throw exception.

Copying values from one object to another existing object is through assignment operator. In the user-defined type class declaration, the purpose of copy constructor and the assignment operator are almost equivalent except that copy constructor initializes new instances whereas the assignment operator replaces the contents of existing objects. The assignment operator can be overloaded in C++ language just like all other operators:

```
class Myclass
{
public int Number;
public Myclass(int number)
{
this.Number = number;
}
public Myclass& operator= (const Myclass &newObject)
{
this.Number = newObject.Number;
return *this;
}
}
```

You can't overload the assignment operator in C#, likewise, you cannot overload operator in Java because it violates one of the principles of Java language design: transparency. The clone method in C# and Java accomplishes the deep copy of one instance to another.

Overloading simplifies the problem when only one method is applicable, such as when the parameter types are mutually incompatible or there are more parameters in one method than another. And even one type may implement multiple interfaces, and potentially implement the same generic interface multiple times with different type arguments.

3.2.10 Iteration

While Not the origin

Boundary philosophy, loop within boundary.

In mathematics, iteration is the process of iterating a function, applying a function repeatedly, and using the output from one iteration as the input to the next. Iterative method is designed for a certain mathematical problem which solution is approximately numerical. In computing, iteration is a block of statements repeating execute for n times, the block of statements can be either inline code and another function, it is iteration, or in a computing term, loop. There are different types of iterations: condition-controlled loop, counter-controlled loop and sequence-controlled loop. Condition controlled iteration is the looping terminates until meet certain condition. Counter controlled loop is iterating a certain number of times and each time the counter increase or decrease. A sequentially controlled loop refers to iterate through each element in a sequence list. When the program iterates, it tracks the step of the iteration and executes the block of statement or jumps to the function. In a computing algorithm, iteration is one of the very important build blocks along with sequence and selection. It can help simplify the algorithm by repeating the steps until terminates. In computer machine itself, the very big advantage of computing is to do the repeated tasks tirelessly and correctly much better than human being does.

For condition-controlled loop, it keeps executing the block of statement when the condition met and jump out of the look when breach the condition, see the below iterative pseudo code:

```
If inputText not equal "i love programming"
Please input text
Print inputText

string inputText = "";
cout << "Please input text:"<<endl;
cin >> inputText;
while (lowercase(inputText) != "I love programming")
{
cout << "Please input text:"<<endl;
cin >> inputText;
}
cout << "You input:" + inputText<<endl;
```

The above code uses while loop, or you can use do while loop. Condition controlled loop starts the test at the beginning of iteration to decide if need go into the loop. If the condition check is true forever, then it goes into an infinite loop.

For counter-controlled loop, it uses a counter to determine how many times the block of statements need to be executed. See the below pseudo code:

```
For inputText times range from 1 to 5
        Please input text
        Print out input text
End
```

```
string inputText = "";
for (int counter = 1; counter <=5; counter++)
{
        cout << "Please input text:"<<endl;
        cin >> inputText;
        cout << "You input: " + inputText<<endl;
}
```

The above code uses for loop to control the times of iteration, it is also a definite repetition loop. A control variable counter has initial value 1 and increase by 1 during each iteration until finally reach 6, then break out the loop. Since counter-controlled loop is definite, it never goes into infinite loop.

For sequence-controlled loop, it tries to iterate each item in the sequence of collection and execute the block of statements. See the below pseudo code:

```
array of numbers arr[] = 1,2,3,4,5,6,7,8,9
For each number in arr
Print out number
End
```

```
int[] arr = {1, 2, 3, 4, 5, 6, 7, 8, 9}
```

```
for(int number : arr)
{
cout << number << endl;
}
```

The above code uses foreach loop to iterate each item in the array without performing initialization, condition checking and increment or decrement. It focuses on traversing and processing each item in the sequence instead of doing n times. The collection of sequence cannot be modified during the foreach loop, otherwise the runtime error of illegal operation will throw.

Iteration is very important in computing, and all high-level imperative programming languages provide loop flow control statement to perform iteration process. Why is it so important? How to achieve this from hardware point of view?

Iteration is the basic mechanism of problem solving. It is a systematic, repetitive, and recursive process in qualitative data analysis. Loop is running code and running code again. An if statement conditionally branches to two different bits of code. If one of those bits of code jump back to the earlier code, or to the if itself, then a loop is formed. A jump statement that can jump somewhere else is needed. A goto is one command that does that in some languages. A way to name or identify where to jump is required, even if it's just by a line number. The below 8086 assembly code depicts this thought:

```
int array[10];
int counter;
for (counter = 0; counter < 10; counter++)
{
```

```
array[counter] = counter;
}
```

```
        ; count = 0, xor: 0 out the count register cx, it executes faster than
        "mov cx, 0"
        xor cx, 0
        ;array[counter] = counter, pointer to array address
label   mov DWORD PTR array[0+cx*4], cx
        ; count++; increment counter by 1
        inc cx
;check counter < 10. If true, repeat the loop.
        cmp cx, 10
        ; jump back to loop
        jle label
```

Further deep into the hardware register for loop structure, we can also use an index register, which holds an offset for an array. So:

```
        ;initialize loop counter
        mov ecx, 10
        ;set index register be 0
        sub esi, esi
        ;initialize array sum be 0
        sub eax, eax
        ;add array address value to eax
top     add eax, [array+esi]
        ;increment index by 4 byte
        add esi,4
        ;iterate again
        loop top
```

Iterative concept has long history. We could trace it back to Miss Ada Lovelace, the student of Mr. Babbage, the first computer programmer, and the author of G-note. Within her first program, we see the term *repetition*. Iteration is currently used in many areas: science, engineering, medical, and marketing, etc. One example in engineering is the plan-do-check-act cycle implementation. Most new product development or existing product improvement programs have an iterative checking loop. Being iterative, you practice the art of iteration. Being iterative, you make a second pass that this time includes a bit more detail. Being iterative, you can only make it once, but you can make it better as many. Being iterative, you make your way through work by repeatedly processing a limited number of steps, with each successive pass bringing you closer to your end goal.

3.2.11 Recursive

Recursion, by definition, is solving the problem via the solution of the smaller version of the same problem, in which the problem is defined in terms of itself. It involves a major routine be part of the program and can be execute multiple times successfully, then back to the convergency. In mathematics and computing, recursive definition, or inductive definition, is used to define a set of elements in terms of other elements in the set. In computing programming, a recursive function is defined as the same function needs be called repetitively but have different input values. Recursive is widely used and is a very powerful computing mechanism to solve the complex problems.

For example, the below calculation:

$0! = 1$

$(n + 1)! = (n + 1)\, n! = (n + 1)\, n\, (n - 1)! = \ldots.$

We can call a function calculating n! by passing different value n + 1, n, n − 1, n − 2, … until finally reach the base 0. So, we can define the following factorial function:

```
int factorial (int n)
{
      if ( n <= 0 )
      {
            return 1; // base case
      }
      return n * factorial (n - 1); // recursive case
}
```

A recursive function always finally stops repeating itself. There are two parts in a recursive function: the recursive case and the base case. The recursive case is that a solution is designed for a problem in such a way that the problem has its sub-problems, such as the same problem for smaller input size that we continue to call the solution until reach the base condition. The base case is terminating condition that function can return a result immediately, which is the smallest version of the problem for the solution. The function finally stops calling itself and prevents infinite loops.

Recursive functions use "the call stack.", or compiler uses a stack data structure to simulate recursion and calculate. When a program calls a function, that function goes on top of the call stack, which is similar to a stack of books. You add stack block one at a time, when you are ready to take block off, you always take off the top item, last in first out LIFO order for recursive calls and return values.

If the number input n is 5, the following call stack is created:

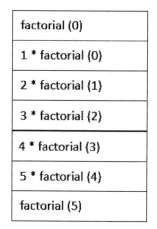

factorial (0)
1 * factorial (0)
2 * factorial (1)
3 * factorial (2)
4 * factorial (3)
5 * factorial (4)
factorial (5)

Figure 3.2.11.1 Factorial call stack

But stack memory space is finite, if the recursive call is too deep, or turns into infinite due to the wrong or missing base case, the stack overflow error will throw. Therefore, recursive function needs be designed in a correct way, the most important is that the recursive step needs to reduce to smaller subproblem so that recursion is converge.

If think about state machine, a finite state automaton can be seen as a program with only a finite amount of memory. For example, a finite state automaton A recognizes the following languages:

$L(A) = \{ab(b+ab)^n \mid n \geq 0\}$, the below is the FSA state transition diagram:

Bing Wang

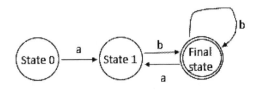

Figure 3.2.11.2 Finite State Automaton for $a^n b^n$

The following assembly snippet shows how factorial (5) works:

```
L0000: push rbp
L0001: push rdi
L0002: push rsi
L0003: sub rsp, 0x30
L0007: lea rbp, [rsp+0x40]
L000c: mov rsi, rcx
L000f: lea rdi, [rbp-0x20]
L0013: mov ecx, 0x4
L0018: xor eax, eax
L001a: rep stosd
L001c: mov rcx, rsi
L001f: mov [rbp+0x10], rcx
L0023: mov [rbp+0x18], edx
L0026: cmp dword [rip+0x9f86b], 0x0
L002d: jz L0034
L002f: call 0x7ffd0cc0ca40
L0034: nop
L0035: cmp dword [rbp+0x18], 0x0
L0039: setz dl
L003c: movzx edx, dl
L003f: mov [rbp-0x14], edx
L0042: cmp dword [rbp-0x14], 0x0
L0046: jz L0053
L0048: nop
L0049: mov dword [rbp-0x18], 0x1
L0050: nop
L0051: jmp L0077
L0053: mov edx, [rbp+0x18]
```

```
L0056: mov [rbp-0x1c], edx
L0059: mov edx, [rbp+0x18]
L005c: dec edx
L005e: mov rcx, [rbp+0x10]
L0062: call C.factorial(Int32)
L0067: mov [rbp-0x20], eax
L006a: mov eax, [rbp-0x1c]
L006d: imul eax, [rbp-0x20]
L0071: mov [rbp-0x18], eax
L0074: nop
L0075: jmp L0077
L0077: mov eax, [rbp-0x18]
L007a: lea rsp, [rbp-0x10]
L007e: pop rsi
L007f: pop rdi
L0080: pop rbp
L0081: ret
```

Recursive demonstrates its powerful in many algorithm designs, such as binary tree search, merge sort, quick sort. It shows more useful in tree-based traversal, such as recursively looping file directories and sub-directories, string pattern search, etc.

Recursion can be implemented in an iterative way. Iteration can be replaced with recursion as long as the difference and conversion are obvious. To convert iteration from recursion, we need find the false conditions and repetitive execute statements. To convert recursion from iteration, we need to find the right base case and make the repetitive calling to smaller version of subproblem and can gradually converge. Recursion generates clear and simple solution while iteration computes faster.

Finally let us think of the famous Tower of Hanoi problem, you will observe the real beauty of recursion.

3.2.12 Delegate

Back to unmanaged C/C++ days, developers always talked about callback function, which is a very useful programming mechanism. C function takes a pointer to a callback function to execute at runtime, the pointer stores the memory address of the function, this address doesn't carry any additional information of passing parameters and returned data type value, it's a very lightweight mechanism but not type safe. The .Net framework introduced a concept of delegate to represent as a pointer to function with type safe and usually the piece of function code being invoked is lazy declared and not known until runtime. In object-oriented programming, delegation refers to evaluate a property or method of one object, the receiver or the sender. When an object receives a request, it forwards the request to another object, the delegate, to process the request doing the work and reply to the sender. A delegate is created in such a way that the delegated object is created to hold the reference to a method, the determination of actually invoking the method is not at compiling time but runtime.

Declare a delegate type:

delegate void Notify (string sender);

Declare a delegate variable:

Notify greetings;

Assign method to a delegate variable:

```
void HelloWorld (string sender)
{
        Console.WriteLine("Hello World: " + sender);
```

}
greetings = new Notify (HelloWorld);
calling a delegate variable: greeting("BingWang");

A delegate variable can store a method and its receiver, but no parameters:

greetings = new Notify (myObj.HelloWorld);

A delegate variable can hold multiple values at the same time:

greetings += new Notify (myObj.Goodbye);

It seems delegate is easy to use to construct instance by new operator and invoke the callback method, however, what's really going on behind the scene is bit more complex. The compiler and CLR need do lots of work. For the above example, when it sees: *delegate void Notify (string sender);*, the compiler actually defines a complete class:

```
class Notify : System.MulticastDelegate
{
public Notify (Object object, IntPtr method);
public virtual void Invoke (Int32 value);
public virtual IAsyncResult BeginInvoke (Int32 value, AsyncCallback callback, Object object);
public virtual void EndInvoke (IAsyncResult result);
}
```

The System.MulticastDelegate class derives from System.Delegate, which derives from System.Object. The Delegate class has static methods Combine and Remove. Because all delegate types are derived from MulticastDelegate, they inherit MutlicastDelegate's field, properties and methods. To make developers' life easier,

C# compiler automatically provide overloads of the += and -= operators for instances of delegate types. These operators call Delegate.Combine and Delegate.Remove respectively, they also simplify the building of delegate chains. Now, .NET framework provides generic delegate as well:

```
public delegate void Action();
public delegate void Action<T>(T arg);
public delegate void Action<T1, T2>(T1 arg1, T2 arg2);
```
.

.

.

In addition to the Action delegate, the .NET framework also provides Func delegates, which allow the callback methods to return value:

```
public delegate TResult Func<TResult>();
public delegate TResult Func<T, TResult>(T arg);
public delegate TResult Func<T1, T2, TResult>(T1 arg1, T2 arg2);
```
.

.

.

It is now recommended that these delegate types be used whenever possible instead of defining delegate type. Lambda expressions are directly related to delegates, when the parameter type is a delegate type, a lambda expression can be used to implement a method that is referenced from the delegate. The above delegate type example can be simplified through lambda operator =>:

```
Action<string> notify = param => Console.WriteLine("HelloWorld" + param);
```

In Javascript function expression const fun = function () {}

Javascript arrow function fun = () => {}

Delegation is dependent upon dynamic binding at run time since it requires that a given method call can execute different segments of code. For example, it makes it possible to use a single OS provided class to manage windows, the OS unmanaged class takes a delegate and can override the default windows behavior as needed. When the top right corner of close box in the windows is clicked, the window manager sends a delegate, a windowShouldClose call. The messages send to the self and the self in a method definition in the receiving object is not statically bound to that object at compile time but at run time. It is similar to the class inheritance that some developers prefer to use delegate rather than inheritance for more readable and understandable of coding. However, the traditional object-oriented class definition is still the mainstream because it is complicate and hard to distinguish between delegation and inheritance. Delegation seems passing a duty off to some other entity or object, it only can be an alternative to inheritance in such a way that an object of another class as an instance variable, it forwards the messages to the instance. So, some cases delegate is better than inheritance in terms of message forwarding. The primary advantage of delegation is flexible at run time because it can easily be changed at that moment, but it does not facilitate dynamic polymorphism. Therefore, understanding the difference, using inheritance when you want to express the relationship is-a, use composition or delegation when a class needs enhanced but it is sealed and no further be sub-classed, and use delegation when functionality of a method needed be invoked to execute instead of being override.

OBJECT-ORIENTED PROGRAMMING SHRUG

Entities should not be multiplied unnecessarily.

– William of Ockham

4.1   Object-Oriented Philosophy

THE PHYSICAL WORLD, THE MATERIALIZED world, the spiritually ontologized world, on one hand, it is in such an inherent oddness that everything is a radically individual segregated from everything else, on the other hand, all objects in universe diaspora flow, merge, fusion and connect fundamentally in which every object may partake. The willingness to countenance counterintuitive metaphysical and embrace the object based ontological is worth being advocated.

4.1.1   Object

So, what's object? From a broad view of sense, objects are things as diverse as anything in the universe. The sun, the moon, we the people, the rain, the ants, the bacteria, and the invisible nucleus. As America philosopher Charles S. Peirce succinctly defines: *"By an object, I mean anything that we can think, i.e. anything we can talk about."* In philosophy, an object is a thing, an entity, or a being located in space and time. This may take in several senses. In a restricted sense, an object is something describing as what it looks like, the properties and relations with other objects. The properties and relations belonging to objects fall into a different logical category. In a further narrow down sense, an object is material excluding anything abstract, such as minds, believes, or ideas. Meinong's controversial *The Theory of Objects*, which insists upon *granting ontological status to every possible object of thought, including those that merely subsist because they do not genuinely exist.* It confronts a challenge to circumscribe all the possible intentional relations to explicitly and metaphysically differentiate between existence and subsistence. So, what is metaphysical? The origin of philosophy, beginning from the pre-Socratics, was metaphysical in nature. Derived from the Greek meta ta physika, after the things of nature, metaphysical refers to an idea and an abstract thought not from human sense perception, it refers to the studies not from the objective purpose of derivation and materialization. The traditional idea of metaphysics is first philosophy, it concerns the nature of being and the world, how to explain some fundamental phenomena and principals, it surrounds and attempts to answer the two basic questions: What is it? What is it like? The metaphysics practiced as philosophy in such a way that one formulates and defends one's most fundamental assumptions, both narrow ontological assumptions and broadly categorial assumptions. The narrow ontological assumptions are about the kinds of things and entities, the broadly categorial assumptions are about a variety of features of these things and entities, such as properties and relations. One task of metaphysics is to carve reality into two major different categories, real and sensation. Real is the fact, and sensation is observing, listening, touching, smelling, tasting and the sixth sense the ontological feeling. An object of engineer has real facts: first name, last name, birth date, social security number, years of working, etc. this engineer also has sensation like experience level: expert with +30 years working experience, advanced with 20 years to 30 years working experience, average with 10 years to 20 years working experience and junior with below 10 years working experience. An object of room has facts: door, window, ceiling, lights, furniture and has sensation as well such as the heat level: freeze, cold, cool, warm, hot and burning. Objects are independent of one and the other representing its unique characteristics and distinguishes from the other. A chemical engineer is different from a mechanical engineer from professional point of view, a chemical engineer Mr. Robert is different from a chemical engineer Mr. Smith from person object point of view. Similarly, an office room is distinguished from a game room. Objects are excess each follows the other through invoking and execution. Execution is purely an act of underlying interact, it transcends both possibility and consequence beyond the limits.

4.1.2 Object relations

What are object relations? In metaphysics, object-oriented relation ontology is the thought of all relations, among humans and nonhumans, bases on the human consciousness on the equal footing, bases on speculative realism, bases on the equality of object relations, it proposes contend that nothing has special status and everything exists equally. Object-oriented ontology rejects the claims that human experience sits at the center of philosophy, it emphasizes that everything is understood through visual and appearance, on the contrary, it uses speculation to characterize objects existence and interact. Relational ontologies believes that both object and property are not empty, object is composite, it has parts, and these parts are not object's properties, instead, they are other objects. Object relations are selective based on their interact effectiveness, the relation can be one to one, one to many and many to many, but objects do not have relations with all other objects in the world. There have been a usual common debate going on for quite a long time for the entity relationship, should the relationship engulf the objects or defend the independent of the objects. An object is in network, an object of person books a hotel room, he will be in the network and have access to the resources to maintain his existence and state transition. Objects have actual properties that yield the potential to produce features, effects, interactions with other objects affecting them and being affected by them at the same time. One example of objects interaction in network is water cycle ecosystem. Water cycle is a circular cycle of evaporation, condensation and precipitation. The complex ecosystem on the earth can be considered as one big object *Eco*, it is a composite object consisting of many different parts, or small objects, like water, cloud, mountain, tree, lake, groundwater, etc. with each object has its own properties and actions. Water object has three states: solid, liquid and gas, it actively connects with all the other objects in the network, the ecosystems. The temperature property of Eco object triggers the water object actions of evaporation, condensation and precipitation. Water object vapors into the sky to form cloud object, cloud object condense to form water object to precipitate back to earth. Water object's actions change its states, from liquid to gas, to solid, and back to liquid, so on, so forth...

Object-orientation ontology opposes the idea that effects of relations on objects are universal with all objects having an effect on each other and object identity should be self-contained. In the above example, we notice some objects are emerged after transition, cloud formed after water evaporation. So, some elements of object-oriented ontology might well be adopted from transcendental ontology. As an object, should it exist as an entity itself? Or can be transformed to produce? If we think about the famous example Darwin's natural selection, the evolution has fundamental three phases: variation, selection and transmission. It always generates new forms: organism, species, etc. From the object-oriented ontology point of view, it is suggested that any kind of object is in evolution change, randomly transform of potential to shift in a given selection environment.

Object orientation, orientation is, according to the philosophy of orientation, the achievement of finding one's way successfully in a new situation. But every situation is somewhat new. Object orientation is, above all, about how we understand the objects, the object relations. To provide a more realistic view of the world as we experience it in everyday life, the philosophy of orientation connects with ongoing research in the sciences and scrutinizes the societal orientation worlds of business, politics, mass media, law, art, science, and so on, which professionalize specific orientation skills and orientation virtues that are rooted in everyday orientation. It investigates these orientation worlds not with respect to their ideals but to their realities.

4.2 Object-Oriented Programming (OOP)

Come out from the philosophy world, back walk into the programming ecosystem, object-oriented programming is a very important distributary channel that fascinated almost all software developers from its very beginning.

4.2.1 Object-oriented programming paradigm

What is paradigm?

A paradigm is a set of conventions we use to understand the world. In software, paradigm shapes the way we formulate abstractions. What does the world contain? Do we divide the world into procedures or categorize it as modules, classes and objects? Procedure styled programming requires you specify statement sequence, define variables with different scopes, do branching, looping and I/O, it is true indeed that procedure programming can solve any of the problem a Turing machine can solve. Early programs had long sequence of labeled statements and the program control movements was through labels, such as FORTRAN's "GO TO". Today, procedure language still remains the fundamental language that exposed to first learner on how to program to solve some basic problems. However, it has its limitation, the very important one is that in the procedure language, there's no concepts to represent the real world. Instead, it only has method and algorithms, the real-world entities function through lengthy long procedures. This fundamental idea isolates the software programming mechanism from the world it actually represents. Philosophy indicates that the subjects of the world is actually in a fusion state that all science fields are related. Another difference is at the program design, look at the below example diagram of client server communication, procedure programming passes numerous parameters when invoking service operations.

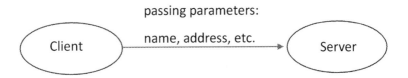

Figure 4.2.1.1 Client server communication in procedure programming

Object oriented programming passes an object encapsulating the data properties inside when invoking the service operation. The object may represent the domain context reflecting the business concept.

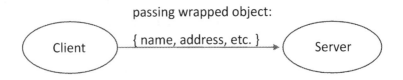

*Figure 4.2.1.2 Client server communication
in object-oriented programming*

The functional and imperative programming paradigms are based on the mathematically exploration in the 1930s with lambda calculus and the Turing machine. The lambda calculus and Turing machines are considered functionally equivalent that anything that can be computed using a Turing machine can be computed using lambda calculus, and vice versa. But there is a common misconception that Turing machines can compute anything computable. Actually, there are many problems and many cases Turing machine cannot compute. Lambda calculus compute adopts a top-down and functional approach, whereas the Turing machine towards a bottom-up and imperative approach. Both imperative programming and functional programming have their base foundations in the mathematics of computation theory, predating digital computers.

Object-oriented programming was coined by Alan Kay circa 1966 or 1967 while he was at graduate school. Alan Kay, the commonly known as the father of object-oriented programming, fascinated by the first object-oriented language SIMULA at 1960s. It was a Norwegian Defense Research project, which the computing scientist Kristen Nygaard was assigned to carry out calculations related to the construction of Norway's first nuclear reactor. Like Nygaard said for himself: *"I had no wish to be responsible for the first nuclear accident on the continent of Europe."* After extensive work on a traditional numerical approach, Nygaard turned to simulation. The necessity of using simulation, the need of concepts and a language for system description and the lack of tools for generating simulation programs drove him to design a simulation language. Along with Nygaard, Ole-Johan Dahl, now widely recognized as Norway's foremost computer scientist, produced the initial ideas for object-oriented programming, which is now the dominant style of programming for commercial and industrial applications. They developed Simula I and Simula 67, Simlula 67 introduced the concepts of class, object, subclass and virtual procedure.

Alan visioned this language could provide a good way for non-specialties to create graphic-oriented applications. In Xerox Parc, the team headed by Alan used Simula as a platform for their development of the first object-oriented language Smalltalk. Smalltalk extends object-oriented programming by the integration of graphical user interfaces and interactive program execution and it still exists to this day. Then in 1970s, Bjorn Stroustrup integrated object-oriented concepts into the C language and created C++, which became the first object-oriented language to be widely used commercially. About ten years later, James Gosling developed a simpler version of C++ called java language, which gained widespread popularity with the booming of the internet. Alan said: *"I made up the term 'object-oriented' and I can tell you I didn't have C++ in mind."* The idea was to use encapsulated simulation in software to communicate via message passing rather than direct data sharing. The simulation breakdowns a monolithic program into separate data structure and procedures. It introduced the class concept for the encapsulation of data structure, code reuse, dynamic or static class instantiation, etc.

Object-oriented programming organizes the program into a number of classes and blocks. It is by far the most popular programming paradigm in the programming language today. If saying, for the procedure programming, application code is placed into totally distinct functions or procedures, it performs like a black box having its input data and output data, these data are placed into sperate data structures, the rules, algorithms, logics to generate the output is in the black-box, then for object-oriented design, the input data, also can be called properties or attributes, and behaviors or actions are contained in a single object.

4.2.2 Object in object-oriented programming

So, in the object-oriented programming paradigm, what is object anyway? In philosophy world, object is defined as entity. In programming space, object is also an autonomous entity, but has its own identity, state and behaviors to represent the real-world object. With object-oriented, we look at the world in a similar way as our brain does, we just not pay too much attention of it. When we vision the surroundings, our brains process the scene we quickly have seen, they strip out the unnecessary stuff and try to capture the important and necessary information. The brains automatically classify all we see into categories, even though the world is not neatly categorized. It happens during our everyday life as long as we observing and thinking. One example is when we go out travelling. Look at the below picture:

Figure 4.2.2.1 The Meeting of Waters (Portuguese: Encontro das Águas)

When I was taking boat fliting on the amazon river, my vision quickly captures two-color (yellow and black) water clearly distinguished by a zigzag demarcation line. My brain quicky processed the image, my mind raised question: how come? Both historically and scientifically. My ears automatically listened intently to the tourist guide. It is *The Rio Negro* and *The Solimões River* meet to form the Amazon River. *The Rio Negro,* visible in black, is the world's largest black-water river. It flows from Colombia and gets it dark color from the leaves and decayed plants. *The Solimões River,* owes its brown color from rich sediment content, flows to meet *The Rio Negro* and together form this important junction. It is interesting, I have bigger impression for the two-color water because of my curiosity, my eager to find out the answer. However, my vision also covered the boat on the river and grass land far away, but my brain just simply ignored it, instead, my brain triggered the signal to see the two-color water line automatically categorizing this one as an object of my sight scenes during my travel. With object-oriented way, our brains keep processing what we observe, categorizing the important and filtering the trivial miscellaneous, then we think, we ponder and eventually we learn. One of the critical learning resources is from life experience, from observing and thinking.

Un-separable, in our career life, we think and solve the problem with the similar way of our daily life. Build architect has thousand years of history, each building has tons of objects to compose its appearance. Church was built solemnly and grandly since the ancient time, office buildings need be spacious and brightness, theme parks need be enjoyable and amusement, residential houses need be comfortable and warm, etc. Just as Christopher Alexander indicates in his book *The Timeless Way of Building*, a building is only be alive when it is governed by the timeless way. Software architects also need architect drawing and planning. With object-oriented, software is built as a community of objects with each object has its role to play, each object provides a service or action that used by or applies on other members of the community. An object of a software is a bundle of variables and related methods. The identity is the property of an object that distinguishes it from all others. In programming, usually we denote the identity as variable id or name, and reference or the pointer to address of object *p. The state consists of the properties and their current values of the object. For example, object employee can be given a set of properties: name, title, social security number, birth date, etc. When the properties values defined, the object state is set at this moment. The behavior is how object acts or reacts to the operations on it. When object acts or reacts, its state changes and it can apply operation on other visible objects. The behavior is also described as message passing, a message to other objects is a request sending for service. The message encodes the request for an operation and is accompanied by any additional information arguments need to carry out the request. The receiver is another visible object to whom the message sent to, it interprets the message and performs some actions to satisfy the request. Object-oriented programming advertises the types of data and types of operations to manipulate the data but hide the implementation from user.

Actually, people already treat the things in life as objects, think of telephone, it has numbers you can dial, but as for the detail implementation of how your voice transmitted over the phone line reaching to the other party, regular users do not know. Telephone, as a very common object, has its properties as a device, has state of quiet or ring, has action of dialing the number through. In language itself, think about stack, A stack has a set of operations: push, pop, check if it is empty, and top. If the stack is implemented as an object, its implementation is hidden from the program. It may be implemented as an array, a queue, or some other data structure. The program does not need to know how the stack is implemented. It only concerns that the stack could provide the specified operations with the desired behavior results. Objects package data and the operations and the operations are only publicly accessible without internal detail implementation. This information hiding made large-scale programming easier by thinking about each part of the program in isolation. Objects may be derived from more general ones by inheriting their capabilities. Such an object hierarchy made it possible for code reuse that defines specialized objects without repeating all. The below picture denotes the object hierarchy component: Computing engineers contains software engineers, software engineers include .NET developers, some .NET developers work on Restful and web api service implementation and maintenance, Bing Wang is one of them. An object is also known as an instance. An instance refers to a particular object, such as Bing Wang is an instance of object .NET restful web api developer, or a developer. The variables of an object are instance variables containing the state of the object. Developer instance BingWang has state information such as name, age, years of working experience, working company name, etc. There're tremendous instances of developer in the world.

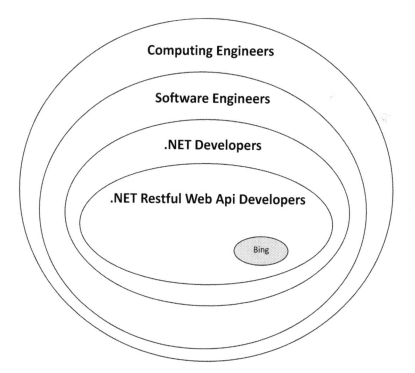

Figure 4.2.2.2. Objects Hierarchy

Object has behavior, in procedure language, behavior is defined as procedure or subroutine. Object behaviors are contained in method that is invoked by another object through sending messages. BingWang has dozens of state attributes, she also has behavior such as work, or communicate with colleagues. Behaviors change the object state, work behavior increase the state of years of working experience. The below state transfer diagram shows the object state change with behavior:

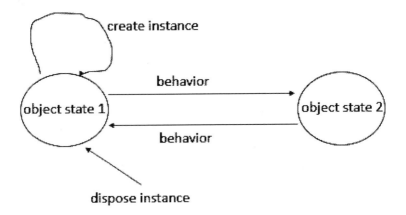

Figure 4.2.2.3 Object state transition

4.2.3 Class in object-oriented programming

In object-oriented programming, what is class? In mathematics, a class is a set, such that any entity falling into specific criteria can be identified to belong to a class. In object-oriented programming, each type of object is defined as an entity containing a set of properties, which may be primitive data types or user defined types. The object-orientation comes from the fact that each such object type completely characterizes the type of real-world object that it represents. The criterion of being in a specific class is that the programmer has defined and named a class having that set of properties and methods. A set of objects having the same behaviors but different states, or a template defining such a group in terms of their common properties and functions. Class and object are tightly connected with each other. Class is a blueprint, a template to create an object. An object cannot be instantiated without class. Restful developer can be defined as a class, it provides the blueprint for what is developer and what developer can do? Developer1,2,3 are the class instances. They can be categorized into one container because they all have restful skills and work on restful related programming projects. See the below picture:

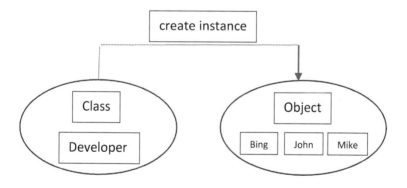

Figure 4.2.3.1 Classes and Objects

The user-defined objects are created using the class keyword, an instance is a specific object created from a particular class. The picture above shows how a developer object can be templated for many other developer instances, here have developer instance Bing, John and Mike. When we are creating a blueprint of class for developer, we need include all the attributes that the program interests, such as for a payroll software, developer class has attributes of name, gender, age, social security number, bank account, home address, contact phone, etc. we also can call them metadata, which is also a concept we can borrow from relational database management. Relational database has schema, table description, column name and data type. Each row in the table is an object. Table needs multi-level of normalization, similar to class, which needs normalization to remove the duplicated attributes. In C++, C# and Java, the keyword *class* is used to begin the definition of an object followed by object name and all its properties definitions are enclosed in {}, below is an example of C#:

```
public class Developer
{
      public string Name { get; set;}
      public string Gender { get; set;}
      public int Age { get; set;}
      public string SSN { get; set;}
      public string AccountNumber { get; set;}
      public string HomeAddress { get; set;}
      public string ContactPhone { get; set;}
}
```

The term *Developer* represents a class or category of all developers. All the fields specified in the *Developer* class are attributes. Each class may define the attributes to store the state of the object. The attribute values change, the state of the object change. Behavior is represented by method, such as for the following:

```
public class Developer
{
```

```
        public void Work();
        public void Join();
        public void Leave();
}
```

Developer object can have behaviors of work, join the company and leave the company. The detail implementations of the methods describe the behaviors. Behavior changes the state of *Developer* object.

Class definition including properties and methods has a concreate relationship with object instances. When a program loads, the memory needs areas to store the major two parts of the program: application code and application data. For C# .NET, how CLR execution model stores the class metadata and objects' data is a very complicated process, even though we do not need worry too much about memory management and garbage collection, but we still need keep them in mind to optimize our application.

When the class *Developer* is compiled, the compiler emits instructions representing the methods and packs them into code segment, which locates on the stack. The codes exist prior to and without any existence of an object instance, they are just part of the *Developer* type and known ahead of time. All instances of *Developer* share the same code segment. At run time, the code segment becomes real data address, the three instances of *Developer* Bing, John and Mike are loaded into memory, their data and *Developer* reference properties are stored in the heap, the pointers to each address are allocated on the stack, the code execution and method table are loaded into app domain until CLR is shutdown.

Below is a simple C# code snippet:

```
public class C {
    public void M() {
        Developer d1 = new Developer();
        Developer d2 = new Developer();
    }
}

public class Developer
{
    public string Name { get; set;}
    public void work(){}
}
```

Below is part of the intermediate language after the above code compiled:

```
.class public auto ansi beforefieldinit C
    extends [mscorlib]System.Object
{
    // Methods
    .method public hidebysig
        instance void M () cil managed
    {
        // Method begins at RVA 0x2050
        // Code size 14 (0xe)
        .maxstack 1
        .locals init (
            [0] class Developer d1,
            [1] class Developer d2
        )

        IL_0000: nop
        IL_0001: newobj instance void Developer::.ctor()
        IL_0006: stloc.0
        IL_0007: newobj instance void Developer::.ctor()
```

```
    IL_000c: stloc.1
    IL_000d: ret
} // end of method C::M
```

```
.method public hidebysig specialname rtspecialname
    instance void .ctor () cil managed
{
    // Method begins at RVA 0x206a
    // Code size 8 (0x8)
    .maxstack 8

    IL_0000: ldarg.0
    IL_0001: call instance void [mscorlib]System.Object::.ctor()
    IL_0006: nop
    IL_0007: ret
} // end of method C::.ctor
```

```
} // end of class C
```

```
.class public auto ansi beforefieldinit Developer
    extends [mscorlib]System.Object
{
    // Fields
    .field private string '<Name>k__BackingField'
    .custom instance void [mscorlib]System.Runtime.CompilerServices.
    CompilerGeneratedAttribute::.ctor() = (
        01 00 00 00
    )
    .custom     instance     void     [mscorlib]System.Diagnostics.
    DebuggerBrowsableAttribute::.ctor(valuetype     [mscorlib]System.
    Diagnostics.DebuggerBrowsableState) = (
        01 00 00 00 00 00 00 00
    )

    // Methods
    .method public hidebysig specialname
        instance string get_Name () cil managed
    {
```

```
    .custom instance void [mscorlib]System.Runtime.CompilerServices.
    CompilerGeneratedAttribute::.ctor() = (
        01 00 00 00
    )
    // Method begins at RVA 0x2073
    // Code size 7 (0x7)
    .maxstack 8

    IL_0000: ldarg.0
    IL_0001: ldfld string Developer::'<Name>k__BackingField'
    IL_0006: ret
} // end of method Developer::get_Name

.method public hidebysig specialname
    instance void set_Name (
        string 'value'
    ) cil managed
{
    .custom instance void [mscorlib]System.Runtime.CompilerServices.
    CompilerGeneratedAttribute::.ctor() = (
        01 00 00 00
    )
    // Method begins at RVA 0x207b
    // Code size 8 (0x8)
    .maxstack 8

    IL_0000: ldarg.0
    IL_0001: ldarg.1
    IL_0002: stfld string Developer::'<Name>k__BackingField'
    IL_0007: ret
} // end of method Developer::set_Name

.method public hidebysig
    instance void work () cil managed
{
    // Method begins at RVA 0x2084
    // Code size 2 (0x2)
    .maxstack 8
```

```
    IL_0000: nop
    IL_0001: ret
} // end of method Developer::work

.method public hidebysig specialname rtspecialname
    instance void .ctor () cil managed
{
    // Method begins at RVA 0x206a
    // Code size 8 (0x8)
    .maxstack 8

    IL_0000: ldarg.0
    IL_0001: call instance void [mscorlib]System.Object::.ctor()
    IL_0006: nop
    IL_0007: ret
} // end of method Developer::.ctor

// Properties
.property instance string Name()
{
    .get instance string Developer::get_Name()
    .set instance void Developer::set_Name(string)
}

} // end of class Developer
```

4.2.4 Object oriented programming principles

The class concept evolved out of the notion of encapsulate, an idea originated in SIMULA. If SIMULA is the start of object-oriented programming, object-oriented concept cannot leave simulation and domain modeling. Philosophy tells us object is any entity in the real world. In the software industry, we rely on running programs to solve problems. The problems have their associated business contexts, which entities are business objects.

For example, in the banking industry, it has concept of *Account, Account Payable, Account Receivable, Account Reconciliation, Investment, Investment Premium, Investment Security,* etc. Further down, account has balance, interest, transaction, and different types of accounts, etc. The account is shapeless, figureless and intangible, we only see our monthly balance fluctuate without knowing what happens and how it works behind the scene, but we know the interactions: deposit, withdraw, open a type of account, and close account, etc. In the banking software, numerous objects and their interactions over the time simulate the business regulations, rules and mathematical theories. In the education industry, we have tangible figures, professors, lecturers, tutors, students, paper exams, homework, courses and grades, etc. Contiguously, these figures and materials can be simulated and modeled in the program through objects and the functions among each other. Simulation provides a rich and vivid platform composing of mounts of objects, these objects sit in numerous modules that coupled into one enterprise integrated system, these objects interact through sending messages to invoke the behaviors, these objects are encapsulated by hiding the important data and detail implementations, these objects have inheritance relationships among some of them that the attributes and behaviors have limited taxonomic inference over their relations, these objects play different roles in modules to reference something, have purpose of doing something and cost effective than real world practice. Simulation is the sub-class of modeling towards analytical and discrete state approach. Mathematics brings the power of analytical equation and calculation, discreate state approach embeds low-level implementation to represent high-level phenomena to accomplish the history data analysis and future predication. Modularity produces cohesive, decoupled and independent abstractions. Classes and objects are the main characters of the object paradigm. Objects are instances of related groups of classes from cohesive data structures. A class is a programming language template and all the instantiated objects simulate the same responsibilities defined in the class and implement those responsibilities in the same way.

The object-oriented program has four principles: encapsulation, abstraction, inheritance and polymorphism. The entity encapsulates the properties of the object because all of its properties are set within the definition of the object. For example, object account has properties account number, owner, balance, interest, etc, they locate in a single "place", users of the account object are not concern with the internal ingredients of the object, and they can only change the properties of the object through object's behaviors. Below is an example in Java language:

```
class Account
{
        private string accountNumber;
        private string owner;
        private decimal balance;
        private decimal interest;
        .
        .
        .
        protected String getOwner() {}
        public decimal getBalance() {}
        public void deposit(decimal amount) { }
        public void withdrawal(decimal amount) {}
        public void changeInterest (decimal interestChange) {}
```

```
    public void close() {}
        .
        .
        .

}
```

Encapsulation describes the idea of bundling data and methods within one unit, a class. The concept also often refers as hiding the internal representation or object state from outside world, information hiding. *Account* object x contains both attributes and behaviors. All the important attributes are defined as *private* access that only object itself behavior can access it, this is also known as data hiding, a major part of encapsulation. Outside world does not and does not need to know the account number, balance and interest. They are the data portion belong to object itself. The access modifier *protected* is that the data or behavior can be accessed within the derived classes. The access modifier *public* is that the methods can perform as API to be invoked by other library or external programs. In C#, there's an access modifier *internal* that the data and methods can only be accessed within the same assembly. Using the different access modifier keyword is one way of implementing encapsulation, another way is through interface. Interface is a fundamental mean for object communication, users of the object class communicate with the other object class through sending message to the other object and invoking the interface. If users of class *Account* object x want to know its balance, they send message to *Account* object x invoking the behavior "getBalance()", but users do not and do not need to know the detail implementation of the method "getBalance()", which is encapsulated inside the class through interface methods defined in the *Account* class. This is very important for security and maintenance concern. For security, we do not want to expose object's critical or sensitive data such as password, social security number. For program maintenance, when anywhere in the program is broken, we do not want to track all the way in the code and may only need change the problematic interface method. In the real world, there are many entities that we only can see the surfaces of them and do not know what is inside and how it works behind the scenes. In the home, what surround us are TV, refrigerator, microwave, etc. What we can touch is the button or door, how they work and what the detail implementation are invisible for us. Therefore, we can say encapsulation and information hiding present everywhere in our daily life.

Abstraction is a center point in many science fields. In philosophy, abstraction is the thought process wherein ideas are distanced from objects. It is the process of generalization by reducing the information content of a concept or an observable phenomenon. Abstracting a grey Toyota car to a car retains only the general information of the car's attributes and behaviors, abstracting an article is to provide a short summary of important information written in the article. Abstraction reduces the complexity of idea to a simple general concept, which allows the understanding of a lengthy explanation of the topic in term of a short and concise description. Things that do not exist in the universal place and time diagram are often considered abstract, a physical object is considered concrete not abstract if it is a particular entity that occupies a particular place and time. That's why in object-oriented language, for abstract class, the language cannot instantiate an instance of it. Our minds process information mostly with abstraction as well. When we are thinking about a car, we do not have in mind a particular car but an abstract impression of car, what a car looks like? So, when we are seeing an object looks like a car, our minds popup immediately that it is a car first, if we know more information of car, we may continue recognize what kind of car it is, its brand, model, possible price, etc. The abstraction in mathematics is that we initially encounter a problem in real world, we analyze the problem based on the mathematical concepts and we may finally distill our idea into a concept, a formular, or mathematical modeling, which are abstract structures to represent the underlying real-world problems.

The abstraction in object-oriented programming is a very important concept, we take an object-oriented language, not to rush to code, we may need understand the object-oriented programming from a top level and learned that the software is actually a community of objects interact with other. Each object provides its service or behaviors to wait for triggered by another object or client. Further down to the next level, we realized that the objects can be grouped into different modules to serve for different purpose. Some Modules are for application user interfaces (GUI), some modules are for middleware, business domain logic, some modules are for services, web services or windows service, some modules are for data providers. In different languages, the modules have different names, library for C++, package for Java, assembly for C#. Then viewing horizontally, we see the abstraction of the interactions among objects. It can be accomplished through messaging integration, API call, client server communication, or consumer published event queuing, etc. Finally zoom into each object class level, we abstract the individual behavior or task to interface and do not need to go to each detail implementation. Therefore, each level from top to down, from horizontal to zoom in, abstraction concepts are the core of software which counterintuitively drive us to design the architect of the software with object-oriented abstraction in mind. In term of the type, abstraction has data abstraction and process abstraction. When the object data is not visible the outer world, it creates data abstraction, access to the object's data is provided through methods, like the below diagram showing the class *Account*:

Process abstraction is the internal implementation hidden like a black box, only the input and output are known, the detail logic, algorithm or business rules are complete dark for the users.

In terms of implementation, abstraction is implemented through abstract class, interface, access modifiers and header files. A class containing at least one abstract method is abstract class. There is difference between abstract class and interface. Abstract class can have both abstract and non-abstract methods, interface only has abstract methods. Abstract class does not support multiple inheritances but interface does. Abstract class can provide the implementation of the interface but interface cannot. Abstract class cannot instantiate an instance but interface can have an instance. Through the abstraction, we can reduce the complexity of the design and implementation process of the software.

Object-oriented programming's inheritance concept derives from the original study of inheritance. The study of inheritance system is aimed at identifying and classifying the various mechanisms to processes the heredity, to pass the hereditary information one by each, to functionally interact between the different systems, and to produce the consequences of these properties. Object-oriented programming is all about real-world objects and inheritance and the way of representing real-world relationship. Inheritance in Object-oriented programming supports one of its powerful features: code reuse. Structure design provides code reuse to a certain context, such as in procedure programming, you can write a routine and call it as many times as the program needs. The object-oriented design takes an important step further, it allows programmer to define relationship between classes to reach not only code reuse but also better design. Inheritance allows one or more classes to inherit some common attributes and behaviors from another class, this is also one of the major designs or code refactor guideline. A class X inherits part of all of the structure and behavior from another class Y, class X is a subclass of class Y, class Y is superclass of class X. A subclass can add those attributes and behavior methods from superclass, it can also replace or modify inherited behavior by its own way of implementation. But how to abstract out the common attributes and methods into the superclass? It needs analysis for the real object itself.

This diagram actually reflects a *is-a* relationship that *Developer* and *QA* are actually employees, they all have name and social security number, they all work during the work day. In addition, *Developer* has programming skill matrix and do programming,

QA has applications need to test and they do application validation. Therefore, the attributes of name, ssn and work method are abstract out into *Employee* super class, *Developer* and QA have their additional attributes and their own implementation of work. We can use the below code sample in C# to denote this relationship:

```
protected abstract class Employee
{
        protected string Name { get; set; }
        protected string Ssn { get; set; }
        protected abstract void Work();
}
protected class Developer : Employee
{
        protected string[] SkillSet { get; set; }
        protected override void Work()
        {
                Doprogramming();
        }
}
protected class QA : Employee
{
        protected string[] TestedApplications { get; set; }
        protected override void Work()
        {
                Dotesting();
        }
}
```

We can also say *Employee, Developer and QA* are user defined types, an object of type *Developer* or *QA* is automatically an object of type Employee too. The practical effect of this is that object of type *Developer* can be assigned to a variable type *Employee*, so in program, it would be legal to say *Employee employee = new Developer()*. The object of *Employee* is actually an object of *Developer*, we can use the *is* operator in C# to determine what type of this object belongs to: *if (employee is Developer)*. On the other hand, the assignment statement *developerObj = employee* would be illegal because employee could potentially refer to other types of *Employee* such as QA, just like for the primitive type compiler does not allow you to assign an int value to a variable type short because not every integer is short number. But you can use type-casting, such as *developerObj = (Developer)employee*. Be noted that type-casting is also need valid, if *developerObj = (QA)employee,* then you will get a cast exception throw. Inheritance could potentially down to multiple level inheritance like a tree, it has single inheritance, multiple inheritance, multiple-level inheritance, hierarchical inheritance. In this example, *Developer* class can be superclass of *NetDeveloper* class, and *NetDevleoper* class can be derived to *UIDeveloper,* and so on... In a complex enterprise solution software system, inheritance is very important for the program design based on the business domain context.

Polymorphism is a Greek word literally means many shapes. Poly is many like polygon, polystyrene, polyglot, etc. Morph is change or form like morphology is the study of biological form, and morpheus is the Greek god of dreams. So, polymorphism is the ability to present the same interface for differing underlying forms, the data types. In biology, polymorphism is a discontinuous genetic variation resulting in the occurrence of several different forms or types of individuals among the members of a single species. In object-oriented programming, polymorphism describes a pattern that class entities have different functional implementations but inheriting from the same interface, it is one kind of inheritance. In an inheritance hierarchical, the child class inherits everything, the attributes and methods from parent class, and child class itself has its own features. Still the *Developer* class example, what kind of the work the employee does? Different employees may have different work, for developer, it is do programming, for manager, it's lead and managing, for accountant, it's payroll, tax and finance related, etc. Therefore, each type of employee has his own way of working, this is what it meant by polymorphism, it is different objects who can respond to the same message in different ways. In C++, Java and C# languages, they use keyword override to replace the superclass implementation. If the superclass method declared as virtual and has its implementation, the subclass can inherit the behavior of superclass if it does not have its own implementation, and the correct implementation for the subclass object is selected on the fly, this is run-time polymorphism.

There are other forms of polymorphism, function overloading, a function can be defined as multiple function signatures with the same name and different parameter types, such as *deposit(float)*, *deposit(double)*, *deposit(decimal) and deposit(object)*. The compiler will automatically select the correct one for the type of argument being passed into, this is compile-time polymorphism. Templates, a feature of type that a function and a class are parameterized by. For example, you can define a generic list template class, and then instantiate it as list of integers, list of strings, or list of user defined types. In the application code, the data structure of the list variable is written in arbitrary element type, and the compiler generates versions of it for the various element types. Polymorphism makes applications more modular and extensible. Instead of complex conditional jump statements describing all kinds of logic, you can create interchangeable objects and implement their corresponding behaviors, this is the basic goal of polymorphism.

4.3   Object-oriented expression

We all know how the class object are expressed in popular C++, Java and C# languages, what about some other languages like Lisp, Perl and Javascript, which I started to learn to implement when I studies at school. Maybe I memorize the old times, right now trying to pick it up with an unexpressive taste yet such enjoyable.

I still use the above example class *Developer* with the name as attribute, below is an expression in Lisp:

```
(defclass developer ()
((name
:accessor name
:initarg :name)
(lisper
:initform nil
:accessor lisper)))

(defvar developer1 (make-instance 'developer :name "Bing Wang" ))
```

In Perl, the class is defined as package:

```
package Developer;
use Class::Property;
```

```
property(
    'name' => { 'get' => undef, 'set' => undef },
);
use Developer;
my $developer = Developer->new();
$developer->name = 'Bing Wang';
```

Javascript expression is more closed to C++ and C#:

```
class Developer
{
    constructor(name)
    {
        this.name = name;
    }
}
let developer = new Developer("Bing");
```

Object expression has a variety of different forms in different languages. Mustache is a simple web template system, which does not have if else loop logic statements and can be described as logic-less template engine. A typical Mustache template: *Hello {{name}}, you are a programmer of {{language}}.* Given the following data: *{"name": "Bing", "language": "C-sharp"}* will produce: *Hello Bing, you are a programmer of C-sharp.* jQuery is a javascript library used to manipulate DOM. With jQuery, we can find, manipulate and traverse html document. The following is a Mustache basic template example in jQuery:

```
<script src="https://code.jquery.com/jquery-3.2.1.min.js"></script>
<script src="https://cdnjs.cloudflare.com/ajax/libs/mustache.js/2.3.0/
mustache.min.js"></script>
</head>
<body>
<div id="container"></div>
<button id="button">Click Me</button>
```

Bing Wang

```
<script>
$("#button").on('click', function() {

var data = {name: "Bing", "language": "C-sharp"};
var template = "Hello {{name}}, you are a programmer of {{language}}.";
    var text = Mustache.render(template, data);
    $("#container").html(text);
});
</script>
```

Json is a lightweight data inter-changeable format. It is good for human to read write and easy for machine to parse and generate. Below is a Json mustache syntax:

```
square": {
    "src": "../images/test.png",
    "alt": "Square Image",
    "width": "300",
    "height": "300"
}
```

The syntax tells you how the attributes of src, alt, width and height nested within a larger container square. If we wanted to use the attributes for the square image in our pattern, we can write:

```
<img
src="{{ square.src }}"
alt="{{ square.alt }}"
width="{{ square.width }}"
height="{{ square.height }}"
/>
```

This is Mustache documentation link: <ins>https://mustache.github.io/mustache.5.html</ins>, it should provide a good beginner's primer.

4.4 The pitfall of object-oriented programming

Is object-oriented programming slowly dying?

With object oriented in mind, you can improve the software maintainability and provide higher quality of the software product. Since design is modular and loosely coupled, part of the system can be modified without a need to make large scale changes. However, we have to recognize that object-oriented programs usually have larger program size running relative slower than procedure program because it requires more instructions to execute. Some problems are not good to be provided solution based on object-oriented concepts, a simple design with some procedures may knock it down. Think about data analysis, machine learning, and parallel programming, those developers truly love functional programming. Language C++ has been keeping adding features since its first commercial release in year 1985. During this period of time, there has been a tremendous growth in the capability of computing hardware. The cost has dropped dramatically of memory, in-core and auxiliary: hard disks, flash cards, CDROM, etc., and processor speed and capability has grown enormously. The popular computer folklore Moore's Law, which gets its name from Intel co-founder Gordon Moore. On his paper published on Electronics magazine on April 19, 1965, Gordon introduced the Moore's Law, he indicated that the future of integrate electronics is the future of electronics itself. He predicates that with the unit cost falling, the number of components in a computer chip would double every year. Moore's Law came to be true, throughout all these years, the number of transistors per chip rose from a handful in the 1960s to billions now. This means the amount of information storable on a given amount of silicon has roughly doubled every year since the technology was invented. CPU is much faster now and memory access speed was improved with lower and lower RAM latency. With object-oriented programming, the classes encapsulate code and data, an instantiated object generally needs contain all data associated with it, it needs more CPU power and memory to run. With modern hardware, excessive encapsulation is bad, even worse for multiple level inheritance transformation.

The object-oriented programming is not dead at all, but it is significantly less ubiquitous than it used to be. JavaScript, for example, is object-oriented by design but strongly supports functional programming approach based on the requirement and portability. The point of programming is to translate ideas from human being. What approach the programmer selects is a judgement call through team members' discussion and investigation based on the project demands. Nothing is ever a clean sandbox and sometimes, a well-designed object-oriented approach might entrench and hold the project back. Thinking a new way for object-oriented programming infusing a functional approach, or other program paradigms, might worth studying and evolving in the software developing community. But object-oriented is neither dead, nor is it truly alive? Actually, it is a long history convoluted creature keep absorbing abstraction and encapsulation ideas to make it an ideological programming philosophy. The debate of functional programming versus object-oriented programming may boil down to this point: is the philosophy of object, object relation, object oriented, object abstraction and encapsulation going to extinct? are we going to propose and enrich functional philosophy? I would like to say, do not throw object-oriented philosophy out of your mind, but make sure that it is not the only perspective implanted.

COMPUTING WORLD
DEVELOPMENT
SHRUG

Every new beginning comes from
some other beginning's end.

- *Lucius Annaeus Seneca*

5.1 Data

DATA COMES FROM A SINGULAR Latin word, *datum*, which originally meant *something given*. Its early usage dates back to the 1600s. Over time *data* has become the plural of *datum*.

We are entering digital era, data was emerged from paper record to digital format, it is a kind of new capital and an economic factor of production for goods and services. It is gaining more and more attention and at the same time it gets more and more popular. Now, data is soil, everywhere, infill to our daily life. When we are out for shopping, the purchased items and their prices shown on the clerk registers' screens, what you see are actually data. When we easily book flight without the need to call, we just go to air flight company web site entering the necessary information and click "Check Out" button and take the web browser returned conformation slip ready to go to, our life becomes easier because of data, all playing is the data. No matter what companies or organizations you work for, they cannot survive without data. Simply for the employers' payroll process, our bank get deposit at certain times, which has turned out being a routine thing because of data, data's existing help payroll process go through easily and smoothly, data's presence supports companies' running and profiting. Data's ubiquitous pushes the development and turning around of economy, governance, humanities, and every corners of our society. It brings endless waves, one tide after another. It seems slowly and slowly, imperceptibly, we are no longer live without data.

In computing, data reflect information structured for transformation and processing. Our vehicles run freely on the infrastructure highway, our data shuttle is back and forth on the information highway. In today's computers and transmission media, data is converted into binary digital form. Claude Shannon, an American mathematician known as the father of information theory, initially proposed binary digital concept based on two-value boolean logic from electronic circuits, on or off. He built the foundation for what data mean in term of computing. Binary digit formats embodied in the CPUs, semiconductor, memories and disk drives, as well as many of the peripheral devices. A computer program is actually a collection of bits translated into instructions to execute in the computer CPU. Data has meaning beyond its use in computing. In electronic network communication, the term data is different from control information or control bits. In science, the term data describes the facts, the analysis and the prediction before a new theory or model is created. In medical, the term data tells you the history, the experience, the body facts, the diagnosis and the healing process. Initially hand papers, then punch cards, then followed by magnetic tapes and the hard disks. A bit 1 or 0 is the smallest unit of data. The storage of memory is measured in megabytes and gigabytes now with bigger data measure to come.

Data is the foundation of knowledge, as the old saying: knowledge is power. There are many ways to classify the data, primary and secondary, qualitative and quantitative. Primary data is data collected or generated at first hand, secondary data is resulting from analysis, research or statistics. Qualitative refers to text, image, video, sound, recording and observations, etc. Quantitative is numerical data. Five main categories that typically can be sorted into for data management purposes: observational, experimental, simulation, derived or compiled, reference or canonical. Observational is data captured from real-time. Experimental is the data from lab tests and analysis. Simulation is the data generated from models which mimic the real theoretical systems. Derived or compiled is the data converged from multiple resources. Reference or canonical is the data integrated beyond collecting and mining, it implements a data model that can help make business decision and improve business strategy. Data is often stored in many different systems with different formats. The data format affects the data share and preserve, open and sustainable data format is the best choice. Data appears in different size and shapes, it can be numerical, text, multimedia, or other types. The data encoded in different way will have different data format. For text file, it relies on the format of Microsoft word doc, plain text file, pdf, rtf, xml, and json, etc. For numerical, it includes the format of IBM SPSS statistics, Stata and excel, etc. For multimedia, it is all about image, audio or video file like jpg, gif, tiff, png, mpeg, mp4, etc. Apart from these, data has a few other formats like software application file, 3D models, instrumental specific formats and specimen collections, etc. Even if information is provided in electronic, machine-readable format, but in detail, there may be issues relating to the format of the file itself.

You can't manage what you don't measure, this explains why the recent explosion of digital data is so important, why the big data emerged. Big data is a term that describes large volumes of data, hard-to-manage, structured and unstructured. It is just what it sounds like, lots and lots of data. It comes in a wider variety of forms than traditional data, and it is collected at a high rate of speed. Whoever are interested on the large data can do the analysis and predication, which help make the business decisions and strategic business moves. The process of accessing and storing large amounts of information for analysis has been around for quite a long time. But in the early 2000s, Doug Laney formally proposed the definition of big data as the three V's: volume, velocity and variety. With the boom and flourish of the internet, the data transfer and collection are at petabytes now. The volume of data cannot be neglect because it is more and more hard to process the data with high volume, low density and unstructured. With the industry revolution and the emerge of more and more mission critical system, capturing the real time data stream with an acceptable speed is even more important than volume. With more and more digitized business activity, more and more flourish of new sources of information, large amount of digital information keeps growing on virtually any topic of interest to business. Social media networks, mobile devices, GPS, electric communication all produce torrent of data. Data scientist and analysts no longer rely on the volume of the data, instead, how to use and analyze it turns to be more and more important, just as Google's director of research, Peter Norvig says: *"We don't have better algorithms. We just have more data."* With big data gets bigger, so does the opportunities and research.

5.2 Database

Human being began to store information very long time ago, it started from the ancient civilizations like the Egyptians and Sumerians, who did try to find a way to keep track of data when they were pioneering the accounting techniques. With the society development, industry revolution and technologies invention, database is a foundational element of the modern world, actually we interact with it during our daily life without even knowing it. From the paper filling cabinets which keep the family files, government files, health record and tax documentation to the computer's born that we entered the digital times. More and more, computer scientists realized the importance of electric database and database management system.

In order to conquer the ever-growing data volume, data management, data governance, and data analytics are crucial to make the data understood and communicated in a common language. A strong management practice and a robust system are essential for every organization, regardless of size or type. A data management solution is more and more critical to provide an efficient way to manage heterogeneous scattered data in a unified way. It relies on the data management platform such as database, data lakes and data warehouse, etc., We can call it data utility which delivers the data management through analytics and algorithms to help users better use the data.

Database management system development has been through dozens of years of history. Pre 1960s' magnetic tapes developed replaced punch cards and paper tapes allowing the search from the first medium tapes. The first generalized DBMS, the GE's integrated data store was built in 1961. IBM developed information management system (IMS) in 1960s. The database technology experienced rapid growth in 1970s, the relational model established by Edgar Codd illustrated in his famous paper *A Relational Model of Data for Large Shared Data Banks*, which laid foundation for database theory, the entity-relationship (ER) model introduced by Dr. Chen. The paper and model coined the term *relational database* sparking a new approach to model data represented as cross relational tables with fixed-length of records that would allow any piece of data to store once after normalizations, instead of being stored as free-form list. Based on his idea, people started to think database as a new way that the database's schema, or logical organization, is disconnected from physical storage, this is also the standard principal for database systems. In 1980s, the relational database model grew rapidly and replaced the earlier navigational model, the database management system developed for personal computers allowed PC users to define and manipulate data. Preliminary SQL standard published allowed the generated application programs to start from a high-level nonprogrammer language interface, at the same time, the rich index concept and implementation make query efficient. In 1990s, the internet booming drove the exponential power growth of the online business and database industry, a notable outcome was the creation of MySQL, along with database system Oracle and SQL server built by software giant Oracle and Microsoft.

Database system design and management technology development is a major critical component of computing world. The data reflects a variety of information, government has data, science research and modeling need data, engineering process data, medicine relies on data, etc. A database is a collection of data, discrete or related. The data is facts, it has implicit meaning and needs recorded. The printed index-based address book is data, the line delimited ascii text is data, the column-based spread sheet is data. It can be stored in file formats, as in mainframe systems using ISAM and VSAM. It can also be stored in database, but the term of database is more restricted. Database is mini-world representing some aspects of the real world, it is a logically coherent data collection, its design, built and data query are for special purpose. Database has data definition meta-data and data itself, database and software together we called it database management system.

Database system with its self-describing nature, not only contains the database itself, but also the definition and description of database stored in system catalog called meta-data, or schema. The insulation between programs and data changes the traditional ways of file processing that any changes to the structure of a file require changing all programs, instead, the structure of data files is stored in database management system catalog separated from the access program. Similar with one of the object-oriented programming principals: abstraction, database approach hides the data storage detail and access the data only through data operations such as insert, delete and update. Database structure has high-level and low-level data models. High-level or conceptual model provides the view of user perceiving the data, the entities, attributes and relationships. Entity represents the real-world object or concept, attributes are their properties, relationship describes the interactions among entities. Low-level or physical data model describes how data stored in the computer. These reveal the entity relation ER model concepts. Relationship type among entities types defines a set of associations among entities. It has one to one, one to many and many to many relationships. One of the methods actively used in a real database structure design is semantic modeling. The somewhat less traditional view of data modeling begins with conceptual data modeling. The system of symbols employed in conceptual data model borrows a number of the basic modeling constructs containing entities, attributes, and relationships. The characteristics of conceptual data models are: the objective of the model, the scope of the model. The objective of the model is to provide and communicate a specific business concepts and domains to all the common users. The scope of the model is using a language to describe the object names, this language reflects the business subject domain context, this language covers the business data points, this language eliminates the data abstract to show the real business intent and discover the complete business concepts. The semantic modeling can be described through ER diagrams. The first version of the entity-relationship model was proposed in 1976 by Dr. Peter Chen. Logical data model is a data model specifying problem domain expressed in the data structure such as relational tables, columns and data types. The physical data model structures the design of a database based on the logical data model after it is validated. Logical model more focuses on capturing the concepts in the business problem domain, whereas physical model builds the structure of the data associated with that business domain.

Database are actually files of records being stored in computer disk. Data is stored in the form of records. Each record consists of a list of related data values, and each value corresponds to a particular field of the record. The data type of value field varies from numeric and text, represented as int, string, boolean and large unstructured objects like images, digitized video audio stream or free text, these are referred to as binary large object (BLOB). A file is actually a sequence of records, it may have fixed-length of records with the record length is fixed, and the variable-length of record with the exact length of some records is unknown, at this time, a special separator character is used to terminate the variable-length field. A file header or file descriptor contains disk address of the file block, record format descriptions, field type codes, etc. When searching for a record on disk, one or more blocks are copied into main memory buffers. For record insertion, the new record is added to the end of the block, for the record update and deletion, the program update and delete in the file block buffer after search and locate the record, then copies back the buffer overwritten to disk. The famous binary search algorithm can be used on the ordered file blocks. Binary search is a search algorithm to find the position of a target value within a sorted list. It recursively starts from the middle elements of the list, left and right, comparing with the targeted value until the targeted value is found or not. The worst case is running in logarithmic time. Binary search can be applied to solve a wide range of problems, such as finding the next-smallest or next-largest element in the array. The index is an access structure used to speed up the record search within certain criteria. The most prevalent types of index are single-level indexes with three different types: primary, secondary and clustering. The primary index is an ordered file whose records are of fixed length with two fields, the first field is the primary key field of the data file and the second field is a pointer to a disk block. The ordering key field is primary key of the data file. If records of a file are physically ordered on a non-key field but does not have a distinct value, this field is called clustering field. A secondary index is also an ordered file with two fields. The first field is the non-ordering field of the data file, the second field is either a block pointer or a record pointer. The multi-level index scheme using B-tree and B+-tree is created to reduce the number of blocks accessed when searching a record.

The database relational concept is thought of as a table of values called relation, a row is called tuple representing a list of related data value, a column header is called attribute, the data describing the types of values in each column is called domain.

Relational model has constraints including domain constraints, key constraints, entity integrity, and referential integrity constraints. Domain constraint specify that the value of each attribute must be atomic value from the domain for that attribute. A relation is defined as a set of tuples, all elements of a set are distinct and all tuples in a relation must also distinct. The entity integrity constraints states that no primary key value can be null. The referential integrity constraint is used to maintain the consistency among tuples of the two relations. In the 1970 article *A Relational Model of Data for Large Shared Data Banks* and 1972 article *Relational Completeness of Database Sublanguages*. Dr. Codd presented the relational database model through mathematic formulas of *Relational Algebra*, which is I think, implemented as relational integrity, and *Reduction*, as normalization process.

The data type of binary large object (BLOB) refers the term big data used to describe large data. Big data-driven business models have evolved which treat data as an asset in itself. The big data is stored separately from its record with only a pointer to the BLOB included in the record. The concept of data itself shaped as qualitative and quantitative. They have been reflected as word expression and number statistics in the database system software. Some data types support word expression such nchar, nvarchar, text and xml etc. Some data types support number statistics such as int, binary, bit, etc. Microsoft SQL is more fit for relative middle size data bank due to its limitation on hardly set maximum disk size per database and the windows CPU requirement. It provides at most they call *large object data type* such as pixeled image. On the contrary, Oracle explored more spaces due to its varieties of server hardware architectures and platforms to support big data type such as BLOB and LONG RAW. In relational database world, it uses tabular format with columns and rows to represent the data and has to go through the normalization steps. But for big data, what should be the new format to represent and store the varieties of data types such as text, voice, audio, video, etc. Even further based on this nature, do we need to normalize the data anymore? Do we need to create new set of commands such as DDL, DML, DTL and TCL?

5.3 SQL Server

Microsoft firstly achieved tremendous success in desktop database product such as Access and FoxPro, when IBM and Oracle have developed full-featured database manager system such as DB/2 and Oracle. The predecessor of SQL server is Ashton-Tate/Microsoft SQL server released in 1998 after Ashton-Tate, Microsoft and Sybase worked together to debut the beta version on OS/2. Years later, in order to survive the PC database market dominated by Ashton-Tate, Microsoft refocused on the core dBASE desktop product. The windows LAN Manager release gave a Microsoft a big boost that they released SQL server version 1.1. At that time, only the system administrator facility can create databases, but regular users can set parameters and run SQL queries. The code base was initially from Sybase, SQL Server 7.0 was largely a rewritten code for an older engine created by Sybase and purchased from them by Microsoft, plus new tools like Query Analyzer showing comprehensive info about SQL Server's processor, new SQL OLAP Services, and new graphical interfaces can help users to create tables, indexes, replication, backup scheduling, etc. After this release, Microsoft gained full control over SQL server product and entered the corporate database world. The success of windows 3.0 release fundamentally changed SQL server development, the window-based database management system. The breakup of Microsoft and IBM on the joined development on OS/2 pushed Microsoft to develop their own windows to compete with OS/2, the windows NT was developing and born under such friendly pressure.

After numerous tests and tortuous on the 16-bit and 32-bit version of SQL server development, Microsoft moved full-speed ahead in developing SQL server for windows NT and it was a huge success. It continued to evolve to be more scalable, more efficient, and more user friendly using. Since SQL Server 2000, it was developed as a high-performance client-server relational database management system supporting high volume transaction processing as well as data warehousing and data analysis. It included more modifications and code base additions such as T-SQL, XML and HTTP support, performance and accessibility features for loading partitions, and advanced management features for automating database work. SQL Server 2005 brought native support for XML data management in addition to relational data handling. SQL Server 2008 introduced backup compression and the ability to track changes to databases via change data capture. SQL Server 14 introduced a new table feature that can fit entirely in memory, regardless of its size and added the ability to back up data to Azure. SQL Server 2016 introduced PolyBase support, which gives the administrator the ability to query CSV data or data stored in Azure or HDInsight. SQL Server 2017 was another step forward, which gave administrators the ability to choose development languages and data types by integrating SQL Server with Linux. SQL Server 2019 includes the Big Data Clusters option, which allows users to work with giant data sets. SQL 2022 introduces new object storage integration to the data platform so that users can integrate SQL Server with S3-compatible object storage and azure storage. Since the initial release in 1989, Microsoft SQL has been gone through dozens of years of the evolution process based on computing hardware technology development, more data goes to cloud and more popular of big data, it is one of the most developed, supported, high performance and popular relational database management system on the database industry market.

5.3.1 SQL Server Architecture

Microsoft SQL Server Data Engine was release to provide an alternative to use the Jet Database Engine (JDE) for Microsoft Access, and focused on the ability to operate on client-server communication application instead of accessing file system on the desktop directly. It's a client-server architecture that client application sends requests and SQL server accepts, processes and replies the data to client.

SQL server is composed of three major components: protocol layer, relational engine and storage engine. The protocol layer supports three types of client-server communication architecture: shared memory, TCP/IP and named pipe. Shared memory supports client and sql server running on the same machine such as sql server express localdb, localhost or 127.0.0.1. TCP/IP provides the capability of client and sql server interacts via network protocol that the server is running in a separate machine. Named pipe is different from TCP/IP, it runs on the intra-network, the LAN, but client and server are still running in different machines. All the three protocols use tabular data stream to exchange data. Tabular data stream is encapsulated in the network packets to transfer between client and server, below diagram shows the SQL server protocol layer components:

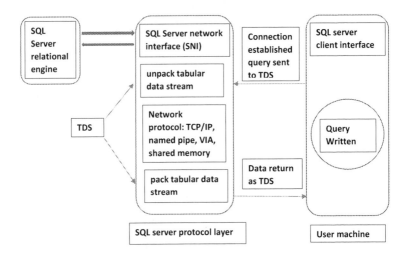

Figure 5.3.3.1 SQL server protocol layer communication

The relational engine is also known as the query processor. The core in this engine is transact-SQL, the Microsoft version of structural query language (SQL). The first component is command parser, it receives the query data sent from protocol layer, parses the SQL syntactic based on the SQL keywords, checks the semantics based on the schema. If command parsing result is error, it returns to protocol layer, if result is ok, it continues to generate different query trees. The query is generated and sent to the second component query optimizer, before it determines an execution plan, it looks at cache to find related existing plan, if it finds the plan, the optimizer retrieve the query and send to run directly, otherwise it comes with the plan based on statements. The statements such as Data Definition Language (DDL) commands that cannot be optimized are compiled into an internal form. The statements of Data Manipulation Language (DML) such as SELECT, INSERT, UPDATE, DELETE will be determined the best way. The query optimization and compilation generate an execution plan, first it normalizes the query that usually breaks down a single query into multiple fine-grained queries, and then optimizes it based on the exhaustive and heuristic algorithm targeting the minimal cost considering memory requirements, CPU utilization and estimated I/O requests. The query optimizer checks the data in the various tables based on the query statement, looks at the index and distribution statistics, the sampling of the data values. From the available information, query optimizer considers various access methods and also use pruning heuristics to produce the most cost-effective plan. The pruning heuristic is that the speed of optimizing a given query tree and executing is not slower than the speed of randomly picking a query execution plan and run it. After the plan is created, it saved to cache for further usage. Below diagram shows the SQL server relation engine running process:

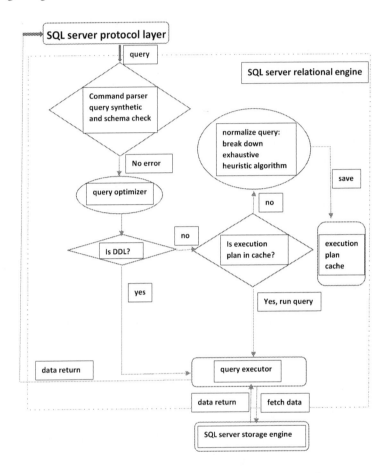

Figure 5.3.3.2 SQL server relational engine running procedures

The execution plan is created and the third component query executor calls the access method to fetch the data and returns to the users. The communication between the relational engine and the storage engine is in terms of OLE DB row sets. The storage engine accesses and modifies the data in disk. A set of operating system files are mapped to SQL server database objects, tables, indexes. Data file physically stores data in the form of data pages with each data page size of 8kb, the smallest storage unit in SQL server.

ASCII Shrug

Every database has one primary file (.mdf) storing the important data related with tables, views, triggers, etc and pointers to the other files in the database objects. Each database may or may not have second file (.ndf) containing user-specific data, but definitely has a log file (.ldf) used for transaction management, recovery and all database modification events. A database can have one or more transaction log files. The data file .mdf is logically divided into pages numbered sequentially from 0 to n. SQL server performs I/O operations at a page level that the storage engine reads or writes the whole data pages during DML operations. Each page contains 96 byte of page header information and one or multiple data rows. If one row exceeds 8060 bytes (8KB), then it is moved to separate text or image page. Extents are the basic unit that space is managed. An extent is 64 KB and has the following two types: uniform extents that owned by a single object and mixed extents shared by up to eight objects. The access methods manager sets up and requests scan of data and index pages. It either sends to buffer manger to retrieve data if query execution plan is *select*, or sends to transaction manager to update data for *update* and *delete*. No matter retrieving or updating, a session opens a table in memory to evaluate the range of rows against the *where* clause. The data parsing has soft parsing if cached, or hard parsing if needs fetch from disk. That's why depending on the purpose and performance, a query plan can be cached in SQL server. Transaction manager is invoked by access method manager. It contains log manager to keep the transaction logs for each commit or rollback and lock manager ensure the data is ACID. The below diagram shows SQL server storage engine components:

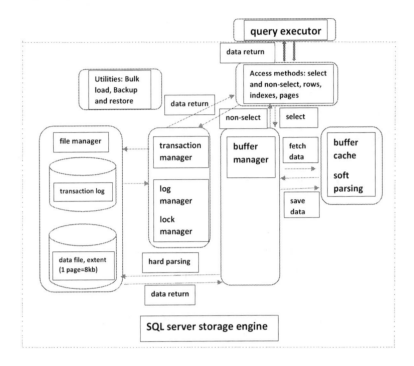

Figure 5.3.3.3 SQL server storage engine components

SQL server enforces the data integrity based on the constraints. Entity integrity, referential integrity and domain integrity, these are the three fundamental aspects of data integrity. SQL server uses primary key constraints to guarantee the uniqueness of values in the designated columns. It enforces logical relationships between tables through foreign key constraints. Each individual data value must meet certain criteria such as matching types and range of datatypes to reach domain integrity. Transaction processing in SQL server ensures all transactions are performed in a single unit of work referring as ACID properties: atomicity, consistency, isolation and durability. Atomicity indicates each transaction either commit or abort. Consistency is that transaction has to enforce data logical correct. Isolation allows data lock and concurrent users to work with data to reach a tradeoff between concurrency and consistency. Durability ensures the transaction effects persist even a system failure occurs. SQL server indexes are the significant data structure and they provide fast access to data when the data can be searched by the index key. An index consists of a tree with a root navigating down to each level, the bottom level is leaf page. The row number decides the level of index tree. The indexes have clustered and non-clustered indexes. The leaf level of a clustered index contains not only the index keys but also the data pages. A table can only have one and better have one clustered index because the data pages can be ordered in only one way. In a non-clustered index, the leaf level contains a pointer to the data row corresponding to the index key. Each table can include as many as 249 non-clustered indexes. However, with more and more indexes, the disk space is increase, which also slows down the data row insertion, deletion or update. A unique index or unique constraint can be created, there is no difference between these two in term of the query optimizer, when a unique constraint is created, a non-clustered unique index is automatically created.

5.3.2 SQL error analysis

5.3.2.1 transaction log

The transaction log for database 'tempdb' is full due to 'ACTIVE_TRANSACTION'

This error could happen when you are using tempdb inefficiently, it could happen when you are doing onerous queries on the DB before a commit performs. Many background processes use tempdb, if it does not perform optimally, all databases are affected and the whole server is slow down that SQL server needs restarted.

In SQL server, the temporary database, tempdb, is a workspace. It is unique in all databases because it is re-created but not re-covered. It is used for temporary tables explicitly created by users. The operations within tempdb are logged so that transactions can be rolled back but cannot recovered due to the limitation of the logged information. All users have privileges to create and use private temp tables and global temp tables nomenclature #localtable and ##globaltable. Temporary tables are useful workspaces used to operate the intermediate data or share work with other connections. Since the logging is minimal, the data modification operation on tempdb is much faster than the operations on other databases. Private temporary table's name starts with a single pound sign #: Create table #mytable, only the connection that creates #mytable can access the table and #mytable exists for the life of connection only. At last, the connection needs drop table: Drop table #mytable to release memory. Since the scoping of the private temporary table is specific to the connection, there will not have naming collision, similar with local variables but not completely the same, the life time of private temp table is for the whole connection session while the local variable lives only within the routine who declares it. Global temporary table's name starts with double pound sing ##: Create table ##mytable. ##mytable can be created from any database any connection and any connection can subsequently access the table for operation, so naming conflict is possible. A globe temp table lives until the creating connection terminates and all current uses of the temp table are complete. Similarly, there have private temporary store procedure and global temporary store procedure the same that the name starts with # and ## respectively.

Temp table is also used for transferring large amounts of data between tables when the amount of memory is not enough to contain the transfer. The tempdb will shrink and grow as the objects use it. Since tempdb operations are minimally logged and its use always be transient, it is not imperative to persist objects permanently. Since memory is also a transient repository for data storage, thetemdb as a result is a perfect candidate for in-memory technologies. When a complicated query is executed with multiple level of conditions through joining, ordering, or grouping, the database engine allocates a certain amount of memory for the operations based on the column and index statistics, sometimes it does not have enough memory to complete the operation if a lot more records than the engine expects. SQL server by default configuration that the tempdb only has a single data file. Microsoft intents to increase the number of data files to maximize the disk bandwidth and reduce contention. Therefore, SQL server 2019 introduces a new feature *memory-optimized tempdb metadata* included in the in-memory optimized database feature set. It greatly and effectively manages the resource contention to handle and scale heavy tempdb workloads.

5.3.2.2 SQL timeout

Besides complicated query run exceeding the default 10 minutes timeout, there are also many possibilities causing SQL timeout. Below are two examples I've seen and investigated.

Mcafee in SQL server

Mcafee auto file scanning cost more CPU processing and memory usage, it interferes with the current processes in the SQL server and slows down the operations in SQL server. We can disable Mcafee AutoScan and manually schedule it.

The stats have not been run recently.

A statistic is a histogram of a column or multiple columns of data in a data table. The goal is to count the number of rows that are in each bucket. For instance, if the column holds the customer's last name, you may get 26 buckets, one for each letter range. The histogram counts the rows that the customer's last name within a certain range value and record that into the range1(letter 'A') bucket and do the same for the rest of name range. When the query optimizer has a predicate on this column, such as *where LastName = 'Allen'*, it will estimate how many rows in the table have the last name starting with letter 'A'. It will check the row count in the range1(letter 'A') bucket. If there are 50 rows, it understands that when retrieving the rows from this table, it will get 50 rows back. Getting the row count is important because it helps the query optimizer better decide which data to retrieve first, especially the optimizer tends to pick the smallest data sets first. A histogram tells you the classification of the values in a data group, it shows the frequency distribution of a data set. Usually, a histogram chart is a very good tool to visualize the histogram data. SQL Server statistics are metadata stored in the form of binary large objects (BLOBs) in SQL Server, the statistics contains the distribution of the column data in a histogram, it stores unique values ratio in the density vector, it also helps the query optimizer calculate row numbers returning based on the cost-effective algorithm, the I/O, CPU, and memory resource desired from the database engine.

Understanding the SQL Server statistics concepts can help you understand how the query plan is generated and subsequently drives you to write optimized query. The query plan is a set of instructions describing how a query will be executed in the database engine, it is created by the query optimizer and require some inputs, which include SQL server statistics, the SQL server statistics plays a key role in the query plan generation process. For example, the statistics might lead the optimizer to choose an index seek instead of an index scan, a potentially more resource-intensive operation. The main functionalities of the query optimizer are generating, updating the distribution statistics on certain columns within a table or indexed view. If a statistics object is defined on multiple columns, the object stores details about the correlation of values across the columns. The correlation statistics, also known as densities, are based on the number of distinct rows of column values. The DBCC SHOW_STATISTICS statement returns the enough information about statistics. In some cases, we need to intervene and update the statistics manually. An *UPDATE STATISTICS* statement can make certain queries have the most up-to-date statistics. *Update Statistics dbo. mydatabase with fullscan,* with fullscan tells SQL server to scan entire column in each statistics object. It provides more accurate statistics but result in more resource intensive operation. There are many different factors affecting table, index or column statistics, one of them is that a huge number of inserts, updates or deletions may impact on the statistics. SQL Server also has option to create and update statistics operations automatically. If the option is turned on, when an index is created, SQL Server automatically creates statistics for the indexed columns. SQL server also has option to auto update statistics or manually update.

5.3.2.3 Deadlock

Transaction (Process ID 829) was deadlocked on lock resources with another process and has been chosen as the deadlock victim. Rerun the transaction.

What is a *deadlock*? Etymologically, they are *dead* and *lock*, a lock that leads to a dead end. In SQL server, a deadlock occurs when two processes are waiting for a resource and neither can continue processing because the other process prevents it from getting the resource. When in this situation, SQL server intervenes automatically. There are two types of deadlock in SQL server, cycle deadlock and conversion deadlock. Cycle deadlock is that process A starts transaction acquiring an exclusive lock on the resource X table1 and requests an exclusive lock on the resource Y table2. At the same time, process B starts a transaction acquiring an exclusive lock on the resource Y table2 and requests an exclusive lock on resource X table1, the two processes deadlock. Conversion deadlock is that for process A and process B, each holds a shared lock on the same resource X page1 within a transaction and each process fails to promote its shared lock to an exclusive lock because other process's lock, the two processes deadlock. There are three types of conversion locks. Shared with intent exclusive, this lock occurs when a transaction that holds a shared lock also has an exclusive lock on some resources lower down in the hierarchy. Red with intent update, this lock occurs when a transaction that holds a shared lock also has an update lock on some resources. Update with intent exclusive, this lock occurs when a transaction that holds an update lock also has an exclusive lock on some resources. SQL server detects deadlock and intervenes through the lock manager, which terminates one process's batch, rolls back the active transaction and releases all the process's locks. SQL server engine has a LOCK_MONITOR thread keeps checking for deadlocks and chooses the lock victim and terminates its transaction. The victim is terminated with an error and has to be run again. The deadlock victim is chosen based on the estimated amount of resource consumption for rolling back. The SET DEADLOCK_PRIORITY <Value> statement can be run to influence the choose of deadlock victim. SQL server uses several locking modes including shared lock, exclusive locks, update locks and intent locks. SQL server can lock user data resources at table, page, or row level. Sometimes, poorly written code or lack of indexes will generate locking conditions.

In relational database management systems, locking is a mechanism that happens every time. A lock can be acquired on different resources and uses different locking modes. SQL server has a couple of locking modes: exclusive locks, shared locks, update locks, and intent locks. All these locking modes are not compatible. Locking model compatibility decides whether a concurrently requested lock is compatible with locks that have been granted. If a resource is already locked by another transaction, a new lock request can be granted only if the mode of the requested lock is compatible with the mode of the existing lock, otherwise the transaction requesting the new lock has to wait for the existing lock to be released or for the lock timeout. No lock modes are compatible with exclusive locks. Shared lock is compatible with update lock, if a shared lock has been applied to a resource, other transactions can also acquire a shared lock or an update lock on that resource even before its completion. Sometimes a lot more complex situations happen involving a session holding multiple locks on multiple resources. Deadlocks are different from blocking, blocking is two processes are waiting for the same resource, deadlock is two processes are waiting for each other's resource, both threads are waiting for a lock that will not be ever released and both are suspended until the other releases its acquired locks. There can be more complicated situations, extended events can be used to collect and monitor various events from SQL Server including capturing details information when a deadlock occurred. From IDERA tool, we can also detect the deadlock incident based on the timing. Deadlocks can also be the result of poor application code combined with a database schema that results in an access pattern that leads to a cyclical dependency. To prevent it from happening, from SQL server side, we can take some prevention measures such as creating better indexes, changing isolation modes, or limiting lock escalation. From the application code side, sometimes when software becomes more and more complex, we should carefully analyze the existing code before applying routines, especially for those routines under transaction block. We should check the routine reference to avoid called from different invokes. The code should also make the transaction block as minimal and fast as possible. For the row update and deletion, if the code is inside transaction scope and some developers prefer object-oriented way to represent the data row as object and update or delete object one by one in a loop, this will drag down speed, instead, a store procedure call by passing the list of ids will be much faster.

5.4 Data Modeling

Data is more and more important playing the pivotal role in the modern world. Its scope is more and more wider covering almost every corner of the world. Nothing can present without data. Data can be machine-readable or human-readable. Data can tell us everything, the business rules, the modeling structure, and the data relation, etc. The customer data is useful for a sales team when they mention specific product sale, an inventory team uses the same sales data based on the product ID when placing order. The warehouse data is a collection of the manufacture's products, how they stored and distributed, it provides the vital statistics to tell company what's the next business strategies. Data is scattered and around, how about data modeling? And what data modeling can help us? Data modeling is the process of cleansing and organizing data into a visual representation or plan that maps out the data relationships and operations, it is a blueprint to create optimal database. A data model un-complicates data into useful information that help businesses for decision-making and running strategies. It is abstract organized through data description, data semantics, data constraints and data relations. Here are several model types: Entity-Relationship (ER) model is based on the concept of real-world entities and relationships among them, it creates an entity set, relationship set, general attributes, constraints and does not require a detailed understanding of the physical properties of the data storage. It emphasizes efficient storage. Hierarchical model arranges the data in the form of a tree-like structure, or parent-child structure with one root or one parent and all the other data is connected. It explains real-time relationships with a single one-to-many relationship between two different kinds of data with each record has a single root or parent which maps to one or more child tables. Network model enables many-to-many relationships among the connected nodes with one child can link to multiple parents. Relational model arranges the data into tables, which have columns and rows, attribute in the entity. Object-oriented database model defines a database as an object collection, or recyclable software components, it works with complex data objects, it is a combination of an object-oriented database model and a relational database model taking advantage of the advanced functionalities of the object-oriented model but with less of the relational data model. The *objects* involved are abstractions of real-world entities. Objects are grouped in class hierarchies with associated attributes. Dimensional data modeling optimizes data retrieval and speeds for analytic in a data warehouse, it has a specific structure to organize data for reporting. Data modeling is the process of creating a visual representation of the information system and the communication connections between data points and objects. The ultimate goal is to illustrate the types of data used and stored within the database management system.

The data models have three types: conceptual data model, logical data model and physical data model. Conceptual data model is a visual representation of database concepts from a high-level user view of data, the view reflects business domain, business rule and business concepts with the corresponding data entity. It establishes business model with entities, business model's attributes with characteristics of an entity, and relationships between data models and the entities. Logical model defines the structure of the data entities and their relationships in the view of a technical map of the data structures and rules to the corresponding data tables. It is less abstract and need provide detail concepts and relationships in the business domain. Physical model is a schema or framework defining how data is physically stored in a database. It specifically designs the database table including the columns, data types and attributes. The internal schema provides how the data will be physically stored within a database. The physical model also offers a finalized design that can be implemented as a relational database, including associative tables with the relationships among entities as well as the primary keys and foreign keys that will be used to maintain the reference integrity. If the logical data model is characterized by the fact that it describes the data, then the physical model does the implementation of the database.

In 1975, ANSI described three kinds of data-model instance: Conceptual schema, logical schema and physical schema. This distinguish allows the three perspectives to be relatively independent of each other.

5.4.1 Guid

As a primary and a reference key, cloud cosmos azure table container's partition key is Guid. More and more data tables' primary keys are Guid. Guid, Global Unique Identifier, or Universe Unique Identifier (UUID) is trying to create almost 100% unique value, but not 100% since Guid can hold the maximum of 3.4 x 10^{38}, or 2^{128} values, but not infinite. When Guid applies to database schema, it has the following pros and cons. The pros are: Overcome the primary key duplicate when data assimilating into one table from multiple tables across databases with primary key as unique identifier. The primary key (Guid) is known before insertion, avoid the client and database round up time during transaction. The reference key (Guid) is known before insertion, avoid additional parent table primary key data retrieval before inserting to child table. Guid, as plain ASCII character, does not reveal data information, good for URL querying and data transmission for security purpose. The cons are: Guid, pseudo random 128-bit numbers, 16 bytes, occupy disk space compared to int 4 bytes and bigint 8 bytes. It needs additional calculation to get Guid before data insertion. If the primary key is as an indicator of unique business data concept but the data resides in different database, Guid brings more overhead on key comparison and data flows in different databases. Considering of the current trend of more and more relative cheap hard disk and more and more fast speed CPU, the future big table data storage across multiple databases will use Guid as the primary key.

5.4.2 Binary Large Object (BLOB)

A binary large object is an SQL object data type, it is a reference or pointer to an object. An SQL BLOB is a built-in type that refers to store structured or unstructured data. Typically, a BLOB is a file, or a large chunk of data, image, video, or some other large objects. In database management systems, such as Oracle or SQL Server, a BLOB can hold as much as 4 gigabytes. SQL locator is used by driver to implement blob, a blob object contains a logical pointer to the SQL BLOB data rather than the data itself. In Oracle, the internal LOB types and external LOB types are two types of LOB with internal LOB types include CLOB, NCLOB, and BLOB types, and the external LOB type is referred as BFILE. The internal LOB types are stored inside the database, the external LOB types are binary data stored in the operating-system files. In SQL server, large value data types are varchar(max), and nvarchar(max), large object data types are text, ntext, image, varbinary(max), and xml.

5.5   OLE DB vs. ODBC vs. ADO

The software applications are written in a specific programming language such as Java, C#, while databases accept queries in database specific language T-SQL, when a software application needs to do data transactions with database, an interface is required to translate languages between application and database. Open Database Connectivity (ODBC) and Object Linking and Embedding Database (OLE DB) are the two interfaces solving this specific problem. Remember ActiveX Data Object (ADO)? Predating ADO was Open Database Connectivity (ODBC). ODBC gives us drivers and ADO have providers. The most compliant provider was the Jet Engine, a part of Access database. ADO dealt with Current Set of Records (CURSOR) at client side, it is a wrapper for OLE DB. OLE DB performs as a group of APIs to accommodate and abstract access to application data of different file storage and formats: spreadsheets, character-delimiter plain text file, structured query language-based database management systems, indexed-sequential files. It is a successor to ODBC. ODBC, developed by Microsoft SQL Access Group in 1992, is an interface making it possible for application to access database management systems, it does not rely on any specific programming language, or a designated database system, or a predefined embedded operating system. ODBC software API applies to both relational and non-relational database systems. It is also a unified generic middleware between a software and a database, if the database specification changes, the software does not need change along with it, maybe only an update to the ODBC driver would be sufficient. ADO is a collection of Component Object Mode (COM) objects that function as an interface to access data. ADO was originally developed in Microsoft as a part of the Microsoft Data Access Components. It is structured as a middleware between software and OLE DB. There is a difference between ODBC and ADO. ODBC is an open interface, it applies to any application to communicate with any database system, while ADO is a wrapper, ODBC is the best choice for the database not support OLE, ADO is the best choice for connecting to multiple databases at once, ODBC can provide connection to only one database. For 16-bit data accessing, ODBC is the only option. ADO can be used for non-SQL.

The OLE DB object model components contain the data source objects, command objects, rowset objects and session objects. Data source objects represent a particular database management system, the tables, or a single file. Command objects wrap the query statement or store procedure to execute commands: SELECT, UPDATE, or DELETE. Rowset objects encapsulate returned rows or tabular data set. Session objects track client session after sending the request to database system. In the application, when the OLE is being initialized, the connection to the data source is established, a command to request access is sent, query is processed at database system and the request results returns. The bridge communication between client applications and a variety of data sources consists of an OLE DB provider, a set of interface and classes binary dll files using the services of an ODBC driver to connect and interact with both relational and nonrelational databases in a uniform manner.

Both OLEDB and ODBC can access relational and non-relational data sources. Microsoft created the OLEDB provider for ODBC, which is ActiveX Data Object (ADO). OLEDB is a Windows-only database API because it refers the component object models (COM) in its library, COM is unavailable on other platforms. On the contrary, ODBC is supported on Windows, Linux, Mac, and UNIX.

Below is an example of using the OLEDB Driver 19 for SQL Server and ODBC Driver 18 for SQL Server.

Provider=MSOLEDBSQL19.1;Integrated   Security=SSPI;Initial Catalog=MyDatabase; Use Encryption for Data=Optional;Trust Server Certificate=True

Driver={ODBC Driver 18 for SQL Server};Server=.;Database=MyDatabase; Trusted_Connection=yes;TrustServerCertificate=yes; Encrypt=yes;

the System.Data.SqlClient namespace is the.NET Framework Data Provider for SQL Server, the System.Data.Odbc namespace is the.NET Framework Data Provider for ODBC, the System.Data.OleDb namespace is the.NET Framework Data Provider for OLE DB.

Eventually, it all evolves to the Entity Framework and Object Relational Mapping (ORM) libraries.

5.5.1 Data Set to Data Model

No matter what kind of provider we use to retrieve or update data, no matter it is OLE DB pre .NET Framework or ADO.NET, we need map the tabular data to the data model and vice versa. Because for multi-tiers enterprise solution, in the front UI and business logic layer, only data model is known and they transfer back and forth. This is also one of the most important components in the data access layer design and implementation. There're many ways to map the data set to the data model. Below lists a couple of mechanisms.

5.5.1.1 Serialization

Json serializer can convert data table to object with the below function call:

```
public class MyDataModel
{
    [JsonProperty("id")]
    public int Id { get; set; }
    .
    .
    .
}
```

```
string serializeddt = JsonConvert.SerializeObject(dataTable, Formatting.
Indented);
```

```
List<MyDataModel> models = JsonConvert.DeserializeObject<List<
MyDataModel>>(serializeddt, new JsonSerializerSettings { NullValue
Handling = NullValueHandling.Ignore });
```

Is it expensive doing through json converter? But at least two lines of code with generic call can accomplish the task. It does not matter whether your data table contains more or less fields than the data model class's property fields, it is not necessarily one to one match and mapping.

5.5.1.2 Linq

Language Integrated Query (LINQ) is a powerful set of technologies based on the transact sql query syntax directly blended into the C# language. LINQ queries are the first-class language construct in C# .NET, just like classes, methods, delegate and events. The LINQ provides linq to objects, linq to sql and linq to xml. Linq to object is constructing queries against collection of objects stored in memory, IEnumerable or IEnumerable<T>. Linq to sql provides the mapping between relational data schema and represented objects, the object receives the attributes of relational data when the object links to the data table. Linq to xml is load xml into memory and manipulate the xml document similar to document object model (DOM) to retrieve the element values in the xml. Therefore, Linq enables the object-oriented approach integrating in C# to provide a single querying interface for different types of data sources: object collection, relational data, document object model, and retrieves the results as objects. The most visible *language-integrated* part of LINQ is the query expression. The basic query expressions patterns are written in a declarative query syntax, which could contain the filtering, sorting, and grouping operations on the different data sources.

Through Linq, we can either create anonymous type for local scope or predefined data model class for global domain model. It is not necessarily all class properties and data field map.

```
var result = from u in mydatabase.Users
            join e in mydatabase.Employees on u.userId equals e.userId
            select new User
            {
```

```
            Name = u.Name,
            Department = e.Department
    };
```

Anonymous type in C# is the type which does not have a name and derives from System.Object class and it is also a sealed class. At the object initialization the data inserted decides the temporary data type. An anonymous type name is not available at source code until at compile time, the type of the anonymous is automatically generated by the compiler according to the value assigned to its properties. It cannot be cast to any other type except an object. An anonymous type array can be created.

5.5.1.3 Reflection

Reflection provides objects that describe assemblies, modules, and types. Through reflection, an instance of a type can be dynamically created, bind the type to an existing object, or get the type from an existing object and invoke its methods or access its fields, properties or attributes.

```
List<MyType> result = new List<MyType>();
foreach(DataRow row in table.Rows)
{
        MyType myObject = Activator.CreateInstance(myType) as MyType;
        foreach(DataColumn column in table.Columns)
        {
            PropertyInfo myPropertyInfo = myType.GetProperty(column.
            ColumnName);
            myPropertyInfo.SetValue(myObject, row[column], null);
        }
        result.Add(myObject);
}
```

Reflection is slower compared to non-reflective code. The important is when its slow. For instance, if the program is web services experiencing high concurrency or embedded system expecting real time critical moment, instantiating objects using reflection is slow. But the time taken to create the object via reflection is still far less than the time it needs to connect to a network. You could still improve the speed through generics by using a wrapper where T: new() and MakeGenericType instead of using object.

5.5.1.4 Attributed Mapping

Business Objects are data entities and data models, each data model class annotated with table name as class attribute. The necessary properties annotated with column name as field attributes. At the start of the service, the application stores the table name, object name and column name, property name mapping in a collection based on table mapping and filed mapping attributes. Data reader returns data columns and values, loop through each object's property to set value based on the mapping in the collection, then finally return the business object. There's no additional third library mapping needed, but need lots of work on maintenance. It is used for complex query and store procedure data read.

```
[Serializable]
[TableMapping("MyTable")]
public class MyDataModel
{
    private string name;
    [FieldMapping("MyColumn1")]
    public string Name
    {
```

```
        get { return name; }
        set { name = value; }
    }

        private string department;
        [FieldMapping("MyColumn2")]
        public string Department
    {
        get { return department; }
        set { department = value; }
    }
}
```

5.5.1.5 Entity Framework

Data entities are transformed to data transfer objects (DTO). DTO can be data contract serialized, property changed event driven and data errored. Auto mapper can easily help map between POCO objects and DTO. It can create map first based on what you need, then simple call the map function passing source and destination object, the underline instance properties values are all copied on the fly, however the field names have to be the exactly same between source object and destination object. It's good for CRUD operations and non-complex query structure, such as WCF Data Service, MVC and Web Api frameworks. Dapper mapper library provides more flexible customized way of mapping, field by field between the source and destination objects. Before call connection.Query function, all the field mappings have to be setup in advance, usually in the Dapper data access layer constructor. You need implement your own mapper inheriting from Dapper's SqlMapper.ITypeMap. Usually, your mapper class contains CustomPropertyTypeMap and DefaultTypeMap. In the CustomPropertyTypeMap, you need implement your way of mapping between properties and column name, such as through the SelectProperty function below. In the DefaultTypeMap, the column names are the object's property names.

EntityFramework Core DbContext class provide lots of async database transaction calls. In the data access layer, the routines can be implemented as async functions:

public async Task<TResult> function (TInput inputObject)

where TInput and TResult are data model class

TInput is transformed from DTO from external layer such as client web call or client call

TResult is going to be transformed to DTO to return to client.

As a lightweight ORM, Dapper provides simplicity, performance and maintenance. Dapper mapper supposes to be optimized and run faster. Entity Framework Core provides more simplified mapping combining automapper and dapper mapper. EF Core is designed as an object-relational mapper by mapping between relational database and the object-oriented application data model and structures. The database table maps to application class, the table columns map to class properties and fields, the rows map to elements in application collections, the primary key unique row maps to unique class instance, foreign key of relationship maps to reference to another class. It allows entity field name be different than column name, then map them through EntityTypeBuilder<TEntity> class, such as the following:

```
public class MyDataModel
{
    public int Id { get; set; }
    public DateTime CreatedDate { get; set; }
    public string CreatedBy { get; set; }
}


public class MyMapping : EntityConfiguration<MyDataModel>
{
    protected override void MapProperties(EntityTypeBuilder<MyData
    Model> builder)
    {
        builder.Property(x=>x.Id).IsRequired().ValueGeneratedOnAdd();
        builder.Property(x=>x.CreatedDate).ValueGeneratedOnAdd();
        builder.Property(x => x.CreatedBy).IsRequired();
    }
}
```

5.6 Windows Desktop Interface

A graphical user interface is an interface through which users interact with the various computer aspects and internet browser. It was first invented in the Xerox Palo Alto research lab in the 1970s, till Microsoft pushed Windows 98 and Windows NT, both of which are 32-bit preemptive multitasking and multithreading graphical operating systems, people started to realize the powerful of windows. Windows possesses a graphical use interface (GUI), visual interface. Usually, an interface consists of a variety of visual elements including a new window, data entry controls, text representation controls, friendly graphical like icons, hyper-links or other graphical representations. Graphical user interface is a relatively simple program with numerous controls event driven routines. Icons are images with clickable feature to represent a programming function, mouse as device input can mouse hoover over the icon or menu to execute a command, such as start a new small program, a new small window. All GUIs make use of graphics on a bitmapped video display. Graphics provide visually rich environment for conveying information, and the possibility of a WYSIWYG (what you see is what you get) video display, which itself becomes a source of user input.

Graphical user interface programming is a completely different framework from old traditional command based, batch oriented, or transaction invoked programming, developers need to know some windows fundamentals. When we write an MS-DOS-based application in C, we need absolutely write a main function, which is the program starting point, from there on, we can use any programming structure to flow to the end. For graphical user interface, we can think of it as a diagram, in the diagram, user controls an input device to flow on the diagram, inputting data, click icon or links to trigger the execution command. If a new window opens, a new diagram display continuing to capture user inputs. To get keystroke, we call the function getchar(), or get through character-based windows library, but in windows based programming, we get device input via messages from the operation system. For data driven programming in MS-DOS, the data has to be either initialize as constant variable or read from a data file, when programming windows, data is in resource file which include bitmaps, icons, menu information, or strings, the linker combines the binary resource file with compiler's output to generate an executable program.

There are four parts ensuring a graphical user interface can be operated smoothly: windows, icons, menu and pointer. Windows, or dialogs either modal or modeless can be toggle back and forth, which is a new small program start to open and run. Icons, a small image on which use click to execute a command either open a new window or access a web browser. Menu, a display bar with text on it to instruct user click different text to execute different command, such as open close save file, open a new dialog, run a function, etc. Pointer, a symbol controlled by mouse either ready to click anywhere on the graphic or hour glass indicating a background process is not complete block the main UI thread.

Microsoft windows graphical user interface programming has been more and more flourish since windows NT went to market. It has been through pre .NET unmanaged programming and .NET managed programming. For unmanaged windows application programming, the technologies were focus on C/C++ programming with Win32 WindowsAPI and Component Object Model (COM). Windows controls are basic building blocks of a Windows application. Controls are called widgets in UNIX. Windows controls are user interface elements in conjunction with another window to enable the user to interact with an application. Controls are windows too. In win32 world, they are created using the CreateWindowW or CreateWindowExW functions. The following are list of controls implemented in Win32 library that are the basic blocks for windows GUI.

Static control displays text and graphics and cannot be selected because it cannot have keyboard focus. You create static child window controls by using *static* as the window class in the

CreateWindow function. Since they do not accept mouse or keyboard input, they do not send WM_COMMAND messages back to the parent window.

```
CreateWindowW(L"Static", "text to display",
    WS_CHILD | WS_VISIBLE | SS_LEFT,
    20, 20, 400, 250,
    hwnd, (HMENU) 1, NULL, NULL);
```

Static image control is a small window by passing SS_BITMAP:

```
imageHwnd = CreateWindowW(L"Static", L"",
    WS_CHILD | WS_VISIBLE | SS_BITMAP,
    10, 10, 200, 200, hwnd, (HMENU) 1, NULL, NULL);
```

Button is a simple small window with a text label. It is used to invoke an action. When a button is clicked, it sends a WM_ COMMAND message to its parent window. The low-order word of the wParam parameter contains the control identifier.

```
CreateWindowW(L"Button", L"ClickMe",
    WS_VISIBLE | WS_CHILD,
    30, 30, 90, 30, hwnd, (HMENU) ID_BEEP, NULL, NULL);
```

Check box control is a window box that you can click to turn an option on or off.

```
CreateWindowW(L"button", L"Show Checkbox Content",
    WS_VISIBLE | WS_CHILD | BS_CHECKBOX,
    20, 20, 200, 45, hwnd, (HMENU) 1,
    NULL, NULL);
```

Edit control is a rectangular child window used to enter and edit text. It can be single line or multiline. The edit class is both the simplest predefined window class and the most complex. When a child window is created using the class name "edit," a rectangle area is defined based on the x position, y position, width, and height called parameters. This rectangle area contains editable text. When the child window control gets the input focus, text can be typed, cursor can be moved, the text portion can be selected, or copy paste.

```
editHwnd = CreateWindowW(L"Edit", NULL,
    WS_CHILD | WS_VISIBLE | WS_BORDER,
    80, 80, 200, 20, hwnd, (HMENU) ID_EDIT,
    NULL, NULL);
```

Slider control is a trackbar window that contains a slider and optional tick marks. The slider is moved by the mouse or keyboard. A trackbar is used to select discrete values from a range of consecutive values.

```
sliderHwnd = CreateWindowW(wc.lpszClassName, L"Trackbar",
    WS_OVERLAPPEDWINDOW | WS_VISIBLE, 120, 120, 320, 200,
    0, 0, hInstance, 0);
```

A tooltip is a common graphical user element, it is hidden most of the time. It is a small box appearing near an GUI object, when a mouse pointer hover over it, it displays a brief message.

```
CreateWindow(wc.lpszClassName, "Tooltip",
    WS_OVERLAPPEDWINDOW | WS_VISIBLE,
    120, 120, 180, 160, 0, 0, hInstance, 0);
```

A month calendar is a complex control used to select a date.

```
dateHwnd = CreateWindowW(wc.lpszClassName, L"Month Calendar",
    WS_OVERLAPPEDWINDOW | WS_VISIBLE,
    120, 120, 300, 300, 0, 0, hInstance, 0);
```

A group box is a rectangle wraps a set of controls, such as radio buttons, checkboxes. A group box has a header label describing the control, it groups related controls.

```
CreateWindowW(L"Button", L"GroupBox",
        WS_CHILD | WS_VISIBLE | BS_AUTORADIOBUTTON,
        30, 30, 120, 30, hwnd, (HMENU) ID_BLUE , g_hinst, NULL);
```

A combo box is a combination of an edit box or static text and a list, it is used an item from a list of available options needs selected.

```
comboHwnd = CreateWindowW(L"Combobox", NULL,
    WS_CHILD | WS_VISIBLE | CBS_DROPDOWN,
15, 15, 150, 120, hwnd, NULL, g_hinst, NULL);
```

A progress bar is a control that is used for processing lengthy tasks. It is animated so that the user knows whether our task is progressing.

```
barHwnd = CreateWindowEx(0, PROGRESS_CLASS, NULL,
    WS_CHILD | WS_VISIBLE | PBS_SMOOTH,
    35, 25, 200, 25, hwnd, NULL, NULL, NULL);
```

A tab control joins multiple windows with corresponding tabs.

```
tabHwnd = CreateWindowW(WC_TABCONTROLW, NULL, WS_CHILD
| WS_VISIBLE,
    0, 0, 250, 180, hwnd, (HMENU) ID_TABCTRL, NULL, NULL);
```

A list box contains a simple list that the user can select one or multiple items from them.

```
listHwnd = CreateWindowW(WC_LISTBOXW , NULL, WS_CHILD
    | WS_VISIBLE | LBS_NOTIFY, 15, 15, 200, 150, hwnd,
    (HMENU) IDC_LIST, g_hinst, NULL);
```

There are many other controls like pen, line, polyline, polygon, rectangle, eclipse, star, etc. All controls in windows form and WPF originally starts from CreateWindow function call in Win32 API library. The Microsoft windows resource compiler is an application development tool used to add UI and other resources to a Windows-based application. Almost every production application needs to use resources. A resource is any binary data that bound into the assembly at build time and become a part of an executable of windows-based application. It can standard or defined. It can contain the data, object, or images. Storing the data in the resource help change the data without recompiling the entire application, it also provides the centralize data resource location shared by multiple applications. A resource file can be text file with string resource in it and converted into binary resource (.resources) file embedded into the executable. It can be an Xml resource file (.resx) defining image and string, and then converted into binary resource the same as text resource file. Visual Studio can help create a resource file and include in the project. In the application code, the System.Resources.ResourceManager class can help retrieve the content of resource based on the running assembly contains the resource file. The resource file does not reside in the executable's data area, the resource manager loads the resource into memory and bound to the executable and shared by multiple application components.

Resource file is very useful for dynamically loading the stream or content at runtime, or multiple assemblies share the same resource. Images no longer need be stored in a separate image files, they are stored in a separate editable file on the developer's computer but are bound into the .exe file during the build process.

Visual styles are specifications for the control appearance. A visual style can customize the overall controls' appearance and provide a standardized mechanism for the appearance in all windows-based applications.

Understanding windows architecture can help us understand how the window, the window class, the window procedure, the message queue, the message loop, and the window messages all fit together in the context of a real windows UI program. For each external event a window needs to respond to, window send a message. How to control the window behaves is through how to handle these messages. After the *UpdateWindow* call, the window is fully visible on the screen monitor's video. It is ready and waiting for the keyboard and mouse input from the external user. Windows maintains a *message queue* for each windows program currently running. When an input event occurs, windows translate the event into a *message* and places it into the message queue. In win32 API, a message is an integer value to communicate in the windows on the very basic levels, message is sent by the system to the windows currently being active. Usually, each window message has two parameters, wParam and lParam. wParam is the notification message and lParam is the window handle to the control which sent message. PostMessage is asynchronous that the message will be placed in queue and may not be processed immediately after it is sent. SendMessage is synchronous sending the message directly to the window and does not return until the window has finished processing. A keep running thread retrieves these messages from the message queue by executing a block of code known as the *message loop*:

```
while (GetMessage (&msg, NULL, 0, 0))
{
TranslateMessage (&msg);
DispatchMessage (&msg);
}
```

The message loop keeps peeking the message queue by calling *GetMessage*. It stops and waits for a new one to come if the message queue is empty. An event sends a message to add to the queue, *GetMessages* returns a positive value indicating there is a message to be processed. Win32 library takes the message and pass it to *TranslateMessage* translating virtual key message into character message and pass the message to *DispatchMessage*. *DispatchMessage* takes the message to find out which window this message should go to and further looks up the window procedure and invoke it. It calls that procedure passing the parameters: the handle of window, the message, the wParam and lParam. The window procedure checks the message and the parameters and execute, then windows procedure returns, the *DispatchMessage* returns back to the beginning of the loop. Think about Node.js event loop, the node.js serves as http web service running on the main thread keep doing event loop. When Node.js starts, it initializes the event loop, processes the provided input script, which may make async API calls. It is singled by event demultiplexer once it receives http requests from any client process. The event loop blocks when no more events to process. Event demultiplexer is a native way to process non-blocking I/O through the concept of auto event of window's threading pool, it replaces the CPU's busy waiting. We call it the reactor pattern.

GUI programming cannot leave from the graphics device interface (GDI) philosophy. The GDI is a core windows component providing functions for drawing points, lines, rectangles, polygons, bitmaps and text. It renders UI elements, window frames and menus. A device context (DC) in GDI defines the attributes of text and images for the output to the screen or device. All drawing calls are through the windows APIs against the device-context object to draw lines, shapes, and text. GDI objects such as bitmaps, brushes, clippings, palettes and pens are selected into the device context before they can be used to display the graphic information. The printer driver converts GDI commands into codes or commands that the various printers understand. The world of graphics output devices is divided into two broad groups: raster devices and vector devices. Most PC output devices are raster devices, which graphics are composed of pixels, they use the rectangular array of pixels to display the images. Vector devices, which graphics are composed of paths, the images are drawn by lines.

Computer keyboard has a positively ancient ancestry beginning with the first Remington typewriter in year 1874. Early computer programmers punch holes in Hollerith cards through keyboard and later used it at dumb terminals to connect with large mainframe computers. In current machine, keystroke input is scanned and sent to window procedures in the format of messages. A user might be typing faster than an application can handle the keystrokes, and some keystrokes have particular functions such as switching input focus. The messages a window receives from keyboard events are different between keystrokes and characters. The keyboard is an input device that generates displayable characters or control characters on the output devices. Keyboard can be thought as a collection of keys, for instance, it has only one key labeled "O", both pressing this key and releasing this key are a keystroke. The "O" key can generate several different characters depending on the status of some function keys such as the Ctrl, Shift, and Caps Lock keys. Without hitting any function key, the character is displayed as a lowercase "o.", with function key toggled like the Shift key or Caps Lock, the character is an uppercase "O".

5.6.1 Windows Form

Windows form (WinForms) is a GUI class library included as part of .NET Framework, it replaces C++ based Microsoft Foundation Class (MFC) library to provide a platform to build client applications on desktop, laptop, and tablet PCs. It wraps Win32 API in managed code so that can provide a more comprehensive abstraction above the Win32 API. Unlike batch processing, WinForms is primarily event- driven. The controls on the form are waiting for user interaction to raise events that handled by program to perform tasks. Like in windows, everything in *WinForms* is a control and itself a type of window. All below controls that can be dragged on forms inherit from the *System.Windows.Forms. Control* class including *System.Windows.Forms.Form* itself. This control class is a wrapper of a set of C++ classes that provides basic functionalities such as set text, location, size, color and events. The controls hosting other controls for reusability also ultimately inherit from the *System.Windows.Forms.Control* class such as user control and layout control, etc.

At runtime, a control declaration translates into a call to *CreateWindowEx* to create a window with the given set of parameters, a control's event translates into a call to *SendMessage*. For example, when you are trying to click a button, you get a handle of the button control:

```
handle = Win32API.FindWindowByPosition(ptr, new Point (posx, posy));
```

Then call SendMessage by passing the handle:

```
[DllImport("user32.dll", CharSet = CharSet.Auto)]
public static extern IntPtr SendMessage(IntPtr hWnd, uint msg, int wParam, int lParam);

private const uint BM_CLICK = 0x00F5;

SendMessage(handle, BM_CLICK, 0, 0);
```

The *SendMessage* puts a click request in the message queue of the button, the button reacts by performing its *OnClick* event handler.

5.6.2 Windows Presentation Foundation (WPF)

.NET framework brings an avalanche of new technologies, new type-safe languages with managed runtime CLR, a new way to connect to database through ADO.NET, a new way of implementing web application through ASP.NET, a new set of classes to build windows application. Windows Forms is a mature toolkit with full features, it is a set of essential bits of wraps of window32 API and rely on Win32 to create the visual appearance of user interface elements such as button, textbox, dropdown, etc. but without customization. For example, if you are creating a stylish glow button, a custom control needs to be created and painted at every aspect of the button through the low-level drawing model. Therefore, there is no easy way to paint in one control and spread to other controls. A standard windows application relies on User32 and GDI/GDI+ of the windows operating system to create its user interface. User32.dll is part of Win32 API, it implements the windows user component to manipulate the standard elements of the windows user interface, it enables the graphics user interface matching the windows look style, it runs as a windows API client library process after loaded into memory, actually many managed-code call the corresponding functions in the library.

GDI/GDI+ provides drawing support for rendering, it is a legacy component of Microsoft windows in charge of representing graphical objects and output them to monitors or printers, but it is hard to render advanced animation due to lacking the hardware rasterization for 3D. GDI+ performs as a bridge between Win32API based applications and hardware, it can also integrate with .NET such as all the components in *System.Drawing* namespace.

The Windows Presentation Foundation (WPF) changes all this by introducing a new model of plumbing. It is more than just a wrapper of Win32API, it is part of .Net framework containing a mixture of managed and unmanaged code. It has three components: a presentation framework, presentation core and mallcore. Like windows forms, WPF includes the standard windows control, it can also draw text, border and fill background color. Unlike windows forms, WPF uses xaml to create controls and provide much more powerful features.

Basically, WPF can build an ordinary windows application with standard controls and a straightforward visual appearance. The new feature WPF rendering engine alters the ways of rendering the contents, all the standard controls can be restyled to the customized look, the objects can also be transformed to rotate, stretch, scale, skew. Underlying WPF rendering engine is a powerful infrastructure based on DirectX, the hardware-accelerated graphics API for multimedia and video. In addition, a very important feature is the improved data binding model through the concepts of view and view model, which cleanly separate the UI layout and data logic.

WPF introduces a new Extendible Application Markup Language (XAML) to construct user interface. XAML document defines the arrangement of panels and controls that make up the windows in WPF. It tackles the complex and rich graphical application to separate the graphical portion from the underlying code. The controls in WPF UI are within different nested containers, each container has its own layout logic. WPF layout takes place in two stages: a measure stage and an arrange stage. WPF replaces ordinary .NET events with a high-level routed event feature. Routed events are events with a traveling power, either tunnel down or bubble up the elements tree. It is basically a CLR event supported by an instance of the Routed Event class. A bubbling event begins with the element where the event is originated then travels up the visual tree to the topmost element, most likely a window. A tunnel event is the event invoked at root and travel down the visual tree through all the child nodes until it reaches the element the event originated. The two events are often implemented as a pair.

WPF data binding is relationship between source and target. The target property is a dependency property, it reflects the updates of data or business model automatically. Data binding has one-way data binding and two-way data binding. In one-way binding, data is bound from its source to its target, in two-way data binding, the source changes while the target control in view updating and vice versa. Similar to WinForms, WPF controls have appearance and their attached behaviors. The control elements have vision bases, user defined, or standard controls, or custom controls. Appearance is attained through the style, which has guidelines such as consistency, arrangement, alignment, grouping and emphasis. Consistency guarantees the control elements look as if they belong together. Arrangement makes sure the controls are grouped horizontally from left to right and vertically from top to down. Alignment forces left alignment so that interface elements are easier to scan. Grouping is grouping related elements together to show related information. Emphasis focuses on drawing user attention through enabling, disabling, font, size, fore color, background color, resolution independent to avoid using pixel for size, template with consistent look among different content of windows.

WPF provides several strategies to personalize and customize the appearance of the controls, styling is one of them. It gives a uniform look or appearance, especially apply an appearance to all the controls of a given type. Styles are defined in the resource dictionary and each style has a unique key identifier and a target type. Multiple setter tags can be defined in one style tag. The style can be reused anywhere in its scope, so it is easy to change the style definition and apply all the control elements who use this style. Style can be defined on the following levels: control level, layout level, window level and application level. Control level defines a style on a control and apply it to this control only. Layout level defines a style applying to a specific layout and all its child elements. Window level defines a style on a window level to make the style accessible to all elements on the window. Application level defines a style on application level to apply the controls throughout the application.

WPF behavior is a piece of functionality attaching to a control element, it specifies when and how the control responds through the action attached to a behavior, there is trigger tag that specify what application should do when the behavior triggered. There are two types of behaviors, the first one is attached behavior, it is implemented through the static attached dependency property and the property registered, it has Get and Set functions needs be invoked. The second one is blend behavior, it is written in XAML referring namespace *System.Windows.Interactivity* which comes from blend SDK (*<i:Interaction.Behaviors>*). Blend behaviors is not static and cannot save state easily but can show up in blends. WPF behaviors can help encapsulate multiple related or dependent activities, plus state in a single reusable unit.

WPF controls are separated into logic, that defines the states, events, properties and template. Each control has a basic appearance supported by the default template, which is shipped together with the control and available for all common windows themes. The appearance of a control changes with the instance of a control template. There are four types of templates, the first one is control template, the default appearance and behavior of the control can be customized by control template, it can completely replace a control's visual tree but the functionality of the control is retained. Through control template, all of the control elements belong to it have the same appearance and behavior. All buttons can look alike a hyper link, all buttons can look alike gradient shaded-colored circle, all buttons can have the same text with the same font and fore colors, etc. The second one is data template, the appearance of data objects can be customized, especially when a collection of objects bind to item controls like list view, list box, or combo box. A data template can contain elements that are bound to a data property, it can also contain markup that describes layout, color and other appearance. Unlike control template, it specifies the appearance of data displayed by a control, while control template styles the control itself. Data template can be applied to content controls or items control, A list of data can display as image and text for each data item, a list of data can show as checkbox or radio button for each data item, etc. The third one is *ItemsPanelTemplate*, the panel can be customized to define a layout of items in item controls like *ListBox* and *ListView*. Every *ItemControl* has its default panel. The fourth one is *HierarchialDataTemplate*, the template of parent *TreeViewItems* as well as their child TreeViewItems can be customized.

In a WPF realistic application, the operations are triggered by a variety of different actions through a set of different user-interface elements, these operations also known as commands to connect controls and no need to write repetitive event handling code. WPF command model consists of four key ingredients: commands, command bindings, command sources, command targets. Command performs as a function pointer and the task is invoked when a control is touched. Command binding links a command to a particular area of the user interface. Command source triggers a command, it is a control element, interacting with it to execute a bound command. Command target is also a control element on which the command is being performed.

WPF supports a single-threaded apartment model in order to interoperable with the earlier Win32, MFC and Winform programming model. A WPF application can create and use as many threads as required to do background processing. The goal of multithreading is to create a responsive user interface, when backend service call is ongoing on a worker thread, the application interface will not freeze. But the UI related work will always need to be managed by the main UI thread, the primary thread or dispatcher. WPF elements have thread affinity that the thread creates them owns them, other thread cannot interact with them directly. WPF objects derives from *DispatcherObject* and have thread affinity. WPF application runs on main UI thread and owns all objects. A dispatcher owns the application thread and manages a work item queue to dispatch one at a time, it can help when a new thread finish loading the data and want to update the control in the view from the other thread. Only dispatcher can update the objects in the UI from non-UI thread, otherwise a run time of thread owning error throws. Dispatcher provides two methods: Invoke and BeginInvoke, executes synchronously or asynchronously. The Dispatcher is not designed to run long blocking operation, such as fetching data from backend service.

5.7 Web Services

Without ASCII, web services are impossible.

The term "server" has been already used in 1960s. That means it can be any kind of entity providing services. The term client was used later on including *user* and *program, user* stands for human user and *program* trying to access resources is truly the client. Client-server model system began to emerge when computers started to transform from large mainframes to distributed processing. The development of UNIX operating system brought the concept of server connection with multiple clients with more stability providence, fault-tolerance and scalability. The evolution of client-server communication relies on many backbone inventions and implementations, the design of the first wide-area packet switch network called the Advanced Research Projects Agency Network (ARPANET), the design and implementation of TCP/IP protocol suite, the booming of internet, more and more improvement of browser's engine. Therefore, the client-server model is also called network computing model or client server network because the client requests and the server responses, all these are delivered over the network. It applies in a wide area, web surfing, e-mail exchange, file transfer, database connection and data transaction. The server is an always-on host listening to the incoming request, fundamentally it is hardware socket receives and delivers network packets. From the architecture point of view, the majority client-server models are based on request-response or request-reply message exchange design pattern, which requires a two-way conversation over a communication channel. It can be in synchronous or asynchronous fashion, which is channel connection keeps open until get response or response returned at some unknown later time respectively. Sometimes we need synchronous fashion to proceed operation only after getting response. The downside of it is if the server machine is down or the server cannot deliver response due to any reason, the client has to wait indefinitely, the system seems gloomed into a dead loop. Asynchronous communication is introduced here to send the request into a queue and continue to operate and not care about the processing of the message in the queue. It is useful in many ways to build a decoupled system.

The open system interconnection (OSI) model is a conceptual model enabling diverse communication system to communicate using the standard protocol. It provides a standard for different computer system to be able to communicate through a universal language. The model includes seven layers, starting from the top to bottom A-P-S-T-N-D-P, which stands for Application layer – Presentation layer – Session layer – Transport layer – Network layer – Datalink layer – Physical layer. The Physical layer is the bottom most layer, where the transfer is 0s 1s bits stream through physical medium, the rate of bits per second is also decided in this layer. The devices in this layer include network hubs, repeaters and Ethernet cable connectors. Data link layer is second from the bottom that combines the bits into bytes and bytes and into frames to transfer the packets, when reaching the other party, this layer receives the signal from the bottom physical layer and decodes it into frames. At this layer, the media access control address (MAC) is used to handle the network components, the devices include layer-2 switch and bridge. Network layer is the third layer from the bottom that accomplish the package routing. It routes the packet through a logical network addressing (IP) and subnetting, the packets are sent from its bottom layer over to the medium. The fourth layer is transport layer that takes the data from upper layer, splits it into smaller packets called segments and dispatch to bottom network layer. The transport layer protocols include Transmission Control Protocol (TCP) and User Datagram Protocol (UDP), a connection-oriented reliable protocol and connectionless unreliable protocol respectively. The session layer is providing a sync in the dialog between two distinctive applications like handshake. The presentation layer presents data to user in an understandable way, the data encryption and decryption, compression and un-compression also happen here. The topmost layer is application layer that communicate with user, or the software plays directly. Therefore, a human-readable information transfer over a network from one device to another, the data must travel down all the seven layers in the sender converting to a bitstream sending through cable or wireless medium, after reach the destination, continue to travel up the seven layers to the top.

The application hosted in the server we can call it service. A service is a unit of operations exposed to the world. Service orientation is an abstract principal to build service-oriented application. As the data proliferation and SaaS application explosion continues, Service-Oriented Architecture (SOA) becomes more relevant than ever, it is a stage in the evolution of application development and integration. Organizations are increasingly realizing the need to have a modern and agile approach to software development. Service-oriented aggregates all the related services into a single domain like a self-contained black-box for its consumers. The services inside communicate with each other through data passing. The box has service provider, service registry and service repository. The service interfaces provide loose coupling reducing dependency, they are service contracts between service provider and service consumer, they can also be defined by Web Service Definition Language (WSDL), an xml based standard tag structure that can be viewed from browser. The services are exposed using standard network protocols such as SOAP, HTTP, Restful HTTP. Service consumer can locate the service metadata and develop the required client components to bind the service.

The web service is a service to provide response through web request. It has been gone through a series of gradually developed technologies. The web service architecture can be viewed both from the service role and the protocol stacks. The web service itself has different roles such as service provider, service registration and service request. The service provider provides service available over the internet, service registration publishes the service in a centralized location so that it can be seen from the world, service request is the client sending requests to the service to perform a certain functionality. Client service communication cannot leave without underline network data transfer protocol. The very bottom is TCP/IP and HTTP, then on each top has different layers based on service channel implementation, which composes the protocol stack.

5.7.1 XML-RPC

Web service implementation has been going through different technologies over the years both in Microsoft world and Java ecosystem. Web service cannot leave XML, a markup language revolution. XML descended from the Standard Generalized Markup Language (SGML) developed by IBM. It is a semantic and structure markup language that is extremely powerful especially for the big success of HTML, which booms the browser and internet. Xml is a lite version of SGML, and it simplifies the SGML structure and support Unicode for different human languages. It was gained immediate popular in the developing world. Xml focus on documentation, it adopts the namespace concepts so that the same element name can represent different category. The nature of describing arbitrary data makes the Xml be a very good container shipping the data across different application processes, boundaries and machine platforms. The paramount possibility of data transfer as Xml format drives many languages develop their own Xml API such as parsing, searching and serialization.

XML-RPC emerged in 1998 right after Xml's born. It was developed by the close collaboration between Microsoft and Dave Winer, an American software developer and entrepreneur. XML-RPC has been established as a new webs service interface protocol.

It provides a http-protocol based mechanism for making service call over network through XML vocabulary. The data model, client request structures and service response structures combine together to decide a remote procedure call. Each component is represented as Xml document. The data model specifies the data element and data type, the request specifies the method name and parameter elements, and the response writes the method response and parameter value element or fault element if remote call failed. The xml document request sent through http protocol as body content payload with new content type text/xml, the response is packed on HTTP and HTTP headers and transfers back with the corresponding response code. XML-RPC emerged along with other distributed communication protocols like CORBA, DCOM, SOAP and Java RMI. More communication protocol technologies developed, recently XML-RPC gained the popularity in Javascript world after the Node.js is implemented.

5.7.2 SOAP

Every time after you login your bank account, you are able to review your bank account detail information, every time you type an address in google map, you are able to see the returned map related with the searched address. There must be a form of agreement between client and service and how they are going to exchange data. The data itself is structured in the message. Right now, there are many ways to build the data exchange architect, one is based on SOAP protocol. SOAP, Simple Object Access Protocol built in 1998, is a lightweight protocol based on XML to exchange data between client and server as textual format. Its specification describes only a single transport protocol binding, HTTP, it initially focused on remote procedure call tunneled over HTTP. SOAP is not based on Microsoft technology, it's an open internet standard, but the SOAP stack implementations are not compatible with one another across language domains. Web service written in .NET is always compatible with .NET clients, Java SOAP stack is applied in Java system. SOAP specification defines three components: envelop, encoding and convention. The message is wrapped in envelop defining the application specific data and failure error returns, it also set the convention and encoding rule to define the data types based on xml schema, and since the communication is one-way or two-way, it needs define the convention for representing remote call request and response. The SOAP specification defines "SOAP message" which is sent between the web service and the client. It is a mere XML document which has the below elements:

```
<?xml version='1.0' encoding='UTF-8'?>
<SOAP-Env:Envelope xmlns:SOAP-Env="http://schemas.xmlsoap.org/
soap/envelope/" xmlns:xsi="http://www.w3.org/1999/XMLSchema-
instance" xmlns:xsd="http://www.w3.org/1999/XMLSchema">

<SOAP-Env:Envelope>
<SOAP-Env:Header>
</SOAP-Env:Header>
<SOAP-Env:Body>
      <SOAP-Env:Fault>
            <faultcode />
            <faultstring />
      </SOAP-Env:Fault>
</SOAP-Env:Body>
</SOAP-Env:Envelope>
```

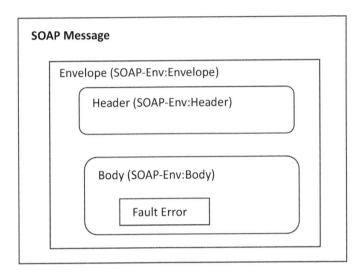

Figure 5.7.1.1 Soap Message

The envelope element is used to encapsulate the entire SOAP message that enables the client application to call the web service and service knows when the SOAP message ends. Each envelop may contain one header element and the header must be the first child of envelope element. The body contains the detail of the actual message, each envelop needs to have at least one soap body element and the body itself may consist of multiple child elements with data structure based on the XML schema. The service response can only have two forms, one is successfully response, one is error response.

5.7.3   WSDL and UDDI

Web services need be defined in a well format so that the services can be discovered or interfaced as an API to integrate with other applications. WSDL, the Web Service Description Language, is a Xml version describing the web service and its network endpoints. WSDL works in conjunction with SOAP and UDDI. Soap provides the network transport data for the web service. UDDI needs publish and locate a web service. A WSDL document describes a web service pretty similar with a type library describing a COM object. It specifies from the four critical pieces of data: interface information, data type information, binding information and address information. The definitions or description element is the root element defining the web service name and all service elements, the type element describes the data types, the binding element specifies the concrete information on how the service implemented, the service element defines the address invoking the services. WSDL defines the contract, the message format and protocol between service and client. Through WSDL, in combination with SOAP and an XML schema, a client can locate a web service and invoke any of the publicly available web methods, the data types are embedded in the WSDL file in the form of XML schema. The client could use SOAP to actually call one of the operations listed in the WSDL through XML over HTTP.

```
<definitions>
<interface name="">
<operation name="">
<input name="" message="" />
</operation>
</interface>
<message name="">
<part name="" type="xs:string">
</part>
```

```
</message>
<service>
<endpoint name="" binding="">
</endpoint>
<binding name="HttpBinding">
<operation>
<input name="" message="" />
</operation>
</binding>
</service>
<binding name="HttpBinding">
<operation />
</binding>
<binding name="SoapBinding">
<operation />
</binding>
</definitions>
```

Web services are self-contained modular applications that can be described, published, registered and invoked over network. The Universal Description, Discovery, and Integration (UDDI) specification describes a way to publish and discover the service information. It was generated along with WSDL. The data captured in UDDI has three main categories similar to telephone book's white, yellow and green pages. It allows businesses to list themselves by their name, product and service they can offer. Therefore, a service provider can explicitly register their service with a web service registry like UDDI, the service consumer or clients can search the web service from internet manually or automatically find out how services and software interact each other over the internet.

5.7.4 NET Remoting

.NET Remoting, a SOAP based remoting call, is a Microsoft developed technology that after the development of technologies: Remote procedure call (RPC), the Component Object Model (COM), the Distributed Component Object Model (DCOM), Common Object Request Broker Architecture (CORBA). It reaches the creation of distributed applications with minimal effort and complexity. It provides a platform supporting data transfer across boundaries. A boundary can be a different process, a different machine, in .NET world, it's an application domain, as illustrated in the following graph:

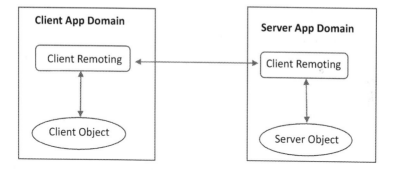

Figure 5.7.4.1 .NET Remoting Client and Service

.NET Remoting enables web services and common language runtime object activation and remoting through http and tcp transport protocols with binary or soap formatter serialization. It communicates between client and server objects via object references. A remote object is a class must derive from System. MarshalByRefObject. During the communication, a proxy represents the actual remote objects on the server. The client accesses the remote methods through proxy: transparent proxy and real proxy. The transparent proxy is the remote object reference returned to the client. The real proxy forwards the messages to the channel down below. The transparent proxy can help client side activate a remote object using the new operator or a System.Activator method. When a remote object's method is called, the transparent proxy calls real proxy's invoke in the namespace of System.Runtime.Remoting.Proxies.RealProxy. with an IMessage interface in the namespace of System.Runtime.Remoting.Messaging. The message is serialized with the formatter depending on the transport protocol. It supports binary and Simple Object Access Protocol (SOAP) serialization. A real proxy is created along with the transparent proxy. You can derive the class of the RealProxy and overrides Invoke method to create customized proxy. The real proxy's primary responsibility is to forward messages to the channel. It first creates a message sink on the channel through calling CreateMessageSink in the namespace of System.Runtime.Remoting.Channels, then process message synchronously or asynchronously. Message sinks are linked together like a linked list into a chain. Each member in the chain retains the pointer to the next sink in the chain. In the application domain at client side, the first sink is a formatter and the last sink is the transport sink, at server side, the order is reversed. You can create a customized message sink and drop in the chain of message sinks and each sink is responsible for calling the respective method on the next sink in the chain. The formatter sinks are to serialize and deserialize IMessage before getting into and after from the stream. The client must implement IClientChannelSink in the namespace of System.Runtime.Remoting.Channels, while the server implements IServerChannelSink in the namespace of System. Runtime.Remoting.Channels. The transport sink supports the transport of serialized message through channel. A channel can one way either receive messages or send messages, it can also be two ways. For HTTP and TCP/IP protocols, each protocol provides a client channel, a server channel, and a combined sender-receiver channel.

Lifetime management are implemented in three ways in distributed applications. The first is to have an open network connection from the client to the server. Server lost memory only when the connection is terminated by client. Second is the DCOM approach, where a combined reference counting and pinging mechanism is used. The server receives messages from its clients at certain intervals. The server frees memory until no more messages are received. The third is like in the internet time, the client request connection is un-predictable. The .NET Remoting lifetime service is customizable as well. By default, an object will get a lifetime assigned to it. It will be contacted just before the lifetime is over and can also increase the object's time to live. This provides the possibility of lifetime service not depend on any specific connection from the client to the server. Singleton and single call are the major two modes of lifetime invocation, where singleton is lifetime with the application domain and single call s lifetime with each remote call.

5.7.4.1. NET Remoting Client and Service

Next, let's look at a code example of server activated object from the web service point of view:

```
namespace ServerActivatedObject
{
//
// Summary:
//    Defines the base class for all context-bound classes.
[ComVisible(true)]
public abstract class ContextBoundObject : MarshalByRefObject
{
//
// Summary:
//    Instantiates an instance of the System.ContextBoundObject class.
protected ContextBoundObject();
}
}
namespace RemoteObjectLibrary
{
[Interception]
public class RemoteObject : ContextBoundObject
{
public RemoteObject() : base() { }
public int Sum(int x, int y)
{
return x + y;
}
}
}
```

The below code is service registration:

```
class Server
{
static void Main(string[] args)
{
```

```
HttpServerChannel http = new HttpServerChannel(8090);
ChannelServices.RegisterChannel(http);
RemotingConfiguration.RegisterWellKnownServiceType(
typeof(RemoteObject),
"RemoteObject.soap",
WellKnownObjectMode.SingleCall);
Console.ReadLine();
}
}
```

The below code is client request:

```
class Client
{
static int Main(string[] args)
{
HttpClientChannel http = new HttpClientChannel();
ChannelServices.RegisterChannel(http);
RemoteObject obj1 = (RemoteObject)Activator.GetObject(
typeof(RemoteObject),
"http://localhost:8090/RemoteObject.soap");
int result = obj1.Sum(10, 20);
RemotingConfiguration.RegisterWellKnownClientType(
typeof(RemoteObject),
"http://localhost:8090/Remote");
RemoteObject obj2 = new RemoteObject();
result = obj2.Sum(100, 200);
}
}
```

obj1 and obj2 are transparent proxy created in different ways. There're no actual communication taking place between the client and the server until method Sum called on the remote object. Server-activated remote objects register in SingleCall mode indicating that there is a new instance with every method call and must remain stateless. Singleton mode remote objects could maintain state because it creates one instance throughout the remote object invokes. That's why SOAP protocol supports both stateless and stateful, .NET Remoting implementation designed on SOAP also supports both stateless and stateful.

The below code example is for client activated object:

```
namespace ClientActivatedObject
{
class Server
{
static void Main(string[] args)
{
TcpServerChannel tcp = new TcpServerChannel(3333);
ChannelServices.RegisterChannel(tcp);
RemotingConfiguration.ApplicationName = "Remote";
RemotingConfiguration.RegisterActivatedServiceType(typeof(Remote
Object));
Console.ReadLine();
}
}
}
namespace ClientActivatedObject
{
class Client
{
static void Main(string[] args) {
TcpClientChannel tcp = new TcpClientChannel();
ChannelServices.RegisterChannel(tcp);
UrlAttribute[] urls = new UrlAttribute[1];
UrlAttribute url = new UrlAttribute(
"tcp://localhost:3333/Remote");
ObjectHandle handle = Activator.CreateInstance(
"RemoteObjectLibrary",
"RemoteObjectLibrary.RemoteObject",
urls);
urls[0] = url;
RemoteObject obj1 = (RemoteObject) handle.Unwrap();
```

```
int result = obj1.Sum(10, 20);
RemotingConfiguration.RegisterActivatedClientType(
typeof(RemoteObject),
"tcp://localhost:3333/Remote");
RemoteObject obj2 = new RemoteObject();
result = obj2.Sum(100, 200);
}
}
```

Activator.CreateInstance() and the new operator are creating instances of RemoteObject. CreateInstance() returns a System. Runtime.Remoting.ObjectHandle, the proxy can only be obtained after unwrap. The server activated objects require a single ObjRef during the lifetime of the server. An ObjRef is marshaled by the server and streamed to the client, where it is unmarshaled to create a transparent proxy. This happens each time the client activates RemoteObject. Unlike server activated objects, client activated objects are activated when Activator.CreateInstance() or new is called.

5.7.4.2 Communication Stack

.NET Remoting channel communication protocol stacks are represented as channel sinks, which support messages passing back and forth between the client and server. The HTTP and TCP channels, in .NET remoting, have two default sinks in the sink chain: a formatter sink and a transport sink. The formatter sink is converting an IMessage into a stream, either in binary or text format, while the transport sink is streaming the data across the wire to reach the other party. They chain together by handing the result to the next sink like a functional linked list. The number of links in a sink chain are not restricted. Customized message sinks

Bing Wang

can be plugged into the chain depending on the problems solving, such as logging and caching, etc. with each sink addressing a single task that is required on the route from the transparent proxy to the remote server object. A sink provider connects channel sinks and a channel, the client channel sink provider implementing the interface of IClientChannelSinkProvider at client side from the namespace of System.Runtime.Remoting.Channels and the server channel sink provider implementing the interface of IServerChannelSinkProvider at server side from the namespace of System.Runtime.Remoting.Channels.

The below code sample is for client sink provider:

```
public class ClientInformationSinkProvider : IClientChannelSinkProvider
{
public IClientChannelSinkProvider Next { get; set; }

public IClientChannelSink CreateSink(IChannelSender channel, string url,
object remoteChannelData)
{
IClientChannelSink nextSink = null;
if (Next != null)
{
nextSink = Next.CreateSink(channel, url, remoteChannelData);
}

if (nextSink == null)
{
return null;
}

return new ClientInformationChannelSink(nextSink);
}
}
```

```
public class ServerInformationSinkProvider : IServerChannelSinkProvider
{
public IServerChannelSinkProvider Next { get; set; }

public IServerChannelSink CreateSink(IChannelReceiver channel)
{
IServerChannelSink nextSink = null;
if (Next != null)
{
nextSink = Next.CreateSink(channel);
}

if (nextSink == null)
{
return null;
}

return new ServerInformationChannelSink(nextSink);
}

public void GetChannelData(IChannelDataStore channelData)
{
// not needed
}
}
```

The last provider is the first to create an actual sink and starts the process where the sinks are chained together. As soon as the provider creates its sink, it could be a candidate for disposal because it has no knowledge of the sink once instantiation is complete. On the client, the first sink must be the formatter sink, and the last must the transport sink. On the server side the order is reversed.

Now the sinks are created, what exactly sink does? Let's see the following example code:

```csharp
public class ServerInformationChannelSink : BaseChannelObjectWith
Properties, IServerChannelSink
{
private IServerChannelSink next;
public ServerInformationChannelSink(IServerChannelSink serverChannel
Sink) : base()
{
next = serverChannelSink;
}

public IServerChannelSink NextChannelSink => next;
public void AsyncProcessResponse(IServerResponseChannelSinkStack
sinkStack, object state, IMessage msg, ITransportHeaders headers, Stream
stream)
{
sinkStack.AsyncProcessResponse(msg, headers, stream);
}

public Stream GetResponseStream(IServerResponseChannelSinkStack
sinkStack, object state, IMessage msg, ITransportHeaders headers)
{
return null;
}

public ServerProcessing ProcessMessage(IServerChannelSinkStack
sinkStack, IMessage requestMsg, ITransportHeaders requestHeaders,
Stream requestStream, out IMessage responseMsg, out ITransportHeaders
responseHeaders, out Stream responseStream)
{
sinkStack.Push(this, null);
ServerProcessing serverProcessing = next.ProcessMessage(sinkStack,
requestMsg, requestHeaders, requestStream, out responseMsg, out response
Headers, out responseStream);
//log request header
LogRequestHeader(responseMsg, requestHeaders);
return serverProcessing;
}
```

```
private static void LogRequestHeader(IMessage message, ITransport
Headers requestHeaders)
{
IMethodMessage methodMessage = (IMethodMessage)message;
string methodName = methodMessage.MethodName;
string header = requestHeaders["CorrelationId"] as string;
//log methodName and header
}
}

public class ClientInformationChannelSink : BaseChannelSinkWithProperties,
IClientChannelSink
{
private IClientChannelSink next;
public IClientChannelSink NextChannelSink => next;

public ClientInformationChannelSink(IClientChannelSink clientChannel
Sink) : base()
{
this.next = clientChannelSink;
}
public void AsyncProcessRequest(IClientChannelSinkStack sinkStack,
IMessage msg, ITransportHeaders headers, Stream stream)
{
}

public void AsyncProcessResponse(IClientResponseChannelSinkStack
sinkStack, object state, ITransportHeaders headers, Stream stream)
{
}

public Stream GetRequestStream(IMessage msg, ITransportHeaders
headers)
{
return null;
}

public void ProcessMessage(IMessage msg, ITransportHeaders requestHeaders,
Stream requestStream, out ITransportHeaders responseHeaders, out Stream
responseStream)
```

```
{
        //add header info to be picked up by the server sink
        //SetRequestHeaders(requestHeaders);
        //log request headers
        next.ProcessMessage(msg, requestHeaders, requestStream, out
        responseHeaders, out responseStream);
}
```

The above explains the basics of constructing a customized sink and provide more functionalities in the ProcessMessage routine.

Sometimes we may encounter an error: *"The input stream is not a valid binary format."* at .NET Remoting message sinks, which both of client and server sides are binary format serialization, when client message sink gets the input stream starting with 3C-21-44-4F-43-54-59-50-45-20-48-54-4D-4C-20-50-55 (translate into string is "<!DOCTYPE HTML PU"), apparently, it's html error response from IIS, but the message sink couldn't translate into a correct corresponding deserialized class instance, it throws exception.

The odd is that this error happens spontaneously. Therefore, I think that it is some issues related with concurrency or environment at that moment. The difficult is that we could not see the complete HTML error message, so we cannot take any action. But one thing we could do is to add some interception codes in the client message sink after binary client format sink and before http transport channel sink and log the complete HTML response stream when error is happening, and hopefully the html response is not generic and could give us some hints on where is the issue.

```
public void ProcessMessage(IMessage msg, ITransportHeaders requestHeaders,
Stream requestStream, out ITransportHeaders responseHeaders, out Stream
responseStream)
{
        next.ProcessMessage(msg, requestHeaders, requestStream, out
        responseHeaders, out responseStream);
        MemoryStream memoryStream = new MemoryStream();
        responseStream.CopyTo(memoryStream);
        byte[] buffer = memoryStream.ToArray();
        string text = System.Text.Encoding.UTF8.GetString(buffer);
        // log response stream (text) to see the detail error if happened
        Stream outStream = new MemoryStream(buffer);
        outStream.Seek(0, SeekOrigin.Begin);
        responseStream = outStream;}
}
```

If error happening such as the IIS app pool is stopped, the html response stream is:

HTML response: <!DOCTYPE HTML PUBLIC "-//W3C//DTD HTML 4.01//EN"http://www.w3.org/TR/html4/strict.dtd>
<HTML><HEAD><TITLE>Service Unavailable</TITLE>
<META HTTP-EQUIV="Content-Type" Content="text/html; charset=us-ascii"></HEAD>
<BODY><h2>Service Unavailable</h2>
<hr><p>HTTP Error 503. The service is unavailable.</p>
</BODY></HTML>
06 Apr 2022 11:41:53.3484521   1 ERROR - *** EXCEPTION ***

System.Runtime.Serialization.SerializationException: The input stream is not a valid binary format. The starting contents (in bytes) are: 3C-21-44-4F-43-54-59-50-45-20-48-54-4D-4C-20-50-55 ...

So at least, we could see some information instead of a generic message "input stream is not a valid binary format."

When building a custom handler, such as for special process of incoming and outgoing contents, customized sink provides a better way to control the actual request. The later web service frameworks also have their own way to provide a customized handler, I'll describe it in later sections. The below code sample represents building a customized message sink:

```
[AttributeUsage(AttributeTargets.Class, Inherited = true)]
public class InterceptionAttribute : ContextAttribute
{
internal const string InterceptionName = "Interception";
public InterceptionAttribute() : base(InterceptionName)
{
}

public override void GetPropertiesForNewContext(IConstructionCall
Message ctorMsg)
{
ctorMsg.ContextProperties.Add(new InterceptionServerProperty());
}
}

public class InterceptionObjectSink : IMessageSink
{
private IMessageSink nextSink;
public IMessageSink NextSink => nextSink;
public InterceptionObjectSink(IMessageSink messageSink)
{
this.nextSink = messageSink;
}
public IMessageCtrl AsyncProcessMessage(IMessage msg, IMessageSink
replySink)
{
return null;
}
```

```
public IMessage SyncProcessMessage(IMessage msg)
{
// customized processing message
}
}
```

The following is the above remote service description metadata through browsing http://localhost:8090/RemoteObject.soap?wsdl:

```
<definitions  xmlns="http://schemas.xmlsoap.org/wsdl/"  xmlns:tns=
"http://schemas.microsoft.com/clr/nsassem/ServiceObject/Service
Object%2C%20Version%3D1.0.0.0%2C%20Culture%3Dneutral%2C%20
PublicKeyToken%3Dnull"  xmlns:xsd="http://www.w3.org/2001/XML
Schema"  xmlns:xsi="http://www.w3.org/2001/XMLSchema-instance"
xmlns:suds="http://www.w3.org/2000/wsdl/suds"  xmlns:wsdl="http://
schemas.xmlsoap.org/wsdl/" xmlns:soapenc="http://schemas.xmlsoap.org/
soap/encoding/" xmlns:ns2="http://schemas.microsoft.com/clr/nsassem/
ServiceObject.RemoteObject/ServiceObject%2C%20Version%3D1.0.
0.0%2C%20Culture%3Dneutral%2C%20PublicKeyToken%
3Dnull" xmlns:ns0="http://schemas.microsoft.com/clr/nsassem/Service
Object/ServiceObject%2C%20Version%3D1.0.0.0%2C%20
Culture%3Dneutral%2C%20PublicKeyToken%3Dnull" xmlns:ns1="http://
schemas.microsoft.com/clr/ns/System"  xmlns:soap="http://schemas.xml
soap.org/wsdl/soap/"  name="RemoteObject"  targetNamespace="http://
schemas.microsoft.com/clr/nsassem/ServiceObject/ServiceObject%2C%20
Version%3D1.0.0.0%2C%20Culture%3Dneutral%2C%20
PublicKeyToken%3Dnull">
<message name="RemoteObject.SumInput">
<part name="x" type="xsd:int"/>
<part name="y" type="xsd:int"/>
</message>
<message name="RemoteObject.SumOutput">
<part name="return" type="xsd:int"/>
</message>
<portType name="RemoteObjectPortType">
<operation name="Sum" parameterOrder="x y">
<input name="SumRequest" message="tns:RemoteObject.SumInput"/>
<output name="SumResponse" message="tns:RemoteObject.SumOutput"/>
</operation>
```

```
</portType>
<binding    name="RemoteObjectBinding"    type="tns:RemoteObject
PortType">
<soap:binding style="rpc" transport="http://schemas.xmlsoap.org/
soap/http"/>
<suds:class type="ns0:RemoteObject" rootType="MarshalByRefObject">
</suds:class>
<operation name="Sum">
<soap:operation soapAction="http://schemas.microsoft.com/clr/nsassem/
ServiceObject.RemoteObject/ServiceObject#Sum"/>
<suds:method attributes="public"/>
<input name="SumRequest">
<soap:body use="encoded" encodingStyle="http://schemas.xmlsoap.org/
soap/encoding/" namespace="http://schemas.microsoft.com/clr/nsassem/
ServiceObject.RemoteObject/ServiceObject"/>
</input>
<output name="SumResponse">
<soap:body use="encoded" encodingStyle="http://schemas.xmlsoap.org/
soap/encoding/" namespace="http://schemas.microsoft.com/clr/nsassem/
ServiceObject.RemoteObject/ServiceObject"/>
</output>
</operation>
</binding>
<service name="RemoteObjectService">
<port name="RemoteObjectPort" binding="tns:RemoteObjectBinding">
<soap:address location="http://localhost:8090/RemoteObject.soap"/>
</port>
</service>
</definitions>
```

5.7.5   ASP.NET Web Service and IIS

After .NET Remoting, web service platform from Microsoft opened a new chapter: ASP.NET, which is a tremendous powerful framework integrated with IIS hosting. Many book and articles described ASP.NET architect diagram, let's delve into the low level of structure as how client web request transfers to the web server routing into ASP.NET runtime and down to the ASP.NET pipeline then come back returning web response. Getting into the innards of underlayers and distilling the insights can help us write better service provider and do quick troubleshooting when production issues occur.

ASP.NET engine is created after ASP, and it is completely built on manage code with the additional extension components built on managed extensions. The WebForm and WebSerivce are two major sophisticated abstractions implemented as http handlers in ASP.NET engine. If saying ASP.NET is an engine, more strictly speaking, it's a web request processing engine. The request enters into the ASP.NET system, routes into the pipeline and reach at the end point, where the current context request stream can be captured and processed.

For ASP.NET web service, when a client request of https://localhost:44320/myservice.asmx?op=GetProducts

It is sent to the host web server, the server's kernel mode driver http.sys gets the request and sends to the internet server application programming interface (ISAPI), a Win32 dll, the lowest layer of ASP.NET and also the first entry point into IIS. ISAPI supports both ISAPI extension and ISAPI filter, which must be registered within the IIS metabase. IIS decides which engine can serve the request. The file extension in the url is asmx, it should map to the default asp.net web service. IIS passes the request to ASP.NET engine. It is routed to the appropriate IIS application pool, then mapped through a script map to the corresponding http handler towards the destinated class specified in the service directive in the .asmx page on disk. .NET runtime CLR and ASP.Net http runtime run in the same process of app pool worker process w3wp.exe (IIS 6 and later). The request is sent from ISAPI extension to Http runtime interface IISAPIRuntime. The ProcessRequest method is the real entry point into ASP.NET pipeline. Once the pipeline is initiated, it creates HttpContext and fire the HttpApplication, like we see in Global.asax file, the Application_ BeginreRequwst and Application_EndRequest start the life cycle of web request processing. The HttpApplication begins processing until to the end of cycle, the new request has to be handled by new HttpApplication object. HttpModules and HttpHandlers are loaded dynamically based on the web. config. The HttpApplication object gives all the registered Http modules to preprocess the request and also decides the type of HttpHandler to handle the request. It looks through the file extension in the url again to dispatch the .asmx default http handler for web service page. HttpModules are event handlers binding with HttpApplication events. It inspects the incoming request, based on the customized processing, it can change the internal workflow of the request. HttpHandlers are the real end point that finally get the request, process and return. An HttpApplication object with its http modules and handlers can only process one request at a time. When another request comes in almost at the same time, the HttpApplicationFactory and HttpHandlerFactory classes pool will dispatch new instance to handle the request. An HttpContext object represents request and response pair throughout the http pipeline.

The below diagram illustrates the above description:

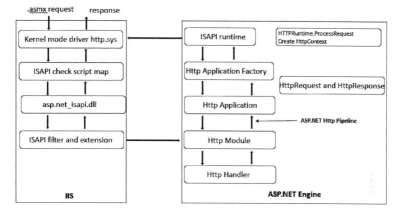

Figure 5.7.5.1 asmx web request goes through http pipeline

When creating a ASP.NET web service now in the Visual Studio 2019, we have to choose .NET Framework 4.0 for a ASP.NET empty web site project, then in Add New item, we could find the asmx web service template.

Client and web services communicate over network using industry standard protocols, like SOAP, HTTP. With soap, the communication is through soap messages, which encapsulates envelop body including the message, the type, in and out parameters as XML. The generated proxy class handles the work of mapping message and parameters to XML elements and sending the SOAP message over the network. The proxy class generation needs service description exists and running. With a service running, a proxy class can be created with the help of wsdl.exe tool. Once the proxy class created, a client can invoke methods in the proxy class, which serializes the parameters and send the SOAP messages to the web service. Upon response back, the proxy deserializes the result and displays at client side. The proxy class uses SOAP protocol by default, however, wsdl.exe can generate proxy classes using either the HTTPGET protocol or HTTPPOST protocol.

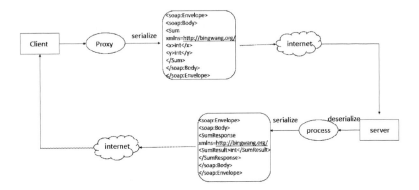

Figure 5.7.5.2 Client Server SOAP Proxy

5.7.5.1 ASP.NET Web Service Sample

The following code sample shows a simple web service:

```
[WebService(Description = "Test ASP.NET Web Service.", Namespace =
"http://bingwang.org/")]
[WebServiceBinding(ConformsTo = WsiProfiles.BasicProfile1_1)]
[System.ComponentModel.ToolboxItem(false)]
[System.Web.Script.Services.ScriptService]
public class MyService : System.Web.Services.WebService, IMyService
{
    [WebMethod(MessageName = "GetSum", Description = "Calculate
    Sum")]
    public int MyMethod(int x, int y)
    {
        return x + y;
    }
}
```

```
public interface IMyService
{
        int MyMethod(int x, int y);
}
```

The below WSDL is for this web service:

https://localhost:44320/Service.asmx?wsdl

```
<wsdl:definitions    xmlns:tm="http://microsoft.com/wsdl/mime/text
Matching/" xmlns:soapenc="http://schemas.xmlsoap.org/soap/encoding/"
xmlns:mime="http://schemas.xmlsoap.org/wsdl/mime/"    xmlns:tns="
http://bingwang.org/"   xmlns:soap="http://schemas.xmlsoap.org/wsdl/
soap/"    xmlns:s="http://www.w3.org/2001/XMLSchema"    xmlns:
soap12="http://schemas.xmlsoap.org/wsdl/soap12/"  xmlns:http="http://
schemas.xmlsoap.org/wsdl/http/" xmlns:wsdl="http://schemas.xmlsoap.
org/wsdl/" targetNamespace="http://bingwang.org/">
<wsdl:documentation      xmlns:wsdl="http://schemas.xmlsoap.org/
wsdl/">Test ASP.NET Web Service.</wsdl:documentation>
<wsdl:types>
<s:schema elementFormDefault="qualified"  targetNamespace="http://
bingwang.org/">
<s:element name="GetSum">
<s:complexType>
<s:sequence>
<s:element minOccurs="1" maxOccurs="1" name="x" type="s:int"/>
<s:element minOccurs="1" maxOccurs="1" name="y" type="s:int"/>
</s:sequence>
</s:complexType>
</s:element>
<s:element name="GetSumResponse">
<s:complexType>
<s:sequence>
<s:element  minOccurs="1"  maxOccurs="1"  name="GetSumResult"
type="s:int"/>
</s:sequence>
</s:complexType>
</s:element>
```

```
<s:element name="int" type="s:int"/>
</s:schema>
</wsdl:types>
<wsdl:message name="GetSumSoapIn">
<wsdl:part name="parameters" element="tns:GetSum"/>
</wsdl:message>
<wsdl:message name="GetSumSoapOut">
<wsdl:part name="parameters" element="tns:GetSumResponse"/>
</wsdl:message>
<wsdl:message name="GetSumHttpGetIn">
<wsdl:part name="x" type="s:string"/>
<wsdl:part name="y" type="s:string"/>
</wsdl:message>
<wsdl:message name="GetSumHttpGetOut">
<wsdl:part name="Body" element="tns:int"/>
</wsdl:message>
<wsdl:message name="GetSumHttpPostIn">
<wsdl:part name="x" type="s:string"/>
<wsdl:part name="y" type="s:string"/>
</wsdl:message>
<wsdl:message name="GetSumHttpPostOut">
<wsdl:part name="Body" element="tns:int"/>
</wsdl:message>
<wsdl:portType name="ServiceSoap">
<wsdl:operation name="Sum">
<wsdl:documentation xmlns:wsdl="http://schemas.xmlsoap.org/wsdl/">
Calculate Sum</wsdl:documentation>
<wsdl:input name="GetSum" message="tns:GetSumSoapIn"/>
<wsdl:output name="GetSum" message="tns:GetSumSoapOut"/>
</wsdl:operation>
</wsdl:portType>
<wsdl:portType name="ServiceHttpGet">
<wsdl:operation name="Sum">
<wsdl:documentation      xmlns:wsdl="http://schemas.xmlsoap.org/
wsdl/">Calculate Sum</wsdl:documentation>
<wsdl:input name="GetSum" message="tns:GetSumHttpGetIn"/>
<wsdl:output name="GetSum" message="tns:GetSumHttpGetOut"/>
</wsdl:operation>
</wsdl:portType>
```

```
<wsdl:portType name="ServiceHttpPost">
<wsdl:operation name="Sum">
<wsdl:documentation xmlns:wsdl="http://schemas.xmlsoap.org/wsdl/">
Calculate Sum</wsdl:documentation>
<wsdl:input name="GetSum" message="tns:GetSumHttpPostIn"/>
<wsdl:output name="GetSum" message="tns:GetSumHttpPostOut"/>
</wsdl:operation>
</wsdl:portType>
<wsdl:binding name="ServiceSoap" type="tns:ServiceSoap">
<soap:binding transport="http://schemas.xmlsoap.org/soap/http"/>
<wsdl:operation name="Sum">
<soap:operation         soapAction="http://bingwang.org/
GetSum" style="document"/>
<wsdl:input name="GetSum">
<soap:body use="literal"/>
</wsdl:input>
<wsdl:output name="GetSum">
<soap:body use="literal"/>
</wsdl:output>
</wsdl:operation>
</wsdl:binding>
<wsdl:binding name="ServiceSoap12" type="tns:ServiceSoap">
<soap12:binding transport="http://schemas.xmlsoap.org/soap/http"/>
<wsdl:operation name="Sum">
<soap12:operation soapAction="http://bingwang.org/GetSum" style=
"document"/>
<wsdl:input name="GetSum">
<soap12:body use="literal"/>
</wsdl:input>
<wsdl:output name="GetSum">
<soap12:body use="literal"/>
</wsdl:output>
</wsdl:operation>
</wsdl:binding>
<wsdl:binding name="ServiceHttpGet" type="tns:ServiceHttpGet">
<http:binding verb="GET"/>
<wsdl:operation name="Sum">
<http:operation location="/GetSum"/>
<wsdl:input name="GetSum">
```

```
<http:urlEncoded/>
</wsdl:input>
<wsdl:output name="GetSum">
<mime:mimeXml part="Body"/>
</wsdl:output>
</wsdl:operation>
</wsdl:binding>
<wsdl:binding name="ServiceHttpPost" type="tns:ServiceHttpPost">
<http:binding verb="POST"/>
<wsdl:operation name="Sum">
<http:operation location="/GetSum"/>
<wsdl:input name="GetSum">
<mime:content type="application/x-www-form-urlencoded"/>
</wsdl:input>
<wsdl:output name="GetSum">
<mime:mimeXml part="Body"/>
</wsdl:output>
</wsdl:operation>
</wsdl:binding>
<wsdl:service name="Service">
<wsdl:documentation xmlns:wsdl="http://schemas.xmlsoap.org/wsdl/">
Test ASP.NET Web Service.</wsdl:documentation>
<wsdl:port name="ServiceSoap" binding="tns:ServiceSoap">
<soap:address location="https://localhost:44320/service.asmx"/>
</wsdl:port>
<wsdl:port name="ServiceSoap12" binding="tns:ServiceSoap12">
<soap12:address location="https://localhost:44320/service.asmx"/>
</wsdl:port>
<wsdl:port name="ServiceHttpGet" binding="tns:ServiceHttpGet">
<http:address location="https://localhost:44320/service.asmx"/>
</wsdl:port>
<wsdl:port name="ServiceHttpPost" binding="tns:ServiceHttpPost">
<http:address location="https://localhost:44320/service.asmx"/>
</wsdl:port>
</wsdl:service>
</wsdl:definitions>
```

Using the below wsdl.exe tool to generate proxy, by default, it's soap protocol.

wsdl.exe https://localhost:44320/service.asmx /out:ServiceProxy.cs

wsdl.exe /protocol:HTTPGET https://localhost:44320/service.asmx / out:ServiceHttpGetProxy.cs

The proxy classes are different for the different protocols, the following is soap protocol:

[System.CodeDom.Compiler.GeneratedCodeAttribute("wsdl", "4.8.3928.0")]
[System.Diagnostics.DebuggerStepThroughAttribute()]
[System.ComponentModel.DesignerCategoryAttribute("code")]
[System.Web.Services.WebServiceBindingAttribute(Name="ServiceSoap", Namespace="http://bingwang.org/")]
public partial class Service : System.Web.Services.Protocols.SoapHttpClient Protocol

The following is Http protocol:

[System.Diagnostics.DebuggerStepThroughAttribute()]
[System.ComponentModel.DesignerCategoryAttribute("code")]
[System.CodeDom.Compiler.GeneratedCodeAttribute("wsdl", "4.8.3928.0")]
public partial class Service : System.Web.Services.Protocols.HttpGetClient Protocol

5.7.5.2 ASP.NET Web Service Security

In ASP.NET web service, security is a major part for web service design and implementation. Unlike client-server communication, which usually happens in private network and the network is secure from outside world. ASP.NET web service is being hosted in the web server opening to the world, some sensitive information need be protected during data transmission to prevent unauthorized access and usage. Security in ASP.NET web service could be implemented in different ways: IP and DNS level restriction, basic authentication, digest authentication, integrated windows authentication, forms and passport authentication, and customized authority implemented.

IP and DNS level restriction has its own pros and cons. HTTP provides a general security framework for authentication through a set of challenge-response schemes. The simplest is Http Basic Authentication, a method that http user agent send user name and password when making a web request. The web server challenges a client web request to provide authentication information with a www-authentication response header containing at least one challenge. From browser, you will see a prompt to ask you enter your user domain/account and password. When the "OK" button is clicked, the authorization header containing the Base-64 encoded user name and password pair: "BASIC: domain\ username:password" will be transmitted to the server. The web server will compare the username/password pair with the windows domain user account database. If the credential matches, status code 200 OK will be sent back to client, otherwise client will receive status 401 access denied response. This authentication is being widely used because all browsers support it and it doesn't need cookies, session, or login page, but one major downside is that the password is utf-8 encoded but not encrypted, which is completely unsecure unless the data transmission and exchange are over a secure channel HTTPS/TLS.

Digest Access Authentication is a negotiable method between server and client on the providence of credentials. It also bases on a simple challenge-response paradigm, but it encrypted the username and password with hash algorithm instead of base64 encoding of the credentials. Message Digest 5 MD5 and Secure Hash Algorithm 1 SHA1 are widely adopted for the encryption. First, client makes the request and gets back a server generated nonce value along with 401 response from server. Then client runs all the fields: user name, realm password, URI request and nonce through MD5 or SHA1 hash method to generate a hash key. Client sends back the hash key along with username and realm. Server receives it and lookup the password either in domain windows user account database or server account database for the sending user name and calculates the hash key by the same method as client, if the key is match with the sending one, it sends back status 200 OK, otherwise 401 access denied. Digest authentication is part of http 1.1 protocol to dedicate to address the issues exist in basic authentication. It is slightly more secure and widely used in more secure applications.

Integrated windows authentication is the extension for NTLM windows challenge response authentication with the more sophisticated hashing. It supports Kerberos authentication protocol. First, the client sends web request to the server, client receives a random number from server. Then client sends user name, domain name and a token containing the encrypted password back to web server. The web server sends these fields to domain controller to verify the credential before sending back response to client. Integrated windows authentication is best suited for intranet network environment where active directory sits as central user account database.

Form authentication faces larger number of users when considering scalability and security. It allows the user authentication against back store database or Active Directory. It is fully customizable with the necessary feature management such as cookies, session, encrypting, decrypting, validating and page redirecting, etc. Usually, it has login page allowing user to enter credential, then send to the server crossing the network. Form authentication requires more computing memory and power. For ASP.NET, the login page can be made the same as the web service page .asmx, which has a "Login" method to validate if the passing parameters use name and password are authenticated. It can also provide a "Logout" method to sign out the form authentication. The following is a sample web.config for form authentication through web service page:

```
<authentication mode="Forms">
<forms name=".LoginForm" loginUrl="Authentication.asmx" protection=
"All" timeout="60" path="/">
<credentials passwordFormat="SHA1">
<!—dummy data-->
<user name="bingwang" password="ABCDEFG1234567890ABCDEFG
1234567890ABCDEF" />
</credentials>
</forms>
</authentication>
```

Besides windows and form authentication, Microsoft also provides passport service to authenticate the application users. After client sends the credential over the network, the web server offloads the authentication duties to passport servers, which verify the user account through an encrypted cookie mechanism. If no cookies stored for this user or cookies expires, the web application redirects to passport server to login, after successfully logged in, the passport server redirects back to the site. Passport authentication is not fit for ASP.NET web service security authentication.

5.8 Secure Communication

Secure communication is a benchmark of internet revolution. It brought the booming of e-commerce, online banking and digital transactions. It started when Dr. Taher Elgamal, an Egyptian cryptographer and also the chief scientist at Netscape, who brainstormed and developed the Secure Socket Layer (SSL) internet protocol. Netscape's version 2.0 is the core of the language for Hyper Text Transfer Protocol Secure (HTTPS), a protocol supporting encrypted transmission between your browser and internet web server. The protocol is correct in theory but the SSL implementation has flaw. Some scientists presented their browser exploit against SSL/TLS(BEAST) showing the problem that an attacker still can break into the secure communication. Transport Layer Security (TLS) is the successor of SSL, it runs on top of transport layer such as TCP, and composes of TLS record and TLS handshake protocols two layers. TLS 1.0 is written by Christopher Allen and Tim Dierks and was an upgrade of SSL v3.0 but without dramatic changes. The later subsequent evolvements and release of TLS version 1.1, 1.2 and 1.3 deprecated SSL entirely. The Transport Layer Security (TLS) protocol was introduced as a major upgrade of SSL v3. A cipher suite is a set of algorithms that support secure a network connection. Suites typically use Transport Layer Security (TLS) or the predecessor Secure Socket Layer (SSL). Each cipher suite has a unique name describing the algorithm content to identify itself. Nowadays almost every web service supports secure connection over TLS to encrypt data transmission. A varies of exceptions or errors may occur when establishing TLS connections, they dramatically depend on the client and server types. Below is one error we got during the SSL/TLS connection.

Sometimes we see the below error:

One or more errors occurred. (The SSL connection could not be established, see inner exception.)

In order to trouble shoot the production issues related with SSL/TLS, let's try to understand how SSL/TLS connections are established.

There are tons of articles explaining the handshake, the message exchanges. At the beginning, it is the client who starts a conversation. Client sends message sort of: "Hello, I would like to talk to you secretly by encrypting the messages. Here is my TLS version and a list CipherSuite from my side." The web server checks whether it supports the same TLS version and also goes through the server's own CipherSuite lists to try to find any matching ones. Then the web server replies: "Hello, we can use your TLS version and I found this CipherSuite from your list at my side. Let's use this TLS version and CipherSuite to connect. Here is my certificate chain with my public key." Client reviews the server's certificate, verify the certificate is not expired, is valid, the issuer is trustable, etc. Once the verification completed and passed, the client creates a random secret and encrypts with server's public key. Client says "OK, we can use the picked cipher, here is the secret key I encrypted with your public key. Could you recognize it?" The message sent from the client can be only decrypted by the server's private key which is privately known to server itself. The server replies: "I can understand, let's encrypt the data transmission through our own secret key." So, the secret conversation starts, which is a series of messy ASCII codes no one could read. Therefore, the handshake is successful after going through a couple of initial HELLO message exchanges in an instant. You could capture network packet using Wireshark, Netmon, etc.

You can see the list of cipher suites in your server by running power shell command:

Run powershell: Get-TlsCipherSuite

Cipher Suite can be edited in the group policy editor in the server, open editor by typing gpedit.msc

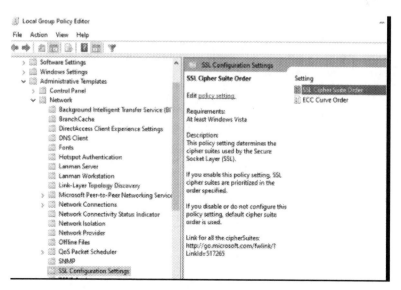

Bing Wang

5.8.1 ASP.NET Web Service Authentication

The following sample codes highlights some ways of customized authentication in web service page:

It goes through custom SOAP header. By adding custom values in the SOAP header and send to web service page to authenticate before continuing to process other requests. It is one simple way:

```
<soap:Header>
    <SOAPHeaderAuth xmlns="http://bingwang.org/">
    <UserName>bingwang</UserName>
    <Password>mypassword</Password>
    </SOAPHeaderAuth>
</soap:Header>

public class SOAPHeaderAuth : SoapHeader
{
    public string UserName;
    public string Password;
}

public class Service : WebService
{
public SOAPHeaderAuth soapHeaderAuth;
[WebMethod, SoapHeader("soapHeaderAuth",Direction = SoapHeader
Direction.InOut,Required = true)]
public bool Login()
{
if (soapHeaderAuth.UserName == "bingwang" && soapHeaderAuth.
Password == "mypassword")
{
    return true;
}
else
{
    return false;
}
}
```

It can also check through backend data store to match the sending account information. The account data is sent along with other client data request:

```
[Serializable]
public class Account
{
        public string username {get; set;}
        public string password {get; set;}
}
[Serializable]
public class ClientRequest
{
        public Account Account {get; set;}
        public int ProductId {get; set;}
}

[Serializable]
public class Product
{
        public int ProductId {get; set;}
        public string ProductName {get; set;}
        public double ProductPrice {get; set;}
}

public class Service : WebService
{
[WebMethod]
public Product GetProduct(ClientRequest request)
{
        // verify the account against database
        If (AccountValid(request.Account))
        {
                // retrieve product from database
                return GetProduct(request.ProductId);
        }

        return null;
}
```

Bing Wang

It can also go through SSL/TLS, data transmitted between server and client is encrypted using public key infrastructure (PKI) techniques. In web server, the SSL certificate is validated against web server certificate store by matching its subject name and expiration status.

```
public class Service : WebService
{
private const string certificateName = "digsn.bingwang.org";
[WebMethod]
public Product GetProduct(int productId)
{
        Product result = null;
        using (System.IO.Stream stream = Context.Request.InputStream)
        {
            if (stream.CanRead && stream.Length > 0)
            {
                Microsoft.Web.Services2.SoapEnvelope envelope = new
                Microsoft.Web.Services2.SoapEnvelope();
                stream.Position = 0;
                envelope.Load(stream);
                XmlDocument xmlDoc = new XmlDocument { Preserve
                Whitespace = true };
                xmlDoc.LoadXml(envelope.OuterXml);
                var nodeList = xmlDoc.GetElementsByTagName("Signature");
                var store = new X509Store(StoreLocation.LocalMachine);
                store.Open(OpenFlags.ReadOnly);
                var subjectFilter = $@"CN={certificateName}".ToLower();
                var certificates = store.Certificates.Cast<X509Certificate2>().
                Where(c => c.Subject.ToLower().Contains(subjectFilter)).
                OrderBy(c => c.NotBefore).ToList();
                store.Close();
                isSignatureValid = // check signature in xml against
                certificates[0]
            }
        }
}
```

```
if (isSignatureValid)
{
        // retrieve product from database
        return GetProduct(productId);
}
else
{
        return null;
}
}
```

5.8.2 ASP.NET Pipeline

Every web request coming into ASP.NET pipeline needs go through http handler. Different http handlers serve to handle different file types. For .asmx, ASP.NET engine has default handler dedicating for web service page. Http modules can help enable some features like caching, logging, and authentication, etc. When sometime we don't want the web request to go through the full processing cycle steps because we are more interested accessing the low-level request and response objects to process our customized processing, we can implement our own customized http handler and http module. Synchronous handler, which implements IHttpHandler interface and Asynchronous handler, which implements IHttpAsyncHandler interface are two type of handlers. These interfaces require to implement the ProcessRequest method and the IsReusable property. The ProcessRequest method handles the actual processing. The intrinsic ASP.NET objects: request, response and server can be accessed through the HttpContext. IsReusable property specifies whether the handler can be pooled for reuse or simply be discarded. HttpModule class implements IHttpModule interface. Through registering the context.BeginRequest and context.EndRequest events, we can add customized processing through the pipeline.

```
public class CustomHandler : IHttpHandler
    {
        public bool IsReusable => false;

        public void ProcessRequest(HttpContext context)
        {
            // analyze request input stream: context.Request.InputStream
            // decide write context response
            context.Response.Write("<h1 style = 'Color:red; font-size:12px;'>
            Sorry, we cannot process this request. </h1>");
        }
    }

public class CustomModule : IHttpModule
{
    public void Init(HttpApplication context)
    {
        context.BeginRequest += Context_BeginRequest;
        context.EndRequest += Context_EndRequest;
    }
    private void Context_EndRequest(object sender, EventArgs e)
    {
            HttpApplication context = sender as HttpApplication;
            // log and process contect repsonse before ending process request,
            such as redirect to new url
            string newUrl = "~/home.aspx";
            context.Context.Response.Redirect(newUrl, true);
    }
    private void Context_BeginRequest(object sender, EventArgs e)
    {
            HttpApplication context = sender as HttpApplication;
            //log context necessry needed property, such as context.Context.
            Request.QueryString
    }
}
```

5.9   Windows Communication Foundation

Window Communication Foundation (WCF), an integrated platform, is Microsoft next revolutionary of the Service Oriented Architecture design. It supports the service implemented as an application with its own App Domain. Client service can communicate through a different platform with service as individual component that has its own boundary, reliability, transaction, security and interoperate with existing web service framework.

Address, binding and contract (ABC) are the three elements of endpoint in WCF. Each service is associated with a unique address so that the message can forward to. The address is represented as Universal Resource Identifier (URI) composing of two elements: the transport protocol and location. The commonly used transport protocols are Http/Https and Tcp. Http and Https are usually for world-wide internet communication with the communication message format as Xml to support platform independent. Net-Tcp is used for intranet communication with message as binary format and relatively fast delivery. The base address can be denoted as [protocol]:[hosting] server domain and name or [dns name]:[port optional]. Binding specifies the communication details for connecting to the endpoints. It contains the protocol, encoding, and transport. These are ordered stack of binding elements. The http or tcp transport layer is the bottom, above it it's encoding to specify the message encoding such as text for supporting interoperability or binary for better performance or Message Transport Optimization Mechanism (MTOM) for large payloads. Above it it's the security mechanism such as reliable message transfer or transaction context flow. Message communication has many patterns, it can be synchronous or asynchronous, can be one way or two-way bidirectional, can be send immediately or queuing. Binding has system binding provided by the WCF framework or developer customized binding. The commonly used system binding includes BasicHttpBinding, an http protocol binding interop with legacy ASP.NET web service-based service. It enables text or MTOM message encoding for crossing machine interoperability. It supports a wide range of client application types and running platforms. Enabling https with wsHttpBinding, NetTcpBinding is a higher performance message binary transmission binding used for intra network but requires both client and service build application on WCF framework. Contract is a standard way of describing the service information and functionality. WCF Contract has service contract, operation contract, data contract, message contract and fault contract. Service contract represents the interface defining the service, which exposed to the client.

5.9.1 Service Contract

It is marked as ServiceContractAttribute at the top of the interface providing the information such as the group of service operations, operation signatures and message data types. Service contract could be publicly expressed in standard XML format metadata, such as WSDL and XML schema that needed by client or other service implementer. A service contract can extend more of other service contract interface, a single class can implement more than one service contract interface. After service contract exposed to the

outside world and client, you can only change the implementation
of service contract but remain the interface intact.

```
[ServiceContract]
interface IMyService
{
}
```

Service contract provides group of operation denoted as operation
contract. It declares the function inside the service contract. It
defines the passing parameters and types and returning result
and types. The binding decides the format of the parameter and
result. It can also be modeled as taking a single message and
returning a message. The OperationContractAttribute needs be
applied to the method operation so that client could recognize
and call it.

```
[ServiceContract]
interface IMyService
{
    [OperationContract]
    Response MyMethod(Request parameter);
}
```

5.9.2 Data Contract

For the message passing back and forth between client and
service, the parameter and return value are the main components.
They need be serialized and deserialized before and after getting
to the wire. In WCF, they represented as data contract and go
through data contract serialization. Certainly, other serialization
mechanism can also be applied such as xml serialization or

binary serialization. Data contract and data member attributes are marked at the top of class type and property fields.

```
[DataContract]
public class Request
{
    [DataMemeber]
    string content { get; set; }
}

[DataContract]
public class Response
{
    [DataMemeber]
    string result { get; set; }
}
```

5.9.3 Operation Contract

The signature of service operation describes the underline message exchange patterns: request-reply, one-way and duplex. Request-reply is message exchange that takes request and deserializes it and proceeds the operation and returns the response after serializing it. It takes a longer communication time, so service fault also is in play. One-way does not have return value similar with the Http method of Post, client does not need wait once the request goes out of the channel.

```
[OperationContract(IsOneWay=true)]
```

```
void MyMethod(Request parameter);
```

Fault contract denotes the error returning to the client when service operation is encountering issue and throwing exception.

The fault is soap fault that modeled as exception in the WCF programming model. One operation contract can have more than one fault contracts to handle the different exceptions and propagate the error to the client.

```
[OperationContract]
[FaultContract(typeof(RequestFault))]
[FaultContract(typeof(OperationFault))]
Response MyMethod(Request parameter);
```

5.9.4 Message Contract

When the exchanged message structure is as important as its content, when sometimes the interoperability is important that the security issue needs be controlled at message level, the message contract is in play to use Soap Xml serialization. The below content and result will specify as the message body. When involving message contract, operation contract can only have one parameter declared as message contract attribute and the return value should also be declared as message contract attribute.

```
[MessageContract]
public class Request
{
      [MessageBodyMemeber]
      string content { get; set; }
}

[MessageContract]
public class Response
{
      [MessageBodyMember]
      string result { get; set; }
}
```

The reader quotas setting can be specified to limit binding as specified in the attributes. WCF will reject the request if the request exceeds any of the limits. The complexity constraints include maximum element depth, maximum bytes per read and maximum string length of the content etc. In network computing, there is a denial-of-service cyber-attack (DOS) that intends to shut down a server or network through flooding the target with traffic or send data triggering a crash. The reader quotas constraints provide protection from DOS attack that attempt to use message complexity to exhaust the processing resources.

Each binding also has security setting. As a service, the security for client service distributed communication is to secure the message during the transmission. WCF security includes three functional areas such as transfer security, access control and auditing. Transfer security touches the functions of integrity, confidentiality and authentication. Transport security mode and message security mode are two main implementations. Transport security happens at transport level protocol such as https that requires client and server reach the cryptographic negotiation. Message security mode is secure soap envelope through WS security. It is transport protocol independent and guarantee the end-to-end security except with a relatively slow transmission due to the nature of Xml and Soap messages.

```
<basicHttpBinding>
    <binding name="bsBinding" closeTimeout="00:02:00" openTimeout=
    "00:02:00" sendTimeout="00:02:00" receiveTimeout="00:02:00" max
    BufferSize="20000"    maxBufferPoolSize="10000"    transferMode=
    "Streamed" messageEncoding="Text" textEncoding="utf-8">
```

```
    <readerQuotas  maxDepth="500000000"  maxArrayLength=
    "500000000" maxBytesPerRead="500000000" maxNameTableChar
    Count="500000000" maxStringContentLength="500000000"/>
    <security mode="Transport" />
  </binding>
</basicHttpBinding>
```

5.9.5 Windows Communication Foundation Behaviors

WCF behaviors enable you to modify default behaviors or add customized extension to modify the runtime behavior. The obvious one is the metadata behavior that ServiceMetadataBehavior implementation controls whether the service publishes metadata. There are four types of behaviors: service behavior, contract behavior, endpoint behavior and operation behavior. Service behavior implements interface IServiceBehavior and its scopes include service, endpoint, contract and operation. Endpoint behavior implements interface IEndpointBehavior and its scopes include endpoint, contract and operation. Contract behavior implements interface IContractBehavior and its scopes include contract and operation. Operation behavior implements interface IOperationBehavior and its scope covers operation.

5.9.5.1 Service Behavior

Service behavior can be implemented through the following mechanisms:

Service class can be denoted a service behavior attribute to participate the construction of the service in run time.

Bing Wang

```
[ServiceBehavior(MaxItemsInObjectGraph = int.MaxValue, Instance
ContextMode = InstanceContextMode.Single, ConcurrencyMode =
ConcurrencyMode.Multiple)]
public class MyService : IMyService
{
}
```

This behavior allows maximum number of items in a serialized object, the default number is 64K. It also creates one service object if not exists and this service object services for all incoming calls and not recycles to subsequent calls. The service instance is multi-threaded but not guarantee thread safe, developers have to handle the thread synchronization by themselves.

ServiceBehavior attribute implements interface IServiceBehavior and Attribute class:

```
[AttributeUsage(AttributeTargets.Class)]
public sealed class ServiceBehaviorAttribute : Attribute, IServiceBehavior
{
}
```

Service behavior also be specified in the configuration as the following:

```
<service behaviorConfiguration="MyServiceBehavior" name="MyService">
<behaviors>
  <serviceBehaviors>
    <behavior name=" MyServiceBehavior">
      <serviceMetadata httpGetEnabled="true" />
      <serviceDebug includeExceptionDetailInFaults="true" />
      <dataContractSerializer maxItemsInObjectGraph="2147483647" />
      <serviceThrottling  maxConcurrentCalls="32"  maxConcurrent
      Instances="32" maxConcurrentSessions="32" />
    </behavior>
  </serviceBehaviors>
</behaviors>
```

Service behavior can also be added at run time through service hosting:

```
ServiceHost host = new ServiceHost(typeof(MyService));
MyServiceBehavior myServiceBehavior = new MyServiceBehavior ();
myServiceBehavior.HttpGetEnabled = true;
host.Description.Behaviors.Add(myServiceBehavior);
host.Open();
public class MyServiceBehavior: IServiceBehavior
{
   public bool HttpGetEnabled  {get;set;}
}
```

Service behavior can also be specified through configuration:

```
<services>
  <service behaviorConfiguration="ServiceWebBehaviour" name="Service.
  WCF.ServiceWeb">
  </service>
</services>
<behaviors>
  <serviceBehaviors>
    <behavior name="ServiceWebBehaviour">
      <serviceMetadata httpGetEnabled="true" httpsGetEnabled="true" />
      <serviceDebug includeExceptionDetailInFaults="true" />
      <dataContractSerializer maxItemsInObjectGraph="2147483647" />
      <serviceThrottling  maxConcurrentCalls="32"  maxConcurrent
      Instances="32" maxConcurrentSessions="32" />
    </behavior>
  </serviceBehaviors>
</behaviors>
```

5.9.5.2 Endpoint Behavior

Contract behavior extends both the client and service runtime across a contract. Endpoint behavior is the primary mechanism

Bing Wang

to modify the client service run time for a specific endpoint. Operation behavior is used to extend both the client service runtime for each operation.

Endpoint behavior is modifying the entire service or client run time for a specific endpoint. It can be created through implementing System.ServiceModel.Description.IEndpointBehavior to inspect the message passing through and response back.

The following code sample adds message inspector at client side, it implements class MyEndpointBehavior inheriting from System.ServiceModel.Description.IEndpointBehavior and class MyMessageInspectorClient inheriting from System.ServiceModel. Dispatcher.IClientMessageInspector:

```
public class MyEndpointBehavior: IEndpointBehavior
{
    public void AddBindingParameters(ServiceEndpoint serviceEndpoint,
    System.ServiceModel.Channels.BindingParameterCollection binding
    Parameters)
    {}
    public void ApplyClientBehavior(ServiceEndpoint serviceEndpoint,
    System.ServiceModel.Dispatcher.ClientRuntime behavior)
    {
        behavior.MessageInspectors.Add(new MyMessageInspectorClient();
    }
    public void ApplyDispatchBehavior(ServiceEndpoint serviceEndpoint,
    System.ServiceModel.Dispatcher.EndpointDispatcher endpointDispatcher)
    {
    }
    public void Validate(ServiceEndpoint serviceEndpoint)
    {}
}
public class MyMessageInspectorClient : IClientMessageInspector
    {
```

```
    public void AfterReceiveReply(ref Message reply, object correlationState)
    {
        //inspect reply Soap message
    }
    public object BeforeSendRequest(ref Message request, IClientChannel
    channel)
    {
        // inspect request Soap message
        return null;
    }
  }
}
```

Before calling the service side method, register MyEndpointBehavior:
channelFactory.Endpoint.Behaviors.Add(new MyEndpointBehavior());

```
public class MyEndpointBehavior : IEndpointBehavior
{
    public void AddBindingParameters(ServiceEndpoint serviceEndpoint,
    System.ServiceModel.Channels.BindingParameterCollection binding
    Parameters)
    {}
    public void ApplyClientBehavior(ServiceEndpoint serviceEndpoint,
    System.ServiceModel.Dispatcher.ClientRuntime behavior)
    {
    }
    public void ApplyDispatchBehavior(ServiceEndpoint serviceEndpoint,
    System.ServiceModel.Dispatcher.EndpointDispatcher    endpoint
    Dispatcher)
    {
        endpointDispatcher.DispatchRuntime.MessageInspectors.
        Add(new MyMessageInspectorServer());
    }
    public void Validate(ServiceEndpoint serviceEndpoint)
    {}
}
    public class MyMessageInspectorServer : IDispatchMessageInspector
    {
```

```
    object IDispatchMessageInspector.AfterReceiveRequest(ref Message
    request, IClientChannel channel, InstanceContext instanceContext)
    {
        // inspect request Soap message
        return null;
    }
    void IDispatchMessageInspector.BeforeSendReply(ref Message reply,
    object correlationState)
    {
        // inspect reply Soap message
    }
}
foreach (var endpoint in serviceHost.Description.Endpoints)
{
    endpoint.Behaviors.Add(new MyEndpointBehavior());
}
```

Endpoint behavior can also be implemented through a custom BehaviorExtensionElement at client side, it implements class MyMessageInspectorClient inheriting from both interface System.ServiceModel.Dispatcher.IClientMessageInspector and interface System.ServiceModel.Description.IEndpointBehavior, it also implements class MyBehaviorExtensionElementServer inherting from class of System.ServiceModel.Configuration. BehaviorExtensionElement.

```
public class MyMessageInspectorClient : IClientMessageInspector, IEndpoin
tBehavior
{
    public void AfterReceiveReply(ref Message reply, object correlationState)
    {
        //inspect message
        string action = reply.Headers.Action;
    }
}
```

```
public object BeforeSendRequest(ref Message request, IClientChannel
channel)
{
    // inspect message
    string text = request.Headers.Action;
    return null;
}
public void AddBindingParameters(ServiceEndpoint serviceEndpoint,
System.ServiceModel.Channels.BindingParameterCollection binding
Parameters)
{ }
public void ApplyClientBehavior(ServiceEndpoint serviceEndpoint,
System.ServiceModel.Dispatcher.ClientRuntime behavior)
{
    behavior.MessageInspectors.Add(new MyMessageInspectorClient());
}
public void ApplyDispatchBehavior(ServiceEndpoint serviceEndpoint,
System.ServiceModel.Dispatcher.EndpointDispatcher    endpoint
Dispatcher)
{
}
public void Validate(ServiceEndpoint serviceEndpoint)
{ }
}
public class MyBehaviorExtensionElementServer : BehaviorExtensionElement
{
    public MyBehaviorExtensionElementServer() { }
    public override Type BehaviorType
    {
        get { return typeof(MyMessageInspectorServer); }
    }
    protected override object CreateBehavior()
    {
        return new MyMessageInspectorServer();
    }
}
```

Bing Wang

On the config at client side:

```
<system.serviceModel>
    <bindings>
        <basicHttpBinding>
            <binding name="BasicHttpBinding_IMyService" />
        </basicHttpBinding>
    </bindings>
    <client>
        <endpoint    address="http://localhost:8080/MySerivce"
        binding="basicHttpBinding" bindingConfiguration="Basic
        HttpBinding_IMyService" contract="IMyService" behavior
        Configuration="messageInspector" name="BasicHttpBinding_
        IMyService" />
    </client>
    <behaviors>
        <endpointBehaviors>
            <behavior name="messageInspector" >
                <myBehaviorExtensionElementClient />
            </behavior>
        </endpointBehaviors>
    </behaviors>
    <extensions>
        <behaviorExtensions>
            <add    name="myBehaviorExtensionElementClient"
            type="Client.Behavior.MyBehaviorExtensionElement
            Client, Client, Version=0.0.0.0, Culture=neutral,
            PublicKeyToken=null" />
        </behaviorExtensions>
    </extensions>
</system.serviceModel>
```

At the server side, implements class MyMessageInspectorServer inheriting from System.ServiceModel.Dispatcher. IDispatchMessageInspector and System.ServiceModel. Description. IEndpointBehavior, also implement class

284

MyBehaviorExtensionElementServer inheriting from System. ServiceModel.Configuration.BehaviorExtensionElement.

```
public class MyMessageInspectorServer : IDispatchMessageInspector,
IEndpointBehavior
{
    object IDispatchMessageInspector.AfterReceiveRequest(ref Message
    request, IClientChannel channel, InstanceContext instanceContext)
    {
        string text = request.Headers.Action;
        return null;
    }

    void IDispatchMessageInspector.BeforeSendReply(ref Message reply,
    object correlationState)
    {
        string text = reply.Headers.Action;
    }
    public void AddBindingParameters(ServiceEndpoint serviceEndpoint,
    System.ServiceModel.Channels.BindingParameterCollection binding
    Parameters)
    { }
    public void ApplyClientBehavior(ServiceEndpoint serviceEndpoint,
    System.ServiceModel.Dispatcher.ClientRuntime behavior)
    {
    }
    public void ApplyDispatchBehavior(ServiceEndpoint serviceEndpoint,
    System.ServiceModel.Dispatcher.EndpointDispatcher    endpoint
    Dispatcher)
    {
        endpointDispatcher.DispatchRuntime.MessageInspectors.Add
        (new MyMessageInspectorServer());
    }
    public void Validate(ServiceEndpoint serviceEndpoint)
    { }
}
```

```
public class MyBehaviorExtensionElementServer : BehaviorExtensionElement
{
    public MyBehaviorExtensionElementServer() { }
    public override Type BehaviorType
    {
        get { return typeof(MyMessageInspectorServer); }
    }
    protected override object CreateBehavior()
    {
        return new MyMessageInspectorServer();
    }
}
```

On the config at server side:

```
<system.serviceModel>
    <services>
        <service       name="Service.WCF.MyService"       behavior
        Configuration="mexBehavior">
            <endpoint address="MySerivce" binding="basicHttp
            Binding" contract="Service.WCF.IMyService" behavior
            Configuration="messageInspector">
            </endpoint>
            <endpoint address="mex" binding="mexHttpBinding"
            contract="IMetadataExchange" />
            <host>
                <baseAddresses>
                    <add baseAddress="http://localhost:8080/" />
                </baseAddresses>
            </host>
        </service>
    </services>
    <behaviors>
        <serviceBehaviors>
            <behavior name="mexBehavior">
                <serviceMetadata httpGetEnabled="true" />
            </behavior>
        </serviceBehaviors>
        <endpointBehaviors>
            <behavior name="messageInspector">
```

```
        <myBehaviorExtensionElementServer />
      </behavior>
    </endpointBehaviors>
  </behaviors>
  <extensions>
    <behaviorExtensions>
      <add   name="myBehaviorExtensionElementServer"
      type="Service.WCF.Behavior.MyBehaviorExtension
      ElementServer, Service.WCF, Version=0.0.0.0, Culture=
      neutral, PublicKeyToken=null" />
    </behaviorExtensions>
  </extensions>
</system.serviceModel>
```

5.9.5.3 Contract Behavior

Contract behavior is to extend both client and service runtime across a contract, the below sample implements an error handler contract behavior. The class MyContractBehaviorAttribute inherits from interfaces of System.ServiceModel.Description. IContractBehaviorAttribute, System.ServiceModel.Description. IContractBehavior and System.ServiceModel.Dispatcher. IErrorHandler.

```
public class MyContractBehaviorAttribute : Attribute, IContractBehavior
Attribute, IContractBehavior,IErrorHandler
   {
      public Type TargetContract => typeof(IMyService);
      public void AddBindingParameters(ContractDescription contract
      Description, ServiceEndpoint endpoint, BindingParameterCollection
      bindingParameters)
      { }
      public void ApplyClientBehavior(ContractDescription contract
      Description, ServiceEndpoint endpoint, ClientRuntime clientRuntime)
      {
      }
```

```
    public void ApplyDispatchBehavior(ContractDescription contract
    Description, ServiceEndpoint endpoint, DispatchRuntime dispatch
    Runtime)
    {
        dispatchRuntime.ChannelDispatcher.ErrorHandlers.Add(this);
    }
    public bool HandleError(Exception error)
    {
        //customize handling error
        return true;
    }
    public void ProvideFault(Exception error, MessageVersion version,
    ref Message fault)
    {}
    public void Validate(ContractDescription contractDescription,
    ServiceEndpoint endpoint)
    {}
}

[ServiceContract]
[MyContractBehavior]
public interface IMyService
{
    [OperationContract]
    string MyMethod(int number, string text);
}
```

5.9.5.4 Operation Behavior

Operation behavior is to extend both the client and service runtime for each operation. It can be implemented through IOperationBehavior and add the operation behavior attribute to the operation contract that you want to apply for. The below is a sample of class MyOperationBehaviorAttribute inheriting from interfaces of System.ServiceModel.Dispatcher.IParameterInspector and System.ServiceModel.Description.IOperationBehavior.

```csharp
public class MyOperationBehaviorAttribute : Attribute, IParameter
Inspector, IOperationBehavior
{
    public void AfterCall(string operationName, object[] outputs, object
    returnValue, object correlationState)
    {
    }
    public void ApplyClientBehavior(OperationDescription operation
    Description, ClientOperation clientOperation)
    {
        clientOperation.ParameterInspectors.Add(this);
    }
    public void ApplyDispatchBehavior(OperationDescription operation
    Description, DispatchOperation dispatchOperation)
    {
        dispatchOperation.ParameterInspectors.Add(this);
    }
    public void Validate(OperationDescription operationDescription)
    {
    }
    object IParameterInspector.BeforeCall(string operationName,
    object[] inputs)
    {
        int number = (int)inputs[0];
        string text = inputs[1] as string;
        if (number < 0 || string.IsNullOrEmpty(text))
        {
            throw new FaultException("Parameter values are invalid.");
        }
        return null;
    }
    public void AddBindingParameters(OperationDescription operation
    Description, BindingParameterCollection bindingParameters)
    {
    }
}

[ServiceContract]
public interface IMyService
```

```
{
    [OperationContract]
    [MyOperationBehavior]
    void MyMethod(int number, string text);
}
```

While operation invoker is associated with interface IOperationBehavior, in fact, it will do with Invoker property of DispatchOperation. Assume that we have defined a MyOperation Invoker class which implements the IOperationInvoker interface, below is a sample of MyOperationInvoker class inheriting from System.ServiceModel.Dispatcher.IOperationInvoker.

```
public class MyOperationInvoker : IOperationInvoker
{}
public class MyOperationInvokerBehavior : Attribute, IOperationBehavior
{
        public void AddBindingParameters(OperationDescription operation
        Description, BindingParameterCollection bindingParameters)
        {
            throw new NotImplementedException();
        }
        public void ApplyClientBehavior(OperationDescription operation
        Description,
            ClientOperation clientOperation)
        {
        }
        public void ApplyDispatchBehavior(OperationDescription operation
        Description,
            DispatchOperation dispatchOperation)
        {
            dispatchOperation.Invoker = new MyOperationInvoker();
        }
        public void Validate (OperationDescription operationDescription)
        {
        }
}
```

5.9.6 Communication Stack

In WCF, communication stack, also channel stack, is an important component to handle message communication during runtime processing. The endpoints communicate with the outside world through the communication stack. The stack has a couple of layers, on which the messages undergo different transformation and pass through. WCF each binding element corresponds to a specific channel in the Channel Stack. The Channel Stack maintains protocol channels and transport channels. The bottom-most is the transport channel using transport protocol to read incoming messages from the wire. The WCF underlying transport protocols have TCP, NamedPipes, HTTP, HTTPS, or MSMQ. The upper layer is message encoding layer, which reads the incoming bytes buffer and deserializes the binary stream into a destinated message business object, mostly through data contract serialization. Then bubbles up to the protocol layer supporting transaction protocol, reliable messaging protocol and security protocol, etc. Eventually, it reaches the WCF dispatcher sending the message to the service app domain. Each client request goes through a channel stack from top to bottom, then an encoded byte stream message travels over the wire to reach the service end, where messages travels from the bottom to the top, which matches the open system interconnection model (OSI).

Svcutil.exe tool can help you create a proxy to designate a communication channel, a channel factory is able to create a communication channel without a proxy. A channel factory is implemented by the IChannelFactory interface, it is a factory for creating service communication channels at runtime to make calls to the WCF services operation contracts.

```
BasicHttpBinding binding = new BasicHttpBinding();
EndpointAddress endpoint = new EndpointAddress("http://localhost:8080/
MyService");
ChannelFactory<IMyService> channelFactory = new ChannelFactory<
IMyService>(binding,
endpoint);
IMyService myService = channelFactory.CreateChannel();
string result = myService.MyMethod(100, "hello");
channelFactory.Close();
```

Channel stack can be built in a custom way by implementing ServiceHostBase directly and also create a custom channel dispatcher by implementing ChannelDispatcherBase. The channel dispatcher interacts with IChannelListener to listen to and retrieve messages from the channel stack. IReplyChannel can be used to support request-reply message exchange pattern. The message processing is also customized implemented. A custom binding can pass additional parameters such as new transports or encoders at a service endpoint to replace WCF system provided binding which could not meet the requirements.

5.9.7 WCF Data Service

OData is the Open Data Protocol (OData). It is an open web protocol to expose data through http, which is based on Representational State Transfer (REST) full architecture. HTTP, AtomPub and JSON are all supported. It is an implementation on top of OData protocol. It allows you to expose tabular data as a set of REST APIs through HTTP verbs such as GET, POST, PUT, or DELETE. WCF data service exposes data resources as sets of relational entities built by entity framework data model. It enables you to retrieve or update data to resources by using well-known transfer formats, such as Atom, XML, JavaScript Object Notation (JSON), or a text-based data exchange format. OData feeds can be created based on common language runtime (CLR) classes or late-bound or un-typed data of custom data source. It is no need to create a proxy service object and you can create your own custom methods and expose it. It is lightweight and can be consumed by any type of client like Windows, Web, mobile, AJAX, and console. However, it is less secure and also some LINQ query operators are not available in OData like Take, Filter, Skip, etc.

5.9.8 WCF Web Service Model

The WCF web HTTP service model allows developers to expose WCF service operations to non-SOAP endpoints. It is designed to be accessed by a wider range of possible clients. URIs play a central role in the web HTTP services, which uses the UriTemplate and UriTemplateTable classes to provide URI processing capabilities. It supports GET and POST operations through the [WebGet] and [WebInvoke] to the associate service operations to accomplish GET, PUT, POST, and DELETE. It can handle multiple data formats in addition to SOAP messages including XML, JSON data object, or streams of binary content such as images, video files, or plain text. It extends the reach of WCF to cover web-style scenarios including web HTTP services, AJAX and JSON services.

Since SOAP is not used, the security features provided by WCF cannot be used, but a transport-based security through hosting as HTTPS can be adopted to accomplish the secure connection. URI templates provide an efficient syntax for expressing large sets of structurally similar URI, e,g. api/v{version}/MyService/product/{id}. The curly brace notation {id} indicates a variable id instead of a literal value. The Bind method with a set of parameters can be produced a *fully-closed URI* that matches the template. The WCF web service model allows developers to control both the URI template and verb associated with their service operations such as the web get and web invoke attributes.

```
[ServiceContract]
public interface IMyService
{
    [WebInvoke(Method = "GET", ResponseFormat = WebMessageFormat.
    Json, BodyStyle = WebMessageBodyStyle.Wrapped, UriTemplate =
    "product/{id}")]
[OperationContract]
    string GetProduct(string id);

    [WebInvoke(Method = "POST", ResponseFormat = WebMessageFormat.
    Json, BodyStyle = WebMessageBodyStyle.Wrapped, UriTemplate =
    "product/{id")]
    void DeleteProduct(string id);
}

[System.ServiceModel.ServiceBehavior(MaxItemsInObjectGraph    =
int.MaxValue, InstanceContextMode = InstanceContextMode.Single,
ConcurrencyMode = ConcurrencyMode.Multiple)]
public class MyService : IMyService
{
    [OperationBehavior]
    public string GetProduct(string id)
    { }
```

```
    [OperationBehavior]
    public void DeleteProduct(string id)
    { }
}
```

the web.config:

```xml
<system.serviceModel>
    <bindings>
            <webHttpBinding>
                    <binding name="webHttpBinding">
                            <security mode="None">
                                    <transport    clientCredentialType=
                                    "None" />
                            </security>
                    </binding>
            </webHttpBinding>
    </bindings>
    <services>
            <service    behaviorConfiguration="ServiceWebBehaviour"
            name="Service.WCF.ServiceWeb">
                    <endpoint address="" binding="webHttpBinding"
                    bindingConfiguration="webHttpBinding" contract=
                    "Service.WCF.IMyService" behaviorConfiguration=
                    "webEndpointBehavior"></endpoint>
                    <endpoint address="" binding="webHttpsBinding"
                    bindingConfiguration="webHttpBinding" contract=
                    "Service.WCF.IMyService" behaviorConfiguration=
                    "webEndpointBehavior"></endpoint>
                    <endpoint address="mex" binding="mexHttpBinding"
                    contract="IMetadataExchange" />
                    <endpoint address="mex" binding="mexHttpsBinding"
                    contract="IMetadataExchange" />
            </service>
        </services>
    <behaviors>
    <serviceBehaviors>
        <behavior name="ServiceWebBehaviour">
```

```
    <serviceMetadata httpGetEnabled="true" httpsGetEnabled="true" />
    <serviceDebug includeExceptionDetailInFaults="true" />
        <dataContractSerializer maxItemsInObjectGraph="2147483647" />
        <serviceThrottling maxConcurrentCalls="32" maxConcurrent
        Instances="32" maxConcurrentSessions="32" />
  </behavior>
  </serviceBehaviors>
      <endpointBehaviors>
              <behavior name="webEndpointBehavior">
                      <webHttp />
              </behavior>
      </endpointBehaviors>
  </behaviors>
  <serviceHostingEnvironment  aspNetCompatibilityEnabled="true"
  multipleSiteBindingsEnabled="true" />
</system.serviceModel>
```

The preceding code allows you to make the following HTTP requests.

GET /GetProduct

POST /DeleteProduct

The WCF web HTTP service model has features to work with many different data formats, the WebHttpBinding can read and write the different kinds of data, such as XML, JSON, Opaque binary streams. Since the WCF web Http service model does not support the WS-* protocols, the only way to secure a WCF web http service is to expose the service over HTTPS using SSL. When calling WCF web http services using a ChannelFactory<TChannel> to create a channel, the WebHttpBehavior uses the endpoint address specified in the configuration file instead of passing in the code of ChannelFactory<TChannel>.

5.9.9 WCF AppFabric AutoStart

WCF is a great choice for applications that communicate over various protocols such as HTTP, TCP, MSMQ etc. One of the major challenges is how to monitor and track a WCF service. Once the service is deployed in the production environment, it becomes essential to track how the WCF service is performing, therefore, a new hosting environment Windows Server AppFabric is created. Windows Server AppFabric extends windows server to provide enhanced hosting, monitoring caching capabilities. It is an extension to the IIS Web server, it provides features like hosting services, configure and monitor WCF services and Workflow Services. Windows Server AppFabric provides two runtime databases: monitoring schema and persistence schema. Monitoring schema provides the functionalities to monitor the activities of the services. Persistence schema provides capabilities to save state of the services running. The WCF service auto start can be configured in IIS. Sometimes, a service operation needs be invoked right after service auto start. The following sample code is one way to reach this purpose:

```
[ServiceContract]
public interface IMyService
{
        [OperationContract]
        void MyMethod(int number, string text);
}


[System.ServiceModel.ServiceBehavior(MaxItemsInObjectGraph = int.
MaxValue, InstanceContextMode = InstanceContextMode.Single,
ConcurrencyMode = ConcurrencyMode.Multiple)]
public class MyService : IMyService
{
```

```
static MyService()
{
        MethodToCallAfterAutoStart();
}

private static void MethodToCallAfterAutoStart()
{
        //declare global variables, or initiate caching
}
}
```

After MyService is auto start, the static constructor will be invoked, thus can initiate the routines that needs to run at the moment of service starting.

5.9.10 WCF Hosting

One outstanding feature of WCF service is its hosting. The service can be hosted in any kind of stand-alone windows process with its own configured identity. A keep-running console application, a windows UI application, or a background running service, all can host WCF service. Like the legacy .NET Remoting service, ASP.NET web service, the WCF service with http and https-based endpoints can also be hosted in IIS, but has one more special new feature, that is Windows Activation Service (WAS). WAS is an underlying component of IIS 7.0 that support hosting WCF service with the bindings other than BasicHttpBinding.

Before IIS 7.0 with WAS, the architecture for Windows Server 2003 and IIS 6.0 fundamentally has two components, the listener process w3svc service and the worker process w3wp.exe. Kernel-mode HTTP stack http.sys gets notice of the message arrival from network and delivers to the listener process. The listener process looks at the request URI and map the request to a specific IIS application pool, then forks an instance of the worker process to process the request. The IIS 6.0 worker process is a lightweight standalone application domain executable. It loads w3wphost.dll, which loads aspnet_isapi. dll to load the Common Language Runtime (CLR) and create a default application domain, then enters managed ASP.NET run time engine. For IIS 7.0 and WAS, WAS is implemented to support non-HTTP scenarios. All the listening, mapping, configuring and routing are also available to non-HTTP-based applications and services. The configuration manager reads the configurations of the application and application pool from applicationhost.config, which replaces the metabase. The process manager spawns new instances of w3wp in response to activation requests. The unmanaged listener adapter interface decides the request of external listeners communication activation to forward to WAS. The listener adapter interface communicates with activation requests received from non-HTTP protocols, namely TCP, Named Pipes, and MSMQ, which are hosted inside of SMSvcHost.exe, the four long-running non-IIS components: NetTcpPortSharing, NetTcpActivator, NetPipeActivator, and NetMsmqActivator. They communicate the corresponding activation request to WAS. During the listener start up, it obtains the necessary addressing information from WAS. WAS assigns to each application a unique listener channel ID to associate each request with the destinated application. After the channel ID is assigned, WAS starts to activate worker process for the coming request.

There are mainly four components in the worker process: process host, application manager, process protocol handlers and application domain protocol. Asp.Net process host loads the CLR into the worker process and at the same time, it initializes the default application domain. The application manager creates a unique application-level domain and manages the lifetime. Process protocol handlers is responsible for the protocol-specific process initialization. Application domain protocol lives inside the activated application domain and does protocol-specific application domain initialization. Each application in its own application domain is independently monitored and recycled. Since WAS is an activation service, it is not responsible for message sending and receiving. Each protocol implementation is responsible for implementing communication between the listener and the worker process.

WCF service WAS hosting needs create a virtual directory, which has to contain three things: a service, a .svc service endpoint, and a web configuration file. The .svc file makes the connection between a URI and a service implementation similar to .asmx files. The @ServiceHost directive inside the .svc file tells the WCF plumbing to create a ServiceHost instance for the type specified in the Service attribute:

```
<% @ServiceHost Service="MyService" %>
```

The entire WCF web configuration takes place in the System. ServiceModel section. When hosting WAS, a base address is not necessary to specify because that address is determined by the web site and virtual directory. Since the WCF metadata can be published by the support of metadata service behavior, the client-side proxy can be generated through tool svcutil.exe or through the "Add Service Reference" dialog in Visual Studio. For WCF with HTTP binding, the request traverses through the ASP.Net IIS processing pipeline (we described the flow for .asmx web service in the above section). There are two modes of operations for HTTP-based endpoints: ASP.NET compatibility and non-compatibility. For WCF hosting by default, ASP.NET compatibility is turned off, the HttpContext.Current is null. The actual activation of the endpoint does not happen in an HttpHandler, instead, it happens at an HttpModule that hands off the request to the ServiceHost. WCF services do not have any ASP.NET host features like session state and authentication. That is why WCF service cannot be tied to a specific hosting environment unless required, then the follow flag can be turned on:

<serviceHostingEnvironment aspNetCompatibilityEnabled="true" />

The ASP.NET compatibility has be to specified in the service class attribute:

[AspNetCompatibilityRequirements(RequirementsMode=AspNet CompatibilityRequirementsMode.Required)]

public class MyService : IMyService { ... }

The requests get dispatched to the WCF runtime using an HttpHandler only when these two switches are turned on, and the whole message flow processing pipeline behaves very much like ASP.NET Web services. WCF services running in ASP.NET compatibility mode support HTTP endpoints only. For non-HTTP endpoints of the WCF service, the protocol listeners are responsible for opening the transport, build communication channel, dispatching the requests to the application domain, and starting to receive the response as well. These protocol listeners are Windows NT services: Net.Tcp listener, listeners for named pipes and MSMQ, in addition, the port sharing service for TCP, these services have to be up and running for non-HTTP activation proceeding. The WAS configuration file applicationHost.config specifies the host name and port configuration for each site. They can also be configured through IIS manager site edit window and protocol can be enabled there as well. Non-HTTP endpoints requests do not pass the IIS processing pipeline and instead get routed directly to the WCF runtime to prevent from using an HttpModule to pre-process or post-process requests. The Application_Start and Application_End events of the HttpApplication class in global.asax file do not fire either. But through the events in the Service Host class, it can help run startup or cleanup code for each service. The lifetime of that WCF service is deterministic if it is self-host. It starts by calling *Open* and stops after calling *Close*. Hosting in WAS is different, WAS demands activation, the process activation gets created when a request message comes in and the process shuts down after a configurable idle period. WAS and the ASP.NET runtime recycle the application domain and the whole worker process periodically. A default is 29 hours to prevent it from happening at the same time of day. The periodically recycling supports the web.config file changes, the bin folder file changes, the recompilation of *.svc or *.aspx files, the modification of physical path of the virtual directory, etc. All in-memory states like sessions or static variables are lost during the recycling. Therefore, WCF WAS hosting is more suited for stateless per-call services instead of session or singleton services.

The WCF ServiceHost type features two events called Opening and Closing, which are the only proper ways to execute code at service startup and shutdown. The handlers have to be wired up for these events between creating a new instance of the ServiceHost and calling Open on it. It is impossible when using the @ServiceHost directive in .svc files. A viable option is to host a custom service host factory:

```
public class MyHostFactory : ServiceHostFactoryBase
{
public override ServiceHostBase CreateServiceHost(string constructor
String, Uri[] baseAddresses)
{
Type service = Type.GetType(constructorString);
ServiceHost host = new ServiceHost(service, baseAddresses);
host.Opening += OnOpening;
host.Closing += OnClosing;
return host;
}
}
```

To make the connection between the already-existing .svc endpoint and the custom factory, Factory attribute has to be added to the @ServiceHost directive:

```
<%@ServiceHost Service="Service" Factory="MyHostFactory" %>
```

5.10 Windows Service, Microservice and Messaging

In windows operating systems, a windows service is a process running in the windows session background, the same as Unix daemon of a long-running executable applications. The services can be automatically started when the computer starts, can be paused and restarted. It does not interfere with user, and it is security context wise. Unlike the regular executable applications that can run in multiple instances in the same machine at the same time, windows service can only be launched in one instance and it runs in administrative privilege. Since .Net was born, .NET windows service is a very popular service design architecture. .Net framework windows service can be created with windows service project template. The service class inherits from class of System.ServiceProcess.ServiceBase and needs override the OnStart and OnStop methods. Each service has a ServiceInstaller, which registers the service in the service control manager. It also associates an event log recording service command. The service is accessed such as started and stopped through the service control manager. The executable loads the service into operating system, the OnStart routine starts the service, any resources declared have to be released in the OnStop. Besides start and stop, commands pause and continue can be enabled from the service control manager's context menu. The windows service is designated to run long, a System. Timers.Timer component is usually used to periodically poll, process or monitor. The timer could be setup during OnStart since OnStart must return to the operating system immediately after the service's operation begins so that the system will not be blocked. Usually, System.ComponentMode.BackgroundWorker threads are invoked to handle the service process. There are many situations that you may need run a long-time service, such as process intensive data, or queuing data item, etc. The below code sample is a .NET framework windows service performs a process in a timely fashion:

```csharp
public class MyWindowsService : System.ServiceProcess.ServiceBase
{
    private const int due = 30;
    private const int period = 20000;
    private System.Threading.Timer timer;

    public MyService()
    {
        timer = new System.Threading.Timer(ProcessDuringElapse, null,
        due, period);
        timer.Change(Timeout.Infinite, Timeout.Infinite);
    }
        protected override void OnStart(string[] args)
    {
        base.OnStart(args);
        timer.Change(due, period);
        }
        protected override void OnStop()
    {
        base.OnStop();
        timer?.Dispose();
    }
        protected override void OnPause()
    {
        base.OnPause();
    }
    private void ProcessDuringElapse(object state)
    {
        timer.Change(Timeout.Infinite, Timeout.Infinite);
        //service process
        timer.Change(due, period);
    }
}

static void Main(string[] args)
{
    ServiceBase.Run(new MyWindowsService());
}
```

In the newly .Net core, a new template worker service can replace the pre-.Net-core way. Your service can inherit from Microsoft. Extensions.Hosting.BackgroundService, which implements interface of Microsoft.Extensions.Hosting.IHostingService, then your service does not only target windows, but also other platforms. The BackgroundService is logging, configuration and dependency inject ready, it needs inherited class to implement ExecuteAsync(CancellationToken) method. This method can loop periodically based on the timer interval. The StartAsync(CancellationToken) defines the start of the background task, the StopAsync(CancellationToken) is triggered when the host is performing ending the background task and a graceful shutdown only after ExecuteAsync is complete. The below is a sample code for a service worker:

```
public static async Task Main(string[] args)
{
    using (var host = CreateHostBuilder(args).Build())
    {
        await host.StartAsync();
        await host.WaitForShutdownAsync();
    }
}

public static IHostBuilder CreateHostBuilder(string[] args) =>
    Host.CreateDefaultBuilder(args)
        .UseWindowsService()
        .ConfigureHostConfiguration(builder =>
        {
        builder.AddJsonFile("hostsettigs.json", true);
        })
        .ConfigureAppConfiguration((hostContext, builder) =>
        {
```

```
    builder.SetBasePath(System.IO.Path.GetDirectoryName(System.
    Reflection.Assembly.GetExecutingAssembly().Location))
        .AddJsonFile("appsettings.json", false)
        .AddEnvironmentVariables()
        .AddCommandLine(args);
    })
    .ConfigureServices((hostContext, services) =>
    {
    services.Configure<HostOptions>(option =>
    {
            option.ShutdownTimeout = TimeSpan.FromSeconds(15);
    })
    .AddHostedService<MyWorkerService>()
});

public class MyWorkerService : BackgroundService
{
        private bool isStartup = true;
        private System.Threading.Timer timer;
        private System.Threading.SemaphoreSlim semaphore = new
        SemaphoreSlim(1,1);
        public override async Task StartAsync(CancellationToken
        cancellationToken)
    {
        if (isStartup && semaphore != null && await semaphore.
        WaitAsync(5000).ConfigureAwait(false))
        {
            try
            {
            }
            finally
            {
                    isStartup = false;
                    semaphore?.Release();
            }
        }

        await base.StartAsync(cancellationToken).ConfigureAwait(false);
    }
}
```

Bing Wang

```
public override async Task StopAsync(CancellationToken cancellation
Token)
{
    await base.StopAsync(cancellationToken).ConfigureAwait(false);
}
protected override async System.Threading.Tasks.Task ExecuteAsync
(CancellationToken stoppingToken)
{
    timer = new System.Threading.Timer(
        async (resetevent) =>
        { await DoWrok(resetevent as ManualResetEventSlim, stopping
        Token); }
        , null
        ,TimeSpan.FromSeconds(10)
        , TimeSpan.FromSeconds(5));
}
private async Task<bool> DoWork(ManualResetEventSlim resetEvent
Slim, CancellationToken cancellationToken)
{
    resetEventSlim.Wait(cancellationToken);
    resetEventSlim.Reset();
    if (timer?.Change(Timeout.Infinite, Timeout.Infinite) ?? false)
    {
        //service process
    }

    timer?.Change(10, 5);
    resetEventSlim.Set();
    return true;
}
}
}
```

With the expand of your windows services, as Nayaki Nayyar (director of Enterprise Architecture and Technology Service at Valero Energy) and Benjamin Moreland (manager of Application Infrastructure at Hartford Financial Services Group) describe "junk drawer of services", creating multiple micro-windows-services integrating with messaging system is one common way of framework architecture of services orchestra. If thinking the service as a cube, with more and more business requirements need be implemented, it can easily expand in all the directions, façade service layer, business logic and data access layer, going to monolithic, convoluted and loose maintenance. Modularity is essential to cast on this cube. If starting from business concept instead of application entity, treat the cube as a business module, can more and more prune to scale the cube to a minimal service by decomposing the business logics based on separate concern and single responsibility. If your service orchestra is for supporting multiple business subdomains, each subdomain can be implemented as a self-descriptive module or microservice, such as account service, order service, inventory service, etc., Or if it's for supporting multiple business customer domains, then each customer domain functionality can be scaled as an individual component or microservice, such as cutromer1 service, customer2 service, etc. Each microservice determines the its own responsibility. The single responsibility principal is stated as "A class should have only one reason to change." by Robert Martin. Consequently, each microservice can be architected only as one reason to design and change.

Along with single responsibility principal and common closure principal, decomposing the monolithic service by business capability, or by subdomain, or designing a microservice from scratch are good techniques. From implementation point of view, Microsoft-way of microservice can be either .Net framework window service, or .Net core background worker. Both service frameworks have the actions of start, stop and dowork that the skeleton can be built in a shared library. The service can be designed as layer structure with business logic layer and database persistence layer, it can also be designed as Hexagonal structure with business logic as the center with additional inbound outbound adapters that receive request and send response. Inbound adapter can be controller forwarding the request to business center. Outbound adapter can be ADO layer for data transaction or message producing to broadcast notification or send the response back. Each microservice has its own source code repository, service hosting and pipeline deployment. It helps the development team autonomous and loosely coupled. It becomes independent scalable and easy to be maintained.

Multiple microservices are built as distributed system, consequently, the inter-process communication (IPC) becomes the major part of the microservices architecture. How the services exchange data between themselves? how the services communicated with client and outside of the world? The following questions are automatically asked during the design: what kind of IPC pattern is more robust and should we use? The microservice expose its endpoint to other service and client, how to guarantee the communication is reliable even though when the destinated service is off line? There are lots of different IPC technologies, synchronous request-response based communication mechanism, Http resource based Restful or gRPC, etc. depending on interaction style: one-to-one, one-to-many, synchronous or asynchronous. A message is a packet of data consists of a header and a body.

The header has name-value pairs containing the information of meta data, the destination address and message id, etc. The body is message payload. Messages are exchanged over channels, or queues, a logical pathway connecting two programs. It has two kinds: point-to-point and publish-subscribe. A sender or producer is a program that sends a message by writing the message to a channel. A receiver or consumer is a program that receives a message by reading it from a channel. The communication uses point-to-point channels for one-to-one interaction styles, and publish-subscribe channel for delivering each message to all the attached consumers.

To avoid the nesh style of multiple microservices, the facade design pattern is an essential mechanism in the design of the distributed system. A central leader service or an API proxy gateway can perform as a service façade accepting a single request from a client and coordinates with other services. The facade service registers all the microservices' endpoint. After receives the request from client, it behaves like forward and forget and routes the message to the destinated microservice. It also functions as a bridge between two endpoint microservices to help exchange the data. The communication security can be implant in the central leader service or API proxy gateway to filter the unsecure connection so that it becomes responsible for auditing, validating and filtering requests. A façade also supports loose-coupling between clients and services by evolving services without disrupting client. The client only knows the endpoint of façade service that it accepts a request, delegate the work to the backend services, gather response and send back result to client. This kind of mechanism can be accomplished by publish subscribe pattern. The leader service starts to run first, then whichever service starts, it registers to the leader service by subscribing the topics. When leader service needs route the request to the backend services, it just publish the corresponding topic. You can build the messaging integration system on top of TIBCO, RabbitMQ, Microsoft MSMQ, or implement your own inhouse system through the web socket protocol.

5.11 RESTful Service

At the time when internet started to boom in 1993, only a fragmented description of the web's architecture, then gradually, professionals called for the standards for web interface protocols. The W3C and IETF together worked on creating formal descriptions of the web's three primary standards: URI, HTTP and HTML. Roy Fielding was involved in the creation of these standards. During his PhD studies, he developed the REST architectural style, tested its constraints based on the web's protocol standards. He defined REST in his 2000 PhD dissertation *Architectural Styles and the Design of Network-based Software Architectures* at UC Irvine. In it, the term REST is denoted as representational state transfer. To create the REST architectural style, Fielding identified the requirements for REST and analyzed many existing architectural styles for network-based applications, it was created as part of the development of the web standards. The REST architectural style is designed for the network-based, the lightweight coupling of the client and the server communication application. It is achieved by creating a layer of abstraction on the server, which defines resource encapsulating and hides the underlying implementation details.

The key abstraction in REST is resource, which is any information: an image, a database query, a temporal service, etc. The resource has its representation, the state contains the data, the metadata and the hyperlinks. The clients access resources through URIs and the server responds with a representation of the resource, a hypertext transferred in the format of message between the clients and servers. The strong decoupling of client and server, the text-based transfer of information, and the uniform addressing protocol communication meet the requirements of the Web. Now REST has been adopted throughout the software industry and is recognized as one of the web APIs for creating stateless, reliable client service communication. An API is a set of definitions or protocols for integrating application enterprises solution. It is referred as a contract between an information provider and an information consumer. A web API obeying the REST constraints formally described as RESTful web API. The most common protocol for the client and server communication is HTTP, which provides operation methods HTTP GET, POST, PUT, and DELETE. Through this stateless protocol and standard operations, RESTful systems are target for reliable, fast, and reusable. This is achieved through the following REST principles such as a client-server architecture, statelessness, cache-ability, a layered system, support for code on demand, and a uniform interface.

Based on Roy Fielding, Representational State Transfer (REST) is started the design in a system as a whole and incrementally emphasizes the constraints and system context. Null state is the starting point for the description of REST, www is a null state without constraints and distinguished boundaries between client and server components. It is a hybrid style gradually added by multiple constrains. The client-server constrains based on separation of concern principal allow each component to evolve independently and improve portability and scalability. Statelessness constrain is added on the client-server communication and becomes client-stateless-server, which makes the data exchange stateless and improve the visibility, reliability and scalability. The cache constrain is added to stateless client server communication and becomes client-cache-stateless-server, which requires the data responses be cacheable and improve the network efficiency while decreasing the reliability. The main feature of REST distinguished from other network-based style is its uniform interface with four interface constraints: resource identification, resource manipulation through representation, self-descriptive message and hypermedia as the engine of application state. Identification of resources is that the resources are different from the representations returned to the client. The manipulation of the resources through representation is that the client can do modification to the resource representation. Self-descriptive message is that the message itself describes enough information to process the message. Hypermedia as the engine of application state is that the hyperlinks from the server contains actions that client can make state transitions. The uniform-client-cache-stateless-server is hierarchical layers that creates bounds on overall system complexity and becomes uniform-layered-client-cache-stateless-server.

REST style focuses on the roles of components, constraints upon the interaction of components and the interpretation of data elements. Components communicate by transferring a representation of resource. The representation can be html web page or jpeg image, it is a sequence of bytes plus representation metadata, the media type describing the data. Client, server, cache, resolver and tunnel are the main connectors to encapsulate the accessing to the resources and the transferring of resource representation. Process view, connector view and data view are the basic three types of view for illuminating the design principals of REST. For the process view, the client-server separation of concerns simplifies component implementation and increases the scalability of pure server component. The connector view concentrates on the component communication mechanism. It examines the resource identifier in order to select an appropriate communication mechanism for the request. The data view reveals the application state as information flows through the components. An application's state is defined by the pending request, the topology of connected components, the active requests on those connectors, the data flow of representation and the processing of those representations after receives. REST architecture treats every content as a resource, which is identified by URIs and represented by various representations. It is similar to object in object-oriented programming or an entity in a database. Its representation is decided using a standard format. The most popular formats are XML and JSON.

For example, a user is a resource which is represented using the following XML format:

```
<user>
   <id>12345</id>
   <username>bingwang</username>
   <firstname>Bing</firstname>
   <lastname>Wang</lastname>
</user>
```

JSON format:
```
{
   "id":12345,
   "usernamename":"bingwang",
   "firstname":"Bing"
   "lastname":"Wang"
}
```

REST does not impose any restriction on the format of a resource representation. It is the responsibility of the REST server to pass the client the resource in the format that the client understands. Roy Fielding laid out the foundation architecture of REST, then subsequentially we have commercial software libraries implementing the RESTful along with the understanding, parsing, and modifying XML and JSON data.

The following is an example of restful api service to hold the data of users. Certain uri dedicates the representation of resource of user:

At server side:

```
public interface IMyService
{
      UsersResponse GetUsers();
      UserDetailResponse GetUser(string userName);
}
public class UsersResponse
{
```

```csharp
[Newtonsoft.Json.JsonProperty("users", Required = Newtonsoft.Json.Required.
Default, NullValueHandling = Newtonsoft.Json.NullValueHandling.Ignore)]
    public ICollection<Models.User> Users { get; set; }
}

public class UserDetailResponse
{
[Newtonsoft.Json.JsonProperty("user", Required = Newtonsoft.Json.Required.
Default, NullValueHandling = Newtonsoft.Json.NullValueHandling.Ignore)]
    public Models.User User { get; set; }
}
public class User : Person
{
    public int Id { get; set; }
    public string UserName { get; set; }
    public string FirstName { get; set; }
    public string LastName { get; set; }
}
```

Controller:

```csharp
[ApiVersion("1.0")]
[Route("api/v{version:apiVersion}/[controller]")]
[Authorize(Roles = "Admin", AuthenticationSchemes = Microsoft.AspNet
Core.Authentication.JwtBearer.JwtBearerDefaults.AuthenticationScheme)]
public class AdminController : ApiController
{
    private List<Models.User> users;
    public AdminController()
    {
        users = new List<Models.User>();
        Models.User user = new Models.User { FirstName = "test", Id = 1,
        LastName = "test", UserName = "testuser" };
        users.Add(user);
    }
    [HttpGet("users")]
    [ProducesResponseType(StatusCodes.Status200OK)]
    public async Task<ActionResult<UsersResponse>> GetUsers()
```

```
    {
        UsersResponse response = new UsersResponse();
        var user = new Models.User { FirstName = "test", Id = 1, LastName
        = "test", UserName = "testuser" };
        response.Users = new List<Models.User> { user };
        return Ok(response);
    }

    [HttpGet("user")]
    public async Task<ActionResult<UserDetailResponse>> GetUser
    ([System.ComponentModel.DataAnnotations.Required][Microsoft.
    AspNetCore.Mvc.FromQuery]string userName)
    {
        UserDetailResponse response = new UserDetailResponse();
        Models.User user = users.Where(u => userName == userName).
        FirstOrDefault();
        response.User = user;
        return Ok(response);
    }
}

public class MyService : IMyService
{
    private const string baseUri = "localhost";
    public UserDetailResponse GetUser(string userName)
    {
        Dictionary<string, string> keyValuePairs = new Dictionary<string,
        string>();
        keyValuePairs.Add("username", "bingwang");
        return InvokeHttpRequest<UserDetailResponse>(@"api/v1/admin/
        user", keyValuePairs);
    }
    public UsersResponse GetUsers()
    {
        return    InvokeHttpRequest<UsersResponse>(@"api/v1/admin/
        users");
    }
    private T InvokeHttpRequest<T>(string uri, Dictionary<string,
    string> parameterValues = null)
```

```
{
    T result = default(T);
    string requestUri = $"{baseUri}{uri}";
    foreach (string parameter in parameterValues.Keys)
    {
        requestUri = $"{requestUri}?{parameter}={parameterValues
        [parameter].ToString()}&";
    }

    string responseText = string.Empty;
    requestUri = requestUri.TrimEnd('&');
    var httpWebRequest = (System.Net.HttpWebRequest)System.Net.
    WebRequest.Create(requestUri);
    httpWebRequest.AutomaticDecompression = System.Net.
    DecompressionMethods.GZip | System.Net.Decompression
    Methods.Deflate;
    using (var response = httpWebRequest.GetResponse())
    using (var stream = response.GetResponseStream())
    using (var reader = stream != null ? new System.IO.StreamReader
    (stream) : null)
    {
        responseText = reader?.ReadToEnd();
        reader?.Close();
        stream?.Close();
        response.Close();
    }
    if (!string.IsNullOrEmpty(responseText))
    {
        result = Newtonsoft.Json.JsonConvert.DeserializeObject<T>
        (responseText);
    }
    return result;
    }
}
```

To summarize, REST stands for Representational State Transfer and an architectural style for distributed hypermedia systems. It has its guiding principles and constraints, and these principles must be satisfied if a service interface needs to be referred to as RESTful. The first principal is the uniform interface, it uniquely identifies the resources. The operation of the resources is through representations from the server response, client has enough information to modify the resources, it is self-descriptive message telling client how to process the message and actions that can perform on the resources, the message itself has enough information on how to process the resources. The second principal is client-server design pattern, it enforces the separation of concerns, encourages the client and the server components evolve independently, it improves the portability of the user interface and scalability of the server components. The third principal is stateless, each client request must contain all of the necessary information to complete the request, it entirely keeps the session state, the server component cannot use any previously stored information. The fourth principal is cacheable, a server response can mark itself as cacheable or non-cacheable. If it is cacheable, the client application can reuse the response data for the equivalent requests for a specified period. The fifth principal is the layered system, it constrains the component behavior and builds a hierarchical architecture layer. The sixth principal is the code on demand. REST allows the server component to deliver in the form of code to have client to execute, the client functionality can be extended by downloading and executing code. A REST API consists of an assembly of interlinked resources, the resource models. It uses resource identifiers to identify each resource involved in the interactions. The resource is self-descriptive. The media type is the data format of a representation, it defines how to process the representation of resource based on the media type without knowing the resource content, it also defines a default processing model without any relation with resource operation methods: GET, PUT, POST, or DELETE. Client can access content in a variety of formats, it communicates with the server through a standardized interface protocol like Http. The exchange and interaction are stateless. All the above principles help RESTful web service applications to be simple, lightweight, portable, fast and reliable.

5.12 WEB API Service

If we say a WCF, or Restful service could easily be extended to become a monolithic application with more and more features and logics need added, then web api service is a lightweight, loosely-couple and standalone application. Application programming interface (API) is a set of routines that allow developers to access specific features or data. API is the core of software development aspects. It's not new and actually started to emerge in the programming world in 60s. If API exposes the features of one software systems to others, then web api publishes its features to the world through endpoints. Endpoints are important as they specify where the resources locate and where the response sent from. Endpoints are static as the location cannot change, otherwise client will see http 404 status error. Endpoints are versional since each service denotes the version number in the uri path when each time upgrades so that multiple versions of services can be accessed simultaneously. Web api is a development concept and framework for building http resource-based services that can be accessed by a variety of clients: web, windows, mobile etc. It is a system-to-system interaction and request-response message pattern, the exchanged data is mostly json and xml format for supporting across different platforms. In an enterprise solution, the service can be modeled as multiple small granular web api services to take each single responsibility, either process it or forward it to other component to process. Web api in .NET is built on top of ASP.Net core framework, which layouts the foundation to build modern, high performance, cloud-enabled, mobile or IoT's applications running in multiple different computer architecture. ASP.Net Web API is an ideal platform for building HTTP services on the .NET Framework.

How does an http request flow through the ASP.Net core web api pipeline? How does the http response return back? Pipeline in simple words is HttpRequest since input goes through and output is HttpResponse.

ASP.NET Core is an open-source framework with the cross-platform capabilities. Its beauty is to enable the developers to ignore the platform barrier and develop the applications for windows, mac as well as for linux. In simple words, .NET Core is the modular version of .NET Framework or a subset of full .NET Framework.

The http request message is converted to an HttpRequestMessage object, which has the following representation:

request-line: is the http request GET uri (http://localhost/WebApiSample/api/v1/admin/users) HTTP/1.1

request-headers: is the http request header part, Accept, Accept-Language, Accept-Encoding, User-Agent, Content-Length

message-body: can be the json formatted request body content

The httprequestmessage object is picked up from the kernel HTTP.sys, which contacts WAS to obtain the information from configuration store applicationHost.config. WWW service receives the configured information such as application pool and site configuration. WAS starts the worker process w3wp.exe in the application pool. The IIS worker process starts to execute ASP. NET core code. ASP.NET core module, a native IIS module, either host your ASP.NET Core app inside the IIS worker process, an in-process hosting model, or forward the httprequestmessage to a backend ASP.NET Core app running the Kestrel server, an out of process hosting model. In the in-process hosting model, ASP.NET core module loads the core CLR and startup to bootstrap the logic. It enters the ASP.NET core web api pipeline starting to handle the lifetime of the httprequestmessage. ASP.NET core module forwards httprequestmessage to HttpServer, which produces HttpContext converting the native HTTP request to managed, then the managed request object starts to traverse in the ASP.NET core web api middleware pipeline.

This happens right in the same IIS worker process, so explicitly specify the in-process hosting model in the web.config file as below:

```
<system.webServer>

    <handlers>

    <remove name="aspNetCore"/>

    <add name="aspNetCore" path="*" verb="*" modules="AspNetCore
    ModuleV2" resourceType="Unspecified"/>

    </handlers>
```

```
<aspNetCore processPath="dotnet" arguments=".\WebApiSample.dll"
stdoutLogEnabled="false"    stdoutLogFile=".\logs\stdout"    forward
WindowsAuthToken="false" hostingModel="inprocess" />
```

`</system.webServer>`

Middleware concept is not new, it first appeared in a report following the 1968 NATO Software Engineering conference in Garmisch-Partenkirchen, Germany. It is commonly known as a component lying between an underline system and the applications running on it. It is essentially function as a hidden translation layer, it enables the communication and data transfer for distributed applications. Sometimes we call it plumbing, or plugin as it connects two systems together so that the data can be easily passed between the pipe. Common middleware examples include application server middleware, message-oriented middleware, web middleware, etc. Since middleware performs communication, the security authentication needs involved. As a broad category, middleware can encompass everything from web servers to authentication systems to messaging systems to data transaction management system.

ASP.NET core web api middleware is a separate component assembled into the web api pipeline to handle requests and responses. Each middleware component can choose whether to pass the request to the next middleware in the pipeline, it can perform work before and after the next middleware in the pipeline. Request delegates are used to build the request pipeline. A middleware, or an individual request delegate can be an in-line anonymous method, or a custom routine defined in a reusable class. They can direct either pass to the next component in the pipeline or short-circuit simply return httpresponse back to the pipeline directly. Once the request is passed to your application's logic as an HttpContext instance, it undergoes the ASP.NET Core middleware pipeline where you write custom code to handle the request and return your expected response. The most important to keep in mind is the order in which the middleware components are added in the Configure method of the Startup class defines the order these middleware components are going to run on the http requests and the reverse order for the http response.

Http request passes through the ordered middlewares and reaches to the http routing dispatcher, then direct to the http controller dispatcher. HttpControllerDispatcher class is related to the delegate handler because whenever the SendAsync(request, cancellationToken) method is called, it calls the inner handler. The web api controller class defines the main logic for handling the http request. All custom controller classes derive from the ApiController class. The right controller is activated by the http request. The action can also be invoked by the request uri. The model binding logic creates values for the parameters of the action for the http request and passed to the action. Model binding is ASP.NET mechanism performing as a bridge between http request and action method, the goal is mapping HTTP request data directly into action method parameters. For example, when a http request for a URL such as "/Admin/User/2" is sent to the server, the framework map the details of the request to the appropriate values or objects as parameters to the action method. A model binder takes the HTTP request and populates a dictionary of key-value pairs, the value providers are the component feeding data into model binders, populating a dictionary of key-value pairs and the model. The action routine is invoked by action invoker, it is a component telling http request which action method to invoke based on the parameters type. The request gets processed in the action routine and the result returned wrapped in the http response object all the way bubbles up back to http server and returns to HTTP.sys, HTTP.sys then sends back to the client.

The structure of HttpResponseMessage format has the below representation:

Status-line: http response status, such as HTTP/1.1 200 OK

Response-headers: the headers in the response stream, like Date, Server, Last-Modified, ETag, Accept-Ranges, Content-Length, Connection, Content-Type

Message-body: the main response stream containing the result mostly in JSON format.

ASP.NET core supports creating web APIs using controllers and some minimal APIs. *Controllers* in a web API are classes that derive from class ControllerBase.

[Microsoft.AspNetCore.Mvc.ApiController]

public class ApiController : Microsoft.AspNetCore.Mvc.ControllerBase

{ }

The class of *Startup* is the entry point of the application. It configures the request pipeline to handle all requests. The inception of *Startup* class can be the Main routine entry of the Program. *Startup* class is mandatory in ASP.Net core application.

The ASP.Net core application is a Console application, which has to configure a web host to start listening. It initializes a new instance of the Microsoft.Extensions.Hosting.HostBuilder class with pre-configured defaults. The final calling hostBuilder. Run method is to add a terminal middleware delegate to the application's request pipeline.

```
public static void Main(string[] args)
{
    Microsoft.Extensions.Hosting.IHostBuilder hostBuilder
        = Microsoft.Extensions.Hosting.Host.CreateDefaultBuilder(args ??
        new string[] { })
    .ConfigureLogging((hostBuilderContext, logBuilder) =>
    {
        // register logger
    })
    .ConfigureWebHostDefaults(webBuilder => webBuilder.UseStartup
    <Startup>());
    .Build();
    hostBuilder.Run();
}
```

Startup class is also responsible for creating two Configure routines: Configure and ConfigureServices. *IApplicationBuilder* is an interface that contains properties and methods related to current environment. In the Configure routine, the application builder adds a list of middleware to the pipeline to do different purposes.

```
public void Configure (IApplicationBuilder app)
{
        //forward proxied headers onto current request
        applicationBuilder.UseForwardedHeaders();
        //add a Microsoft.AspNetCore.Routing.EndpointRoutingMiddleware
        middleware to the applicationBuilder.
```

```
    applicationBuilder.UseRouting();
    //allow cross domain request
    applicationBuilder.UseCors();
    //enable authentication
  applicationBuilder.UseAuthentication();
    //enables authorization capabilities
    applicationBuilder.UseAuthorization();
    //sets the X-Frame-Options header
  applicationBuilder.UseXfo(options => options.SameOrigin());
    //sets the X-Xss-Protection header
  applicationBuilder.UseXXssProtection(options => options.EnabledWith
  BlockMode());
    //sets the X-Content-Type-Options
  applicationBuilder.UseXContentTypeOptions();
    //sets the Referrer-Policy header
  applicationBuilder.UseReferrerPolicy(options => options.StrictOrigin
  WhenCrossOrigin());
  applicationBuilder.UseEndpoints(routeBuilder => routeBuilder.Map
  DefaultControllerRoute());
}
```

ASP.net core has built-in support for Dependency Injection. IServiceCollection is used to add to DI container. Before registering the middleware to add to the http pipeline, ConfigureServices is to add the resources to the dependency injection service collection.

```
public void ConfigureServices(IServiceCollection services)
{
    //create service provider from the dependency injection service
    collection
    var serviceProvider = serviceCollection.BuildServiceProvider();
    //add cross-origin resource sharing services to the dependency
    injection service collection
    serviceCollection.AddCors(options => {});
}
```

You can also write your own middleware component to register in service collection and add to the http pipeline to process. Your middleware component needs to implement InvokeAsync method taking HttpContext as a parameter.

```csharp
public class HealthCheckMiddleware
{
    private readonly WebApiHealthCheckOptions healthCheckOptions;
    private readonly Microsoft.AspNetCore.Http.RequestDelegate next;
    public HealthCheckMiddleware(Microsoft.AspNetCore.Http.Request
    Delegate requestDelegate, Microsoft.Extensions.Options.IOptions<Web
    ApiHealthCheckOptions> options)
    {
        next = requestDelegate ?? throw new ArgumentNullException
        (nameof(next));
        healthCheckOptions = options?.Value ?? throw new Argument
        NullException(nameof(options));
    }
    public async System.Threading.Tasks.Task InvokeAsync(HttpContext
    httpContext)
    {
        if (!string.IsNullOrEmpty(healthCheckOptions.HeartbeatUrl) &&
        httpContext.Request.Path == healthCheckOptions.HeartbeatUrl)
        {
            var heartbeatResult = new WebApiHealthCheckResult(health
            CheckOptions.Name, HealthCheckStatus.Online, "OK");
            httpContext.Response.ContentType = !string.IsNullOr
            Empty(heartbeatResult.ContentType) ? heartbeatResult.
            ContentType : "application/json";
            httpContext.Response.StatusCode = heartbeatResult.StatuCode;
            await httpContext.Response.WriteAsync(heartbeatResult.
            Message);
            return;
        }
        await next(httpContext);
    }
}
```

You can add customized attributes on the controller class or on the action method to inspect the http request or http response message. Action filter is one way that modifies the way in which the action is executed. The ASP.NET MVC framework includes several action filters, such as OutputCache, HandleError and Authorize. The ASP.NET MVC framework also supports four different types of filters, like authorization filters, action filters, result filters, exception filters. For example, you can create an add request header filter attribute to change the action behavior to add a request header in the http request message.

```
public class AddRequestHeaderFilter : ActionFilterAttribute
{
    public void OnActionExecuted(ActionExecutedContext context)
    {
    }
    public void OnActionExecuting(ActionExecutingContext context)
    {
        var request = context.HttpContext.Request;
        request.Headers.TryAdd("x-correlation-id", Guid.NewGuid().ToString());
        request.Headers.TryAdd("Action", $"{request.Method}:{request.Path}{request.QueryString.Value ?? ""}");
    }
}
```

The below design diagram shows the data service model for multiple service modules representing multiple business concepts:

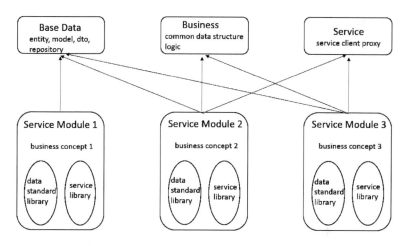

Figure 5.12.1 multiple service modules supporting multiple business concepts

5.13 Miscellaneous

5.13.1 MIME Type and Content Type

The media type is known as Multipurpose Internet Mail Extensions or MIME type, it indicates the format of a document and file. The Internet Assigned Numbers Authority (IANA) is in charge of providing all the official MIME types. The client sends web request from browser, in the server response, the Content-Type header contains the MIME type, through which the client browser determines how to display the content to the end user. A MIME type has type and subtype two parts, which separated by a slash (/), like type/subtype. The type represents the broad category of the data type, it is text, or image, or video. The subtype identifies what kind of data the MIME type need represent. Each type has its own subtypes, and an optional parameter can be added to provide detail information, type/subtype;parameter=value.

Discrete and multipart are the two main classes of types. Discrete types are types representing a single file or medium, such as a single text, video or music file. Application is any kind of binary data requiring a specific application to execute, for generic binary data: application/octet-stream, for other common examples: application/pdf, and application/zip. Image or graphical has bitmap or vector, like image/jpeg, image/png. Text data convey human-readable content like source code, or any text based: text/plain, text/csv, and text/html. A multipart type is the type representing a document which is consists of multiple component parts, the document is broken into category pieces with different MIME types. Message and multipart are two types of multipart, a message encapsulates other message and breaks a large message into smaller pieces and reassembles at the recipient side. The data in the multiple components usually has different MIME types, like multipart/form-data and multipart/byteranges. Some common MIME types web developers know are text/plain, text/css, text/html, text/javascript, image/gif, image/jpeg, image/png, etc. A completed HTML form is sent from browser to server, the request body consists of different parts delimited by a boundary, a string starting with a double dash --.

Content-Disposition and Content-Type for file uploading fields.

Content-Type: multipart/form-data; boundary=aBoundaryString

--aBoundaryString
Content-Disposition: form-data; name="file"; filename="img.jpg"
Content-Type: image/jpeg

(data)
--aBoundaryString
Content-Disposition: form-data; name="field"

(data)
--aBoundaryString
(more subparts)
--aBoundaryString--

The MIME type indicates that the document is composed of multi-parts separated by boundaries into each Content-Type, a Content-Type header indicates its actual type and a Content-Range. If the MIME type is not in the server response, sometimes the client browsers may perform some guessing of the correct MIME type with the help of the bytes of the response content.

5.13.2 Serialization and Deserialization

In computing, serialization and deserialization are the processes of converting an object or data structure into a stream in binary or text format that can be stored in file, memory, or transmitted over the network, then extract from the stream back into the object or data structure with the same content as the original one. The main purpose is to save the state of the object for later usage. The serialization and deserialization target object only, marshal an object. They provide many benefits for data storage in the disk or database system, for data transfer through the wires, for remote procedure calling through SOAP protocol, or for trying to detect any changes in the data along the time line.

When serializing an object into a stream and transmitting over the wire, and deserializing back into the same object, the important feature is the portability, independent of computer architecture and endianness. At client computer, the bytes order of serialization result should be the same as the byte order of deserialization at receiving server computer, it requires additional effort if two sides use different programming language to represent data with different computer architecture. This linearity is very important because it enables a common I/O interfaces to read write passing the state of the object. But on the other side, serialization extracts the object state into a series of bits, which is a low-level technique but violates object's encapsulation. Objects accessed by reference should be properly restored during deserialization in term of composition and one level or multi-level inheritance. Object collection like list, generic list or dictionary should also be covered for serialization or deserialization. At the present time, the serialization format has text based and binary based format. Text format includes raw text format, JavaScript Object Notation (JSON) and Extensible Markup Language (XML). Binary format is not standardized, but more efficient and faster than text considering the memory usage, data buffer size and timing. Text format is human readable, such as Json and Xml text stream, they are self-descriptive and support the easy parsing tree-like data structure. Text stream is easier for developers to add inspection operations during the serialization and deserialization process so that for large complicated object, it has ways to monitor the process.

Machine portable and language portable are two main contexts for portability. Two main issues surrounding the machine portable, one of them is endianness when storing and reading number in two machines with big-endian and little-endian, the other one is the size of memory representation. The incompatible formats represent numerical values storing in the memory that commonly in use are: a big-endian, where the most significant byte is stored first at very left side the smallest memory address, little-endian, where the most significant byte is stored last at the very right side the biggest address space. Big-endian is the common format used in data networking, while little-endian is popular present in microprocessors, like Intel x86 and its successors.

For the other issue on memory representation, various languages differently define their primitive integer type. For example, languages like Java or C# define int as 32-bit variable disregarding execution platform architecture, but the integer type in C and C++ can be 16 bits, 32 bits, or 64 bits depending on the platform architecture the application run on, usually it is 32 bits, so it may produce data in one machine but not recognizable in another machine unless we have additional type size information. The string serialization relies on character encoding and variable-length optimization. Some programming languages force default encoding of character string, others rely on platform architecture or user settings. The character strings can have variable length, that is why string serialization process needs store string length. The size of the array is stored using 1 byte, the elements in the array are addressed by index and size of the elements. Copying the contents of memory that a data structure is stored directly is the fastest and easiest way of serialization, but various platforms have different memory alignments, this in turn makes the same data structure occupy different amounts of bytes in different machines. No matter of what, a deserialized data structure should be a clone copy of its source with all the references in the data object in place.

The object-oriented languages allow reference an object with its parent class pointer. During marshaling, the complete object referenced by pointer should be stored, this requires access to complete class inheritance hierarchy and runtime type information. Multiple inheritance is more like a problem when serializing an object containing some data collections, like lists, dictionaries. The data serialized in C++ could lose some of its information when deserializing in Python, lost in translation. The software constantly upgrades, in the new version of the software, it is usually required to read data saved by the older version. Supporting both backward compatibility and forward compatibility is necessary for object serialization and deserialization, it sometimes requires the ability to skip unknown fields in the input data.

In .Net, different options of serialization technologies are analyzed from the following aspects: range, accessibility and callback, objects that contain circular references, objects that contain dictionary. Range is the property or field, accessibility is public or private, callback refers to OnSerializing, OnSerialized, OnDeserializing, onDeserialized these callbacks. Three main types are optimized for various serialization scenarios: data contract serialization, Xml serialization, Binary or Soap runtime serialization. Any given object type can support none, one, or more of the serialization technologies. When objects need to be persisted to disk or database system, better consider data contract serialization. When need more control or manipulation over the Xml format, better consider

Xml serialization. When the data stream need transfer across .NET Remoting boundaries, better consider runtime serialization. When need create or change serializable types such as adding properties or fields, better consider backward and forward compatibility. Implementing IExtensibleDataObject interface to allow convert back and forth between different versions of the object types, this interface enables the feature of data round-tripping. The ExtensibleData property shares the data contracts across different service versions. The class being serialized must have a parameter-less constructor, this is because the first operation of the deserialization process is to create an empty instance, and then gradually get its properties assigned from reading them from the file or stream. One thing to mention is that no need to serialize everything, such as .Net controls and color classes cannot be serialized. Serialization includes several attributes, such as [XmlIgnore], [Serializable], [XmlAttribute("Name")].

5.13.3 Http Basic Authentication and Digest Authentication

The http basic authentication is the simplest implementation of http protocol security. The client sends request to the server, along with it also sending the user-name and password as non-encrypted base64 text, and waiting for server to send back response. Without the SSL/TLS in place, http basic is not secure at all, but it is very simple to implement. The syntax is:

Value = username:password
Encoded Value = base64(Value)
Authorization Value = Basic <Encoded Value>
In the header, Authorization: <Authorization Value>

The http digest access authentication is a bit more complex authentication, it is an encrypted communication with two request credentials sending to the server, it applies a hash function to the username and the password. The web server returned a nonce value, the http method and the requested URI. Basically, the authentication starts from the first request that the client sends over to the server, it gets the server responds to authenticate, the responds include a special code, a nonce, a number used only once, another string representing the realm, and a hash. The client sends the second request with this nonce and an encrypted form of the username, password and realm. The server checks if the encrypted hash from the client matches those in the server, if match, server sends back the requested information. The whole communication process is secure and there is no plain text. Therefore, at this point, the SSL/TLS is not required, which makes each call slightly faster, but client has to make two communications for each web request, it subsequently makes the call a bit slower than basic authentication. The http digest is vulnerable to a man-in-the-middle security attack, it prevents the use of the strong password encryption, which may easily cause the passwords stored on the server be hacked. The syntax is:

```
Hash1=MD5(username:realm:password)
Hash2=MD5(method:digestURI)
response=MD5(Hash1:nonce:Hash2)
```

The basic and digest schemes are dedicated to the authentication using a username and a secret. But the bearer scheme is dedicated to the authentication through a token. Since OAuth 2.0 is a widely implemented public specification, the data included in an OAuth

2.0 authorization endpoint does not follow some rules, but the payload shape does not change with implementation even though the naming conventions may slightly different.

Secure Sockets Layer (SSL) and Transport Layer Security (TLS) are the two major cryptographic protocols in use today for securing in-transit data from malicious eyes in the middle of any network. SSL was originally designed by Netscape in the mid-1990s. All major web browsers today show a lock icon in the URL address bar when a website's communication is properly secured via SSL or TLS. The HTTP specification offers HTTPS or HTTP Secure, which requires a URI-scheme of TLS/SSL to be present before transferring any data over the network. When an HTTPS request is sent from browser that support HTTPS, it will display a warning to the end user if TLS/SSL connections are compromised.

5.13.4 Bootstrapping

Bootstrapping comes from the term *pulling yourself up by your own bootstraps.*, in computing, it was originated in the early 1950s referred to a bootstrap load button that was used to initiate a hardwired bootstrap program, or smaller program that executed a larger program in programming. In current computing, it is a small starting and loading programs one at a time, each program in the loading process is laced or connected to the next program to execute. This self-starting process proceeds automatically without any external input. In the computing operating system, it is the first piece of codes to run when machine starts. It is stored in ROM and is responsible for loading the operating system. During the boot process, it runs the diagnostic tests, routine testing for configurations of devices, the peripherals connections, hardware and external memory devices. For window operating system, the NT loader, a bootloader for Microsoft Windows NT OS usually run from the hard drive. In .Net Framework, the bootstrapper is responsible for the initialization of an application which built from the composite application library, through it, how the composite application library components are wired up to the application can be well controlled.

For windows desktop application, especially WPF application, there's a shell concept. WPF application is designed as a composite application but loosely coupled with individual parts can be developed, tested and extended independent from other components. The application starts as a blank painting, the shell is a canvas, or a container integrating everything together as a coherent whole. The shell consists of one or more regions with their placeholders that the views of content controls are fit into, the same design principal applies to ASP.Net ContentPlaceHolder web control. The content controls help the shell side along with multiple modules as well as all the interfaces for shared services. Therefore, Prism library comes into play, it helps design and build rich WPF client applications that are flexible and easy to maintain, it builds the architecture that allows multiple modules of the WPF application to be independently developed, later updated or loaded on-demand separately, coupled yet isolated. It relies on the composite design pattern to promote reuse and a clean separation of concern between the application's horizontal capabilities and the vertical capabilities. It has logging and security components across the variety of modules, it also has business and data layers specific to each module.

Prism bootstrap classes and routines help the composite application's registration and configuration during the startup process. It includes creating and configuring module catalog, creating a unity container with dependency injection, configuring default region adapter for UI composition, creating and initializing the shell view, and initializing the modules. The prism library includes a default abstract bootstrapper base class, from which the methods can be override to fit custom needs. Dependency injection pattern plays a very important role in Prism library, it works with the unity application block or managed extensibility framework, just like in the framework of ASP.Net MVC and ASP.Net core web api, the dependency injection pattern helps multi-components wire up into one unity. Mostly the types are represented by interfaces that need register in the bootstrapper and can be retrieved by the service locator at any moment during runtime. Unity application block and managed extensibility framework have MefBootstrapper or UnityBootstrapper base classes that can be derived to implement the CreateShell and InitializeShell method for shell specific initialization.

For web application, responsive UI in web development loosely correlates to a design that can adapt itself to various screen sizes. Today, most internet sites are no longer viewed on large screen desktops only, from mobile devices like smartphones with a variety of screen sizes. The web application is expected to be able to handle all these screen sizes gracefully and adapt to them. Bootstrap provides a whole barrelful of components that can be easily included in our web applications, like dropdowns, forms, navigation bars, buttons, tables. Adding eye-catching design elements to our applications easily help us assure that all of the components will look the same no matter the screen size or device used to view them. Bootstrap has its own grid system predefined, and the containers can be filled gracefully with the required content with responsive, the CSS can be adjusted for the UI display. Bootstrap's customization page can help create and tweak custom theme. Bootstrap is written in file bootstrap.css and boostrap.js, they need be registered in ASP.NET MVC application when the application starts:

```
protected void Application_Start()
    {
        AreaRegistration.RegisterAllAreas();
        FilterConfig.RegisterGlobalFilters(GlobalFilters.Filters);
        RouteConfig.RegisterRoutes(RouteTable.Routes);
        BundleConfig.RegisterBundles(BundleTable.Bundles);
    }

public static void RegisterBundles(BundleCollection bundles)
    {
        bundles.Add(new ScriptBundle("~/bundles/jquery").Include(
            "~/Scripts/jquery-{version}.js"));

        bundles.Add(new ScriptBundle("~/bundles/jqueryval").Include(
            "~/Scripts/jquery.validate*"));

        // Use the development version of Modernizr to develop with and
        learn from. Then, when
        // ready for production, use the build tool at https://modernizr.
        com to pick only the tests.

        bundles.Add(new ScriptBundle("~/bundles/modernizr").Include(
            "~/Scripts/modernizr-*"));
```

```
bundles.Add(new ScriptBundle("~/bundles/bootstrap").Include(
    "~/Scripts/bootstrap.js"));

bundles.Add(new StyleBundle("~/Content/css").Include(
    "~/Content/bootstrap.css",
    "~/Content/site.css"));
}
```

It displays the default layout page for ASP.NE MVC web application:

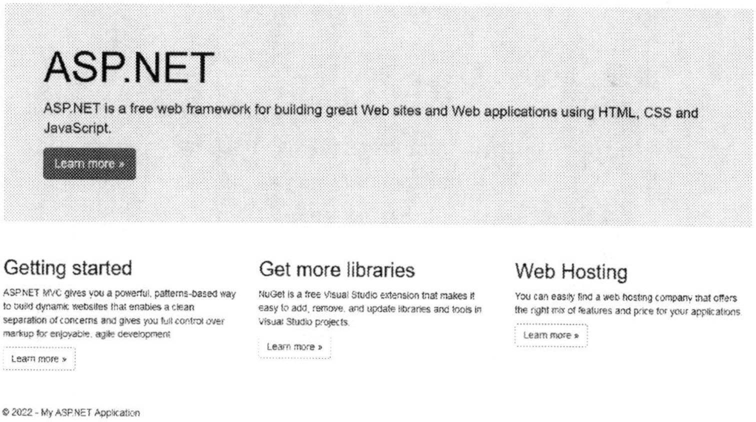

ASP.NET

ASP.NET is a free web framework for building great Web sites and Web applications using HTML, CSS and JavaScript.

Learn more »

Getting started

ASP.NET MVC gives you a powerful, patterns-based way to build dynamic websites that enables a clean separation of concerns and gives you full control over markup for enjoyable, agile development

Learn more »

Get more libraries

NuGet is a free Visual Studio extension that makes it easy to add, remove, and update libraries and tools in Visual Studio projects.

Learn more »

Web Hosting

You can easily find a web hosting company that offers the right mix of features and price for your applications.

Learn more »

© 2022 - My ASP.NET Application

Figure 5.13.4.1 ASP.Net MVC web application starts with bootstrap.css

The default template uses a set of <div> elements to render a top navbar and the main body of the page. A <div> with a class of "container", and then within that, two more <div> elements: "navbar-header" and "navbar-collapse". The main navigation menu is rendered by the <ul> element within the second div with the included links. The main body of each page is rendered in another <div>, marked with the "container" and "body-content" classes, and then a simple <footer> is added to the end of the <div> element:

```
<!DOCTYPE html>
<html>
<head>
    <meta charset="utf-8" />
    <meta name="viewport" content="width=device-width, initial-scale=1.0">
    <title>@ViewBag.Title - My ASP.NET Application</title>
    @Styles.Render("~/Content/css")
    @Scripts.Render("~/bundles/modernizr")
</head>
<body>
    <div class="navbar navbar-inverse navbar-fixed-top">
        <div class="container">
            <div class="navbar-header">
                <button type="button" class="navbar-toggle" data-toggle="collapse" data-target=".navbar-collapse">
                    <span class="icon-bar"></span>
                    <span class="icon-bar"></span>
                    <span class="icon-bar"></span>
                </button>
                @Html.ActionLink("Application name", "Index", "Home", new { area = "" }, new { @class = "navbar-brand" })
            </div>
            <div class="navbar-collapse collapse">
                <ul class="nav navbar-nav">
                    <li>@Html.ActionLink("Home", "Index", "Home")</li>
                    <li>@Html.ActionLink("About", "About", "Home")</li>
                    <li>@Html.ActionLink("Contact", "Contact", "Home")</li>
                </ul>
            </div>
        </div>
    </div>
    <div class="container body-content">
        @RenderBody()
        <hr />
        <footer>
            <p>&copy; @DateTime.Now.Year - My ASP.NET Application</p>
        </footer>
    </div>
```

```
   @Scripts.Render("~/bundles/jquery")
   @Scripts.Render("~/bundles/bootstrap")
   @RenderSection("scripts", required: false)
</body>
</html>
```

For web api core service, it has build-in bootstrap process. it must include *Startup* class, which is like Global.asax in the traditional .NET application, it is executed first when the application starts. The *Startup* class can be configured using UseStartup<T>() method at the time of configuring the host in the Main() method of Program class. The name *Startup* is by ASP.NET core convention, it can be specified as the generic parameter in the UseStartup<T>() method. For example, to name the *Startup* class as *MyStartup*, specify it as .UseStartup<MyStartup>(). *Startup* class must include a Configure method and can optionally include ConfigureService method. The Configure method is a place where you can configure application requested pipeline using IApplicationBuilder instance that is provided by the built-in IoC container. ASP.NET core introduced the middleware components to define a request pipeline, which will be executed on every request. The dependency injection pattern is used widely in ASP.Net core web api architecture, it includes built-in IoC container to provide dependent objects through constructors. The ConfigureServices method is a place where all dependent interfaces and classes are registered through the built-in IoC container. The life scope functions AddTransient, AddScoped and AddSingleton help register the depended types that later can be retrieved anywhere and anytime in the application. ASP.NET core refers some dependent class as a service, the service has its own business logic and data model. At runtime, the ASP.Net core web api host passes an instance of IApplicationBuilder to the Configure method, and the ConfigureServices adds the services to the built-in container:

```
public class Program
    {
        public static void Main(string[] args)
        {
            WebApiHostBuilder
                .Create<Startup>(args)
                .Build()
                .Run();
        }
    }
}
public class Startup
    {
        public void ConfigureServices(IServiceCollection services)
        {
            //Write code to add services to the container here
        }
        public void Configure(IApplicationBuilder app)
        {
            //Write code here to configure the request processing pipeline
        }
    }
```

CHALLENGES OF TOMORROW PROGRAMMING

It is not in the stars to hold our
destiny but in ourselves.

– William Shakespeare

TOMORROW IS COMING, WHEN SUN rises again, it is much sooner than you image. Various technologies will emerge when tomorrow comes, at the same time, the running of tomorrow's clock pushes technologies forward and when a new day comes, something new again. The cycling pushes the world volve, it changes our lives, breaks new boundaries to protect and advance humanity, from deep sea to star and space, from deep underground to cloud and sun, from microorganism to macro universe. In the computing chapter, the innovations kept on going for hundreds of years and is continuing to happen and will prevail. Artificial intelligence, robots reading minds, data soil, massive and various programming languages, more nature and close to human languages. Computing, faster, faster, and much faster, user interface, more allusive and it is hard to distinguish whether it is the real and virtual. The technology is shifting, evolving, and adapting to the world changing trends faster than ever before. Below I have picked some areas that I know one or two and have been fascinated with.

6.1 High-level programming language

We all know that for fashion industry, it is a big transmigration after dozens of years. That's why you look the same attractive as your Mom if you wear your Mom's beautiful dress she bought when she was young. Does the same apply to high-level programming language development? From functional programming in 1950s, to procedure programming, to object-oriented programming, high-level programming languages haven been going through years of study and development. Right now, huge number of programming languages present in the software community, compiled languages, interpreted languages, languages through just in time compiler. For the majority of languages, one common feature is that they are imperative programming, and more focus on how to solve the problem, through simple or complicated algorithm, through iteration or selection, through software design principals. What will be the next generation of programming language? Something new or another big transmigration from the very beginning of the languages in 1940s and 1950s.

I would like to say that the future programming language is more abstract, nature, amenable to formal analysis and friendly to developers with a relatively narrow functionality scope, like T-SQL. One way for writing language is to write down prose paragraphs for the expression allowed and evaluated, this way readers can quickly absorb the ideas but difficult to extract the details, and the prose is hard to formal analysis. Another way of writing language is to implement an interpreter, which has a formal meaning in the language and can be analyzed. The future way of writing programming language is that the grammar is more nature and easy to be understood. It more concerns on what the problem needs to solve? what the condition needs be satisfy? For example, when we are sorting a list of numbers, traditional algorithms have bubble sort, quick sort, or merge sort, the algorithm explicitly tells us what the steps are and how to proceed the execution of each step, such as through iteration, recursive, or swap. For the future programming language, we no longer need algorithm, we just input to computer that we have a list of numbers need to sort, and computer calculates and return us the execution result. We are blind with the detail execution process, it is similar with the functional programming started from 1950s, such as Lisp. It was in 1997 that I first programmed lisp in Unix, 25 years passed, I almost forget Lisp programming, but the impression of such easy to learn and understand engraved to my mind, I believe that I can pick it up quickly if I need program Lisp again.

Talking about functional programming, we need back to Church's λ-calculus. The λ-calculus has such as great historical and foundational significance, the simultaneous development of Turing machine and λ-calculus led to the Church-Turing thesis, it states that those computable functions are equivalent in the λ-calculus and exactly can be implemented by Turing Machines. In the ordinary mathematical algebra course, functions are ubiquitous, like we can define $f(x) = x + 1$, we state what happens during the $f(x)$ execution by applying the argument of x

Bing Wang

instead of stating what f actually is, this is λ-abstraction. Besides λ-calculus, functional programming intercepts many study areas in mathematics: abstract algebra, grouping theory and category theory. From the language design point of view, functional programming has unique feature than imperative programming and object-oriented programming, such as the following:

OOP: developer.program("C#");
where developer is an instance of *Developer* class
Functional: program (developer, "C#");
where developer as a parameter passes to function *program*, we do not concern about how the program function works, we only know there is a function notation program that takes "developer" and "C#" as parameters.

Here is other example: for the following data object, find the developer name whose skill is "C#":

```
const developers =
{
      {name: "Bing Wang", skill: "C#"},
      {name: "Mike Lewis", skill: "Java"},
      {name: "Adam Smith", skill: "SQL"}
}
```
For imperative programming, we may need loop:
```
for (int i = 0; i < developers.length; i++)
{
      const developer = developers[i];
      if (developer.skill == "C#")
      {
            return developer.name;
      }
}
```

For functional programming: we break the task into subtasks, pure function and no state

```
const result = developers.filter((d) => d.skill == "C#").map((d) => d.name);
```

Functional programming belongs to structure programming, it aims to put the execution process into a series of nested functions and call them one by one and finally get the return value. For example, see the below mathematic expression:

$$(10 - 20) / 30 + 40$$

The below imperative programming focuses on the execution process:

```
int x = 10 - 20;
int y = x / 30;
int z = y + 40;
```

but functional programming solves this problem through different functions call, very similar with Lisp:

```
int z = add (divide (subtract (10,20),30), 40);
```

Function is first class and it is equivalent with other data types that can assign to variables and can pass to another function as a parameter, or as a return result from another function:

```
var output = function(i) { console.log(i); };
[10,20,30,40].foreach(output);
```

Functional programming consists of expressions instead of statements since statement is execution without return value, but expression has return value. Every step of functional programming is purely calculation with return result because it is for computation instead of system I/O and it limits the I/O to the minimum possibility. Functional programming keeps referential transparency, the function execution only relies on input parameter instead of external variable or state. We can see from the above example that functional programming is more reliable, easy to develop and test. The current languages of Haskell, F#, Clojure are all have the similar features.

Quantum world is abstract, thus functional. Recent research of quantum computing involves the functional programming which applies to quantum structures. Some research groups are designing framework for specifying and solving the computation problems in standard quantum mechanics through the purely functional, lazy languages Haskell, which permits to manipulate formal quantum structure. Some research group developing functional languages for quantum computation on finite types, the languages integrate reversible and irreversible quantum computations in one language through first order strict linear algebra logic. The strict program guarantees and improves quantum parallelism through decoherence and preserve superpositions and entanglement.

6.2 Database development

We can never and will ever ignore data. For software developing, the first important and critical field all developers need to tackle with is database. I once almost became a SQL DBA but I stopped and continued doing programming. Database is a smartly driven data container, a knowledgeable data bank. With the more and more upgrade and advanced features in-place for database system giant like SQL server, Oracle, with more and more algorithms implementation to process big data, doing analysis, forecast and predication, with more and more mechanisms designed for data migration, data mining and data warehouse to accomplish the data history archive and batch reporting, with more and more data loading to cloud and internet based data lake, have we ever crossed our minds that there still exists numerous legacy software with plain text based data file systems? Those legacy systems are still playing important roles in a variety of industries, some even support real-time, such as traffic control and transportation industry, power supply industry, and automobile industry, etc. Usually, the important part of the real-time system is a central controller with its own embedded operating system, the file system is supported by their own operating systems. The hosted data bank is just purely the group of plain text files, or their own customized file types, either binary or ASCII, but the application has to retrieve, overwrite, flush, pattern searching all the text data as a whole like a mini database management system but may not have implementation for concurrent access, memory usage, logging, or undo-redo. The software connected to the file system has to contain a special file parser. The file system-based database is very limited only fit for the special needs. But, have we ever thought about how to efficiently and smartly support these legacy data file systems? Or how to install the regular operating system in the controller and ETL the data to more advanced database system? Those special needed file systems usually reside in non-window system, so can we also design a suitable database system to replace the purely file system. I would like to say that this special kind of database system performs as a managed wrapper of the underline file system so that some of the necessary action on the files can be implicitly invoked.

Most of the relational database management system like Microsoft SQL and Oracle were designed based on E. F. Codd's ideas presented in the 1970 article *A Relational Model of Data for Large Shared Data Banks* and 1972 article *Relational Completeness of Database Sublanguages*. Dr. Codd, the English computer scientist, presented the relational database model through mathematic formulas of *Relational Algebra* while he was working for IBM. The concept of data itself shaped as qualitative and quantitative. With big data, its new feature of 3V defined by industry analyst Doug Laney, a renowned author and advisor on data analytics strategy. 3V as volume, velocity and variety, is gradually replacing the traditional data nature. The first, volume. Our universe is more and more toward to digital universe, it has unprecedented data explosion reaching 180 zettabytes very soon. The challenge is not data storage but useful data identification. Data comes from myriad sources: smart devices, social media posts, sensors, terminals, electronic records, etc. how to filter the garbage and collect what we need are becoming more and more challenge. The development of volume data filtering techniques is on-going, outlier detection is one. Outliner detection is trying to find out those data who have a big difference than the main cluster of data sets. If not filter them out, they will highly affect the performance of the data classification and analysis model. Build a qualify outlier detection is difficult because we need build a normal data modeling first, and sometimes it is hard to determine the normal data properties from the big volume of data collection, so it is hard to distinguish between the normal and outlier. For example, the handling of noise data, the nature of noise makes the data poor, which is a huge challenge to select outliers. Currently one of the industry-leading data filter and integration tool is IBM DataStage, an ETL tool for the data evoke, measure and transformation. Signal extraction and decomposition is another one, real-life signals from vibrating structures are hard to investigate, how to decompose non-stationary signals into their constituent amplitude and frequency modulated components? Although the theory and algorithms for stationary signals are well developed, it is almost nonexistent for non-stationary signals.

The second, velocity. Data not only comes as huge volume, but grows fast, it comes as lighting speed and need be processed instantaneously. Streaming data keeps flowing into the server real-time makes it hard to do the data batch processing. Tools for real-time data collection are developing and facing challenge as well, especially for signal demand sensing. Apache Storm is a streaming data processing engine for real-time data analysis and computation, it is hugely scalable for highest ingestion rates of data processing with fault tolerance. The third, variety. Data comes in different forms and unstructured, extremely diverse, social media posts, audio, video, stream, images, it is more difficult to manipulate and extract and it is constantly changing. In order to meet the data variety requirements, many calculation models have been emerged in the big data community. Apache Hive, a distributed and fault-tolerant data warehouse system allows user analyze large-scale of data from batch-processing. Apache Hadoop, a software framework allows the distributed processing of large data sets across clusters of computers. Pregel, a vertex-centric computation model and large-scale graphs processing, the scale of this graph supports billions of vertices and edges, which result in efficient processing challenges. SAP Hana, high-performance analytic appliance, is an in-memory multi-model database supporting easy data gathering and analysis so that it helps make better business decision. The design and development of these tool help data scientists extract information from large volume of data sets, further analyze and predicate, at the same time, they expose the deficient and pending for the continuing research and study of the big data.

6.3 Windows operating system

Somehow, I keep the conviction throughout my programming career that I just do not touch the system applications because I feel they are very sensitive and not easy. The research of operating system carries on in many fields throughout the history such as time sharing, multitasking, distributed and fault tolerance, etc. However, as a software developer, after implemented a varieties of application types, especially the web services, the most touching acknowledgments I have for system programs are two points. One is kernel itself and one is the memory management. The ultimate gauge for software is its performance, make it faster through improving throughput and demanding without delays. The developers of the major framework libraries like Microsoft .Net and Java Core are trying to improve user applications' throughput as much as they can. They designed and implemented the concepts of mutex control for multi-process and semaphore for multi-threading in their concurrency library, which ultimately invokes system application. The system application contains the scheduling algorithm managing to dispatch to which CPU core to execute.

It's true that the well-known framework API work perfectly, but sometimes I was thinking, with the advanced hardware technology development on multicore and hyperthreading CPU, should we need to go down the base level of the kernel scheduling algorithms to enhance it so that it applies to all the advanced CPU types. In addition, the CPU chip makers keep technologies renovating, but the memory slots on machine's motherboard remains unchanged. Due to the limitation of RAM and user process's running requirement of loading it into the user space in RAM, should we need to revisit the user process loading mechanism in memory management? Under the situation that RAM is not enough to afford many user processes to swap into to run, we may need to redesign the concept of process in the windows operating system. For example, a process executable file may need refer multiple libraries *.dll, when the user process is being swapped into RAM, is it possible that only the single executable file of small size loaded into RAM and the associated library routines are invoked in disk? I don't know if this is the right approach, but the sure thing is that lots of algorithms in operating system software need to be revisited so that more user processes can be run simultaneously or loaded faster upon immediate demanding.

Today's Windows operating system has strenuously designed the way bottom-up, starting from the hardest part kernel first, then gradually upwards process, memory, disk, displays, it performs as an efficient storage manager. With bottom-up, the operating system is in charge of system resource usage and management, it emphasizes the time multiplexing that each application program gets a slot of time to use resource, the same for space multiplexing that each application program gets a part of the resource. What will be the next generation of windows operating system? Top-down starting from user and ignoring underlying components? It might not be as efficient as the current one, but it focuses on tracking user, moment by moment and thought by thought, it needs a convenient user interface. With top-down, the operating system hides the complicated components that still must be performed, it presents user with virtual machine look that easier to use, so everything relies on the windows interface. Maybe the next generation of windows operation system interface will be the 3D models of spacetime. The operating system is just a middleware, a container, it provides services to the user applications, the services include executing the program, access I/O, get to file system and communication. In addition, the future information management becomes more narrative, all documents become digital lying out in a narrative stream like a documental movie with past, present and future. When user tries to search one document, the returned result might not only the one document, but also all the related documents.

6.4 Windows user interface

I love to work on user interfaces in my programming times, both web interface and windows interface. I do work on web services and data access backend as well, but the software product's final display is interface, which is my face as well I would like to say, so every time interface crashes or hangs in production, I feel I was slapped. Human-computer interaction has been going through a series of milestones: batch interface, command line interface, text interface, the demonstration of oN-Line System by Douglas Engelbart (an American engineer and inventor) in 1968, which is the first system involving the invention of mouse, pointer and windows, then all the ways to the Microsoft windows system. What will be the next generation of user interface to break through the prevalent pixel and vector graphics? We know the computer graphic has two kinds, the pixel composed called raster like bitmap image and the path composed called vector graphics with curves and shapes. But how the image processing works and how the vector is generated given two dimensions of geographic location are the original sources we need trace back to find out. For the next generation of user interface graphic, more dimensions I think, a new file format need be created to embed both pixel elements with color depth and more points' vector-based matrix rotation transformation that can rotate along any axis. Multimedia may need have new element of timing to reflect the media transmission stereoscopically. Should we need to enhance the vector mathematics to be the matrix mathematics to represent more directions such as geographic or space location and timing? How are we going to display the graphics to user because it is no longer static flat picture, it will involve streaming, multimedia, motion, and the most important I would like to say, is to demonstrate the real time. Interface design has been evolved rapidly within recent decades, but it is still a long way to go to astound us in many aspects. User interface is interacting with user, it is also interacting with technology. It started with first text-based command, then the prevalent GUI based Windows and Apple operating system, the GUI allows us use mouse, keyboard. Now we have touching screen and hand gestures, we also witness the voice input like smart speaker enabling a more immersive interaction with GUI.

Below I will give short descriptions of some GUI design examples that currently on going and may potentially be the future GUIs look like. One of the interface designs is gesture recognition, user hand movement to touch the interface, such as tapping, pinching, shaking, etc. This interface is mainly reading the hand movement through sensors or cameras, sending the movement data to computers to recognize, process and in return the computers react by the interfaces. Xbox 360 Kinect is one of the products based on gesture recognition. It has no controller and has a built-in camera to give you control over an attached Kinect. No matter what this product future will be, I believe the idea and technology will be carried on. Others like Multi-Touch, Microsoft Surface technology, in addition to touch gesture recognition, surface has object recognition capabilities, it allows users to place physical objects on the screen to invoke different digital recognition response.

Second of the interface designs is voice-control-based interface that control a computer through voice command, this interface facilitates the communication between a user and a device. One of the current features is google voice search, or search by voice, it allows users speak on a mobile phone or computer and have the device search for data, this way, it can capture speech much faster than typing, it helps those who have difficulty in sight. Speech recognition technology has been progressed within recent years, it performs as an additional layer to transform voice signals into text and ultimately still does the google query through text, delivering the search result back to voice to be heard by users. Machine learning and Artificial intelligence technologies assist the voice recognition by better understanding the human language, consequently better understand voice command to give back to users.

The third of the interface designs is mixed reality combining augmented realty and virtual reality. Augment reality is a recent emerging technology that superimposes digital information over user's view through a smart device. Virtual reality is another technology that users wear a head device, VR headset, his sight is obstructed as if he is in a virtual environment. Mixed reality is a combination of these two. Computer generated objects becomes perceptual simulated contents in the real world around us that we can interact with them performing some professional tasks. It started to enter different industries: healthcare, entertainment, hospital, education, retail, etc., especially in hospital, augmented reality more and more becomes a big thing. In others like some furniture companies, they created augment reality application to visualize what your future house will look like by placing those generated furniture objects into your home environment to help you have a real look and feel. It happens to virtual reality as well, you will see a 3D artificial environment surrounding you when you wear the headset so that you can feel and explore, like googling in the environment that encourages you to keep learning and fumbling. Mix reality helps us understand how we can live as humans, it drives us to explore the real world, it enables businesses of all types to provide a wide range of experiences and solutions.

Besides the above three interface designs, there are more areas professionals are studying and researching. Brain computer interface is the one to understand more about the brain neurotransmitters and brain waves so that future devices can more understand the humans' thinking and behaviors. Biometric interface is the one creating biological marker that unique to each individual person, we have fingerprint scanner and retina scanner, they will continue to evolve. Interface designs for universal control system, space exploration and control, and more and more.

REFERENCES

1. Michael R. Williams, *History of Computing Technology*, 2nd edition, Los Alamitos: IEEE Computer Society Press, 1997

2. Daniel I. A. Cohen, *Introduction to Computer Theory*, New York: John Wiley & Sons, Inc., 1986

3. John L Hennessy & David A Patterson, *Computer Architecture A Quantitative Approach*, San Mateo: Morgan Kaufmann Publishers, Inc., 1990

4. George Boole, *The Law of Thought*, 1st edition, Cambridge: Macmillan and Co., 1854

5. Joseph Albabari & Ben Albabari, *C# 5.0 IN A NUTSHELL*, 5th edition, Sebastopol: O'Reilly, 2012

6. Peter Wolfendale, *Object-Oriented Philosophy the Noumenon's New Clothes*, Windsor Quarry: Urbanomic Media Ltd, 2014

7. Matt Welsfeld, *The object-oriented thought process*, 3rd edition, Upper Saddle River: Addison-Wesley, 2008

8. Christopher Alexander, *The Timeless Way of Building*, New York: Oxford University Press, 1979

9. Ramez Elmasri & Shamkant Navathe, *Fundamentals of Database Systems*, 2nd edition, Redwood City: The Benjamin/ Cummings Publishing Company, Inc., 1994

10. Kalen Delaney, *Inside Microsoft SQL Server 2000*, 1st edition, Redmond: Microsoft Press, 2001

11. Jeffrey Richter, *Programming Applications for Microsoft Windows*, 4th edition, Redmond: Microsoft Press, 1999

12. Adam Nathan, *WPF 4 Unleashed*, 1st edition, Indianapolis: Pearson Education, 2010

13. Ingo Rammer, *Advanced .NET Remoting*, Berkeley: Apress, 2002

14. Juval Lowy, *Programming WCF Service*, 3rd edition, Sebastopol: O'Reilly, 2010

15. *0* - Wikipedia: *https://en.wikipedia.org/wiki/0*

16. John McCarthy, *The LISP Programming System - http://www-formal.stanford.edu/jmc/recursive/node4.html*

AFTERWORD

Now, I am almost done with my book, my compacted developer notes. Doing topics research and writing is such an enjoyable journey. It is a voyage of learning, solidify, summarizing and exploring. Sat back and pondering myself, what will be my next goal, next journey? I have not decided yet, but I am pretty certain that back to zero again, because many fields I still have not touched and many areas I still do not have experience, because it is still a long way to go, for my daughter, for my family, and the most important is, because I know one thing, that is I know nothing!

The End

Oct. 1st, 2022

Printed in the United States
by Baker & Taylor Publisher Services